outledge Studies in Development Economics

Special Economic Zones in South Asia
Structural Change, Competitiveness and Growth
Aradhna Aggarwal

Infrastructure Policy and Inequality
Michael A. Cohen

Responsible Business and Sustainable Development
The Use of Data and Metrics in the Global South
Edited by David Mhlanga and Mufaro Dzingirai

nlocking Economic Development
he Unlearning Process of Nations
hmed Tahiri Jouti

onomic Shocks and Globalisation
tween Deglobalisation and Slowbalisation
ited by Elsabé Loots

e Economics of Financial Inclusion
ted by Firdous Ahmad Malik and Tarika Singh Sikarwar

ancial Sustainability of Local Governments in Southern Africa
ursuit of Sustainable Cities and Communities
ed by Nirmala Dorasamy and Tonderai Kapesa

Political Economy of Underdevelopment in Sub-Saharan Africa
topher E.S. Warburton

rmation about this series, please visit: www.routledge.com/Routledge-Studies-in-
-Economics/book-series/SE0266

The Political Economy of Underdevelopment in Sub-Saharan Africa

This book provides a unique combination of history, politic rationalize the progression of underdevelopment in Sierra Leon of economic growth and development confronting some countries. It concisely presents the internal frictions that are the underdevelopment of Sierra Leonean since 1961, while a performance of the country with some countries in the subre Latin America, and Asia. It highlights the external threats th stifling the economic growth and sustainable development o sovereign debt, the paucity of human capital, the use of external shocks.

The central concepts of analysis include the premise contexts for business strategies and rivalry in an ur economic growth, productivity, sustainable developmen threats to macroeconomic stability in the form of volatile competitiveness, inaccessible foreign markets, deficien the cost of unsustainable sovereign debt, and the viabilit

The book has been intentionally developed for all thos in the political economy of Sub-Saharan Africa (with p Leone), empirical work on economic growth and devel on international political economy, international organi

Christopher E.S. Warburton is an internationa international economics from Fordham University. F in Economics, and International Political Economy Fordham University in New York. As a graduate University of Sierra Leone, he holds a BA (Hons) published peer-reviewed papers in economics ar Economics and law. Two of his most recent pub *Development of International Monetary Policy* (2 *Law* (2021). He currently teaches Economics an program at Berkeley College in New Jersey, US

5.

6.

7.

8. T
A

9. E
B
Ed

10. Th
Ed

11. Fin
In F
Edi

12. The
Chri

For more inf
Developmen

The Political Economy of Underdevelopment in Sub-Saharan Africa

This book provides a unique combination of history, politic
rationalize the progression of underdevelopment in Sierra Leor
of economic growth and development confronting some
countries. It concisely presents the internal frictions that are
the underdevelopment of Sierra Leonean since 1961, while a
performance of the country with some countries in the subre
Latin America, and Asia. It highlights the external threats th
stifling the economic growth and sustainable development o
sovereign debt, the paucity of human capital, the use of
external shocks.

The central concepts of analysis include the premise
contexts for business strategies and rivalry in an ur
economic growth, productivity, sustainable developmen
threats to macroeconomic stability in the form of volatile
competitiveness, inaccessible foreign markets, deficien
the cost of unsustainable sovereign debt, and the viabilit

The book has been intentionally developed for all thos
in the political economy of Sub-Saharan Africa (with p
Leone), empirical work on economic growth and devel
on international political economy, international organi

Christopher E.S. Warburton is an internationa
international economics from Fordham University. H
in Economics, and International Political Economy
Fordham University in New York. As a graduate
University of Sierra Leone, he holds a BA (Hons)
published peer-reviewed papers in economics ar
Economics and law. Two of his most recent pub
Development of International Monetary Policy (2
Law (2021). He currently teaches Economics an
program at Berkeley College in New Jersey, US

The Political Economy of Underdevelopment in Sub-Saharan Africa

Christopher E.S. Warburton

Routledge
Taylor & Francis Group
LONDON AND NEW YORK

First published 2025
by Routledge
4 Park Square, Milton Park, Abingdon, Oxon OX14 4RN

and by Routledge
605 Third Avenue, New York, NY 10158

Routledge is an imprint of the Taylor & Francis Group, an informa business

British Library Cataloguing-in-Publication Data
A catalogue record for this book is available from the British Library

Library of Congress Cataloging-in-Publication Data
Names: Warburton, Christopher E. S., author.
Title: The political economy of underdevelopment in Sub-Saharan Africa / Christopher E.S. Warburton.
Other titles: Routledge studies in development economics.
Description: New York : Routledge, 2024. | Series: [Routledge studies in development economics] | Includes bibliographical references and index.
Identifiers: LCCN 2024027522 (print) | LCCN 2024027523 (ebook) | ISBN 9781032855004 (hardback) | ISBN 9781032855028 (paperback) | ISBN 9781003518464 (ebook)
Subjects: LCSH: Economic development—Sierra Leone. | Sierra Leone—Economic conditions—1961–
Classification: LCC HC1065 .W38 2024 (print) | LCC HC1065 (ebook) | DDC 338.9664—dc23/eng/20240618
LC record available at https://lccn.loc.gov/2024027522
LC ebook record available at https://lccn.loc.gov/2024027523

ISBN: 978-1-032-85500-4 (hbk)
ISBN: 978-1-032-85502-8 (pbk)
ISBN: 978-1-003-51846-4 (ebk)

DOI: 10.4324/9781003518464

Typeset in Times New Roman
by Apex CoVantage, LLC

To my family – Conrad, Denise, and Nabia Warburton

Contents

Figures

Tables

Abbreviations

ACRM	Anti-Corruption Revolutionary Movement
ADB	African Development Bank
ADR	Alternative dispute resolution
AFRC	Armed Forces Revolutionary Council
APC	All People's Congress
ARI	Acute respiratory illness
ARIPO	African Regional Intellectual Property Organization
BSL	Bank of Sierra Leone
CAST	Consolidated African Selection Trust
CFCs	Chlorofluorocarbons
CH_4	Methane
CME	Chicago Mercantile Exchange
CMS	Church Missionary Society
CO_2	Carbon dioxide
COLA	Cost-of-living adjustment
CPI	(a) Consumer price index, (b) Corruption perception index
DELCO	Sierra Leone Development Company
DSM	Dispute settlement mechanism
DSU	Dispute settlement understanding
ECOMOG	Economic Community of West African States Monitoring Group
ECOWAS	Economic Community of West African States
ELG	Export-led growth
FBC	Fourah Bay College
FDI	Foreign direct investments
GATS	General Agreement on Trade in Services
GATT	General Agreement on Tariffs and Trade
GDP	Gross domestic product
GHGs	Greenhouse gases
GNI	Gross national income
GoSL	Government of Sierra Leone
HFCs	Hydrofluorocarbons
HPAEs	High-performing Asian economies
HS	Harmonized Commodity Description and Coding System

HTC	Higher Teacher Certificate
IADP	Integrated Agricultural Development Program
ICOR	Incremental capital–output ratio
ICSID	International Convention on the Settlement of Investment Disputes
IHR	International Health Regulations
IMF	International Monetary FUND
IPA	Investment Promotion Act
IPO	Initial public offering
IREA	International Renewable Energy Association
ISI	Import-substituting industrialization
IT	Inflation tax
ITO	International Trade Organization
LFPR	Labor force participation rate
MFN	Most favored nation
MMCET	Milton Margai College of Education and Technology
N_2O	Nitrous oxide
NPRC	National Provisional Ruling Council
NRA	National Revenue Authority
NRC	National Reformation Council
NTBs	Nontariff barriers
OGP	Open Government Partnership
PAP	People's Action Party
PFCs	Perfluorocarbons
PCIJ	Permanent Court of International Justice
PTAs	Preferential trade agreements
RUF	Revolutionary United Front
RSLMF	Royal Sierra Leone Military Force
SDR	Special Drawing Rights
SLE	Sierra Leone
SLPMB	Sierra Leone Produce Marketing Board
SLPP	Sierra Leone People's Party
SLST	Sierra Leone Selection Trust
SMRC	Sherbro Mineral Rutile Company
SSA	Sub-Saharan Africa
SSL	Statistics Sierra Leone
TC	Teacher Certificate
TFP	Total factor productivity
TOT	Terms of trade
TRIMs	Trade-Related Investment Measures
TRIPs	Trade-Related Aspects of Intellectual Property Rights
UAE	United Arab Emirates
UK	United Kingdom
UNCITRAL	United Nations Commission on International Trade Law
UNCTAD	United Nations Conference on Trade and Development
UNESCO	United Nations Education, Scientific, and Cultural Organization

UNFCCC	United Nations Framework Convention on Climate Change
UNICEF	United Nations International Children's Emergency Fund
US DoS	US Department of State
USTR	US Trade Representative
VAT	Value-added tax
WAEC	West African Educational Council
WASSCE	West Africa Senior School Certificate Examination
WDI	World Development Indicators
WFP	World Food Programme
WHO	World Health Organization
WIPO	World Intellectual Property Organization
WTO	World Trade Organization

Introduction

This book serves a growing need to understand the historical context of economic growth and development in Sierra Leone. It also illustrates interventions that are needed to reposition the country on the trajectory of economic growth and development. Therefore, the book is more than a rendition of the economic and development challenges confronting Sierra Leone. It also speaks to some of the broader developmental challenges confronting a substantial number of African countries after several decades of political economy.

Partial analysis of the colonial past fails to explain the deterioration of the Sierra Leonean economy and the eventual underdevelopment of the country. Significantly, countries with comparable adversities of colonial experiences have accomplished impressive socio-economic gains because of intentional public policies and strategic management of economic and financial resources to move out of a state of backwardness to economic prosperity and development. I specifically allude to Singapore in Chapter 4 of this book. The foregoing assertions call for introspection and alternative forms of conversation about the latent capacities of the country to grow and develop.

This book extensively lays out the bases for alternative forms of conversation beyond the familiar colonial hypothesis – the theory that ascribes underdevelopment of some African countries to the encounter with colonialism. Development strategies are intentional strategies that defy the persistence of primitive preconditions. Therefore, primitive preconditions are insufficient preconditions for perpetual backwardness, especially when humans have a latent capacity to overcome adversities that are not overpowering. That is, humans also have obligations to pull themselves by their proverbial bootstraps to attain successes (personal and national), precisely what the Singaporeans did after their encounter with colonialism.

The steady state of perpetual backwardness or human decadence cannot be a preference for (ab)normal human existence. Therefore, it is incumbent upon policymakers to intentionally pursue social policies that maximize the human welfare of their countries while also eschewing inhumane and destabilizing kleptocratic tendencies. This book traces the path of underdevelopment in Sierra Leone after 62 years of independence, marked by the insidious progression of impoverishment and no quantifiable developmental metric or strategies to improve the welfare of its people.

DOI: 10.4324/9781003518464-1

Infrastructural and human development occur when a country achieves long-term growth and development by measurable indicators of healthy existence, educational access and affordability, infrastructural developments, equitable use of environmental resources, and guarantees of fundamental rights and liberties. Invariably, development encapsulates ethical distributional issues and recognition of fundamental human rights more than the acquisition or accumulation of national income or the lack thereof, though per capita income may be positively correlated with levels of happiness within a country (Warburton, 2022).

In short, development is a hallmark of socio-economic progress that is also driven by ethical awareness rather than socio-economic individualism. It is usual for well-distributed socio-economic gains to result in national happiness (another measure of human progress or development that is contingent on ethical awareness) rather than human misery (Warburton, 2022). Hence, a country that cannot show, for multiple decades, quantitative and apparent physical and human progress in any of the measurable and critical indicators of development cannot be classified as developed or developing in absolute or relative terms. The title of this book is derived from inherent historical experiences. The expectations of the UNDP in 1990 and thereafter are revealing of the motif and motive of this work.

The 1990 Human Development Report introduced a new approach for improving human welfare. Human development is broadly defined in terms of the robustness of human life rather than national income. The dimensions of human development are multifarious, and they must be intentionally pursued. The report provides for the decompositions of human abilities and the prerequisites for achieving those abilities, notable of which are health, knowledge, standard of living, and fundamental rights. That is, the attainment of development is policy driven – human development is not a chance occurrence. Anah (2023) summarizes the key indicators of human development articulated by the UNDP in a schematic representation (Figure 0.1).

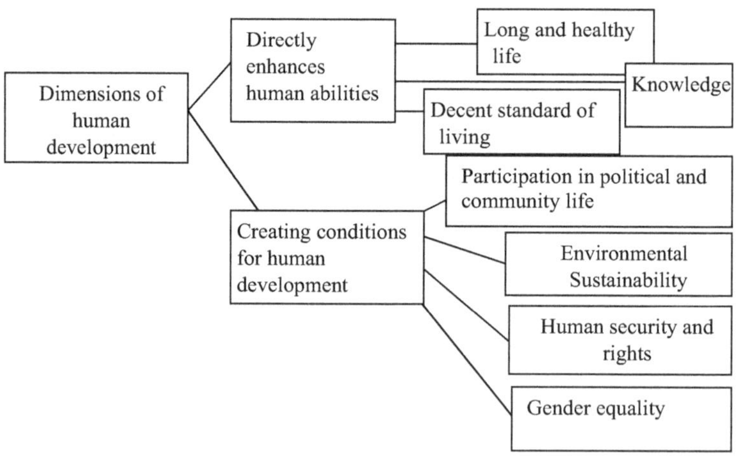

Figure 0.1 The human development approach.

Source: UNDP Human Development Report (1990) and Anah, p. 3

Access to affordable education and health care provides the most basic criterion for human development.

> *It is not only the case that, say, better education and health care improve the quality of life directly; they also increase a person's ability to earn an income and be free of income-poverty as well. The more inclusive the reach of basic education and health care, the more likely it is that even the potentially poor would have a better chance of overcoming penury.*
>
> (Sen, p. 90)

After some countries attained growth targets but failed to account for the stagnation of the welfare of their people, the concepts of development and underdevelopment opened up terminological inexactitudes in the 1970s. Accordingly, during the progression of the 1970s, economic development came to be redefined in terms of the reduction or elimination of poverty, inequality, and unemployment within the context of a growing economy (Todaro and Smith, p. 17). Implicitly, development meant increasing output and reducing social undesirables that were related to improper or ineffective redistribution of the gains of economic growth (redistribution that was conceptually inconsistent with a Pareto optimal outcome or redistribution that does not compromise economic growth). The looming conundrum then becomes, what happens when there is neither increases in per capita income nor a reduction of the social undesirables in a country over extended periods of time? For the purposes of this book, the author has liberally characterized this anomalous situation as "underdevelopment" – what would otherwise be characterized as "least developed," assuming that development is taking place. Of course, the characterization of underdevelopment is not unlike Goulet's forceful portrayal of underdevelopment when socio-economic conditions are shockingly deplorable.

> *Underdevelopment is shocking: the squalor, disease, unnecessary deaths, and helplessness of it all!. . . . The most emphatic observer can speak objectively about underdevelopment only after undergoing, personally or vicariously, the "shock of underdevelopment" . . . . Chronic poverty is a cruel kind of hell, and one cannot understand how cruel that hell is merely by gazing upon poverty as an object.*
>
> (Goulet, p. 23)

Perhaps the indicators of underdevelopment are less controversial: high birth rates, high infant mortality, a large agrarian sector, a small or no industrial sector, low per capita GDP, high levels of illiteracy, and low life expectancy. Since the 1990s, the United Nations Development Programme (UNDP) has been tracking human development, and countries are ranked on a scale of 0 (lowest human development) to 1 (highest human development) based on three targets of development: *a long and healthy life* (life expectancy at birth); *knowledge*, measured by a combination of average schooling by adults, and expected years of schooling for school-age children; and decent standards of living, measured by national income adjusted by varying purchasing power parity of each country's currency to reflect cost of living and diminishing marginal utility of income.

Might a country be developing from a backward situation? *A developing country is a sovereign state with a less-developed industrial base and a lower Human Development Index relative to other countries* (O'Sullivan & Sheffrin, 2003, p. 471). Classifications of "developing" and "underdeveloped" do not necessarily have universal appeal, but there must be a quantifying metric beyond abysmal ocular manifestations to comparatively show when one country is significantly lagging behind others on the most critical indicators of human progress. The fluidity of these expressions makes their usage more convoluted and objectionable than it might seem, but the indicators are contextually necessary to separate achievers from underachievers. The interchangeability of developing and underdeveloped generically shows that some countries are not performing well in industrialization, technological achievements, and international trade. As such, authors do justice to their work when they contextually outline the parameters of their analyses. Obviously, since the concept of "developing" must indicate some evidence of progress or long-drawn progress that is manifest in the lives of people, this book relates to underdevelopment. As such, I specifically allude to the historical lack of progress and the deterioration of human welfare in ocular and quantitative terms.

Accordingly, this book does not subscribe to any of the many nebulous theories of development, including their evolution and omitted variable biases. Rather, it focuses on the requirements for economic growth and human development, and the mechanisms or channels through which growth and human development could be achieved.

Chapter 1 provides the macroeconomic bases for underdevelopment in Sierra Leone. It traces the history of the country, alludes to the propitious climatic and geological conditions for economic growth and prosperity, incorporates the interface of pre-colonial and colonial administration, including some turbulent relationships, and discusses the rise and fall of the acquisition of human capital, which defines the specter of economic growth and decline respectively. The chapter revisits discussions of the colonial railway infrastructure and its effacement. It concludes with the monetary policy choices that have resulted in inflation and the threats of hyperinflation if macro-policies do not urgently and significantly address the issue of price instability in the country. The chapter also reveals missed opportunities for political stability, national cohesion, and economic growth and development. In effect, the chapter establishes the fractious foundations upon which the socio-economic destruction of the country was built.

In Chapter 2, I discuss the context for business strategy and rivalry in an underdeveloped economy. Porter's diamond model is used to frame the discussion of the chapter in terms of factor conditions, demand conditions, and the regulatory environment for doing business. The chapter introduces unfamiliar readers to market structure and business classifications. The inadequacy of sophisticated local firms shifts the focus to foreign firms that are operating in the country for an analysis of innovation and competitiveness.

Theories of economic growth and an examination of economic performance occur in Chapter 3. The chapter opens with an examination of volatile growth patterns and the conventional theories that are most responsible for the economic performance of countries. The theories provide a basis for rationalizing growth in Sierra Leone or the lack thereof. Factors that drive economic growth are examined together with the viability of the most productive sectors in the country. The Markov chain algorithm is utilized to evaluate the productive sectors in the context of some limiting parameters like environmental protection. The chapter also looks at the latent capacities of Sierra Leone to diversify its sources of energy by exploring the uses of solar energy and wind.

Chapter 4 is dedicated to international trade and the importance of international trade for economic growth and development. Integral to the chapter is the discussion of net exports, the most important variable to examine trade imbalances and national expenditure for imports. Excessive imports have implications for fiscal soundness, social spending, and the performance of the local currency. Important theories of international trade, including the gravity theorem, export-led growth, and import-substituting industrialization are explored in the chapter. The effects of preferential trade agreements and tariffs are also explored in the context of economic growth.

The final chapter delves into the threats to macroeconomic stability which come from abroad. These threats take the form of volatile commodity prices, pandemics, the precariousness of long-term investments, and unsustainable sovereign debts. The chapter highlights the need to urgently address these threats for macroeconomic stability and economic growth and sustainable development.

Further reading

Anah, C.I. (2023). *Development and underdevelopment*. ResearchGate.

Goulet, D. (1971). *The cruel choice: A new concept in the theory of development*. Atheneum.

O'Sullivan, A. & Sheffrin, S.M. (2003). *Economics: Principles in action*. Pearson Prentice Hall.

Sen, A. (1999). *Development as freedom*. Knopf.

Todaro, M.P. & Smith, C.S. (2015). *Economic development* (12th ed.). Pearson.

UNDP. (1990). *Human development report 1990*. Oxford University Press.

Warburton, C.E.S. (2022). Why are they so happy when others are so unhappy? The theology and ethics of economic development. *Applied Econometrics and International Development*, Euro-American Association of Economic Development, 22(1), 5–18.

1 Background to open macroeconomics

1.1 Historical background

Between 1460 and 1500, Sierra Leone obtained its name from Portuguese ship captains who considered the coastal area of Sierra Leone to look like lion mountains (*Serra lyoa*) from afar on the sea. Various tribes had moved into the country that is Sierra Leone today during the fifteenth and sixteenth centuries. For example, coastal Sierra Leone was occupied by the Bullom, Krim, Baga, Kissi, Gola, and Nalou. Some Limbas were found in the northern interior (Fyle, 2006, p. xvii).

From the sixteenth century to about the last two decades of the eighteenth century, commercial relations between the Europeans and the Africans on the West Coast of Africa were generally based on the slave trade. However, by the second half of the eighteenth century, the heinous trade in slaves had started to wane. In 1787, some 411 freed black slaves and their white friends from England landed in Freetown of Sierra Leone, a portion of the country that subsequently became a colony of Britain. They found a "Province of Freedom," and the new settle was called Granville Town, a tribute to the work of Granville Sharp (1735–1813), a philanthropist and abolitionist member of the British Parliament who founded the Province of Freedom for the resettlement of former slaves (Fyle, 2006, p. xvii). The shift to industrialization and torment of human conscience made the human cargo less attractive.[1]

The Province of Freedom was burnt down in 1789 because the suzerainty of King Tom, the local chief who had provided land for the settlement, was not recognized by the leader of the settlement. In 1791, the Sierra Leone Company, consisting of British philanthropists and businessmen, reestablished Granville Town but renamed it Freetown (Fyle, 2006, p. xviii).

Various groups of settlers were repatriated from Nova Scotia after the American War of Independence or interdicted on the high seas and sent to Freetown as Liberated Africans or "Recaptives."[2] In January 1792, about 1,200 freed slaves arrived in Sierra Leone from Nova Scotia (Foray: xxxviii). In 1800, a new group of freed slaves, the Maroons, arrived from Jamaica via Nova Scotia (Fyle, 2006, p. xviii).

The settlers naturally had different levels of exposure and sophistication that made some of them susceptible to discrimination because of their perceived cultural inferiority. For example, the "Recaptives" never made it to America or the Canadian province of Nova Scotia and were deemed to be less sophisticated.

DOI: 10.4324/9781003518464-2

However, as the settlers intermingled and intermarried feelings of superordination and subordination dissipated in the circumstance of status crystallization, status crystallization gave rise to a unique group of hybrid settlers known as the *Creoles* or *Krios*, generally used interchangeably, sharing a language consisting of English and Indigenous vocabulary (patois).

> *From 1800 and thereabout, the British Parliament voted annual subsidies as grants-in aid for the Colony's civil establishment and defense (Foray: xxxix). However, financial challenges, and external threats made it extremely difficult for the company to manage the settlement, even with its laudable goal of ending slavery and embarking on a civilizing mission. The overwhelming problems and financial challenges confronting the company eventually caused the company to cede its political functions to the British Crown and Sierra Leone became a Crown Colony on January 1, 1808.*
>
> (Warburton, 2021, p. 6)

The colonial administration depended on the Creoles to be an integral part of the colonial administration until the 1898 Hut Tax rebellion fomented distrust between the colonial administrators and the Creoles, on the one hand, and the indigenes and the Creoles, on the other. By the end of the nineteenth century, the foundation of ethnic dissension had destructively simmered into the body politic of the country with adverse socio-economic connotations. For example, ethnic dissension created political instability in the 1960s and the ensuing socio-economic disaster that followed shortly thereafter. Nepotism, favoritism, and corruption became the order of the day.

Because of their level of education and exposure to Western civilization, the Creoles functioned as lawyers, educators, doctors, missionaries, and civil servants of the colonial administration. As such, they became the foundational instruments/harbingers of the spread of Christianity and human capital in Sierra Leone. Various schools and the institution of higher learning, Fourah Bay College, emerged as the logical outgrowth to rehabilitate former slaves and spread Western civilization in the tradition of Christianity and Western education. The dynamism of the rise and fall of human capital will be subsequently discussed in this chapter.

Notably, Sierra Leone was ruled as two entities under colonial rule, the Colony and the Protectorate, until independence was forged in 1961 under the notion that the Colony and Protectorate are territorially inseparable as one country – though anachronistic laws still consider the two entities to be legally and judicially separate. The evolutionary implications of political dissonance and macroeconomic mismanagement are sprinkled throughout this book.

1.2 Climatic and geological conditions

Sierra Leone has varied climatic conditions. The dry season, which starts in mid-November, has relatively higher temperatures and humidity. The dry season is followed by a nightly cooling period. The Harmattan, which brings dry winds from the Sahara, ends in mid-February. Hot, humid, and rainless days are experienced till April, after which the wet/rainy season is expected to set in. Recent changes in climatic and weather patterns have reduced the intensity and regularity of rainfall, which increases temperatures and threatens food production.

The southern half of the country lies within the heavy tropical rainforest belt. The northern interior has open savannah woodland (because of relatively less rainfall) with estuaries of major rivers. The climatic and weather conditions have been fortuitous for agriculture; for example, farmers produced over 90 percent of the country's rice consumption in the 1970s (Government of Sierra Leone, 1980, p. 30). The shift from local production to the importation of rice has unfavorably affected the balance of trade of the nation and its reserve position.

The climatic conditions are propitious for the growth of several cash crops, including cocoa, coffee, oil palm, and ginger. Tobacco, cashews, sugarcane, and citrus have constituted great cash crop (domestic consumption) combinations with great external revenue potential. Wild oil palm is extensively grown throughout the country.

In 1978/79, coffee accounted for Le 39.5 million in earnings for the country (Government of Sierra Leone, 1980, p. 48). Coffee has been cultivated in the eastern and southern regions of the country, with impressive yields of robusta and liberica, Cocoa, which requires moisture-retentive soils, is grown in the southeastern part of the country.

Cattle rearing does well in the northern savannah region of the country. In the late 1970s, crossbreeding of the N'dama and the Kenyan Sahiwal led to increased yields of milk production. Sheep, goats, and pigs are also reared in the areas conducive to animal husbandry.

Timber exports have a long history in the country, dating back to the nineteenth century when much of the country was covered by virgin forests. The forests of Sierra Leone can produce mahogany, scented guarea, red ironwood, and afzella africana (hardwoods). However, the Forest Department was formed to promote conservation of the remaining forest. Conservation reduces the rate of soil erosion, which could also be very costly and detrimental to human lives otherwise. The increasing population of the country and the need for food and energy have resulted in some amount of dangerous deforestation, leading to landslides and loss of human lives and property.

The point of salience is that the country has tremendous import-substituting capacities to ensure its development without considerable loss of income and reserves. Nature has provided the country with abundant opportunities to grow and develop without undue national suffering. The country does not only have the agricultural resources to do well, but it is also well endowed with subterranean mineral resources. Until recently, minerals accounted for more than 80 percent of exports and contributed 2.7 percent to GDP. Additional information about mining will be provided during the discussion of the railway infrastructure in this chapter. The next section looks at the rise and fall of human capital in Sierra Leone.

1.3 The rise and fall of human capital

The Christian missionaries laid the foundation for Western human capital in Sierra Leone, and they became responsible for several schools in the suburbs of Freetown and beyond. The fortunes of education were insured by the Governor of Sierra

Leone, Gen. Sir Charles MacCarthy, who ruled from 1814 to 1824 in the capacity of Governor. Prior to the advent of the Governor, Gen. Sir Charles MacCarthy, the relationship between governors and the governed had strenuously deteriorated in Sierra Leone. The governor saw the problem of resettlement in Sierra Leone not in terms of profit maximization but as a matter of administrative and humanitarian reconstruction.

Accordingly, the Governor devised a scheme for reorganizing the liberated Africans (Recaptives) into Christian Communities and vigorously tried to obtain funds from the British treasury. He forged alliances between the British government and the Church Missionary Society (CMS) so that the church can provide the personnel for clergy work and teaching. The Governor divided the colony into 13 parishes, which were supervised by CMS clergymen who were paid by the government (Foray, p. 125).

The British government provided funds for churches, schools, and personages in response to the pressure by the Governor to provide funds or subsidy for the colonial personnel. The Governor also introduced several reforms to break down racial barriers and increase settler participation in the governance of their affairs. Foray writes:

> *In terms of length of tenure, in terms of promoting the welfare of the Recaptives, in terms of establishing cordial relationships between government and the governed, his governorship, if somewhat extravagant in expenditure and visionary in some of its aims, was second to none in 19th-century Sierra Leone.*
>
> (Foray, p. 126)

The CMS and other Christian denominations responded to the call for education expansion in Sierra Leone.

> *Up to 1900, there were three secondary schools for boys and three for girls. The boys' secondary schools were: (1) Sierra Leone Grammar School founded by the Church Missionary Society [C.M.S.] in 1845; (2) Wesleyan Boys' High School founded by the* Wesleyan Methodist Church in 1874; *(3) Leopold Educational Institute, founded by the Rev. L.J.* Leopold in 1884. *The girls' secondary schools: (1) Annie Walsh Memorial School founded by the C.M.*S. in 1845; *(2) Wesleyan Girls' High School opened in 1880 by the Wesleyan Methodist connexion; (3) St. Joseph's Convent, begun as a primary school in 1866.* From 1900 *to 1916 the following additional secondary schools were opened: (1) Albert Academy, founded by the* United Brethren in Christ Mission in 1904; *(2) A.M.E. Seminary opened by the* American Methodist Episcopal Church in 1908; *(3) United Methodist Collegiate [later the W.A.M. Collegiate]*[3] *School founded by the* United Methodist Free Church in 1911.
>
> (Sumner, p. 150)

The country's original institution of higher learning, Fourah Bay College (FBC) started as a Christian institution founded by the Church Missionary Society (CMS) in 1827 to train prospective Anglican priests. In 1876, FBC was granted university college status and affiliated with the University of Durham in England. Many leaders from British West Africa and beyond attended FBC (Fyle, p. 54).

In 1950, the CMS relinquished responsibility for the college and turned its operations over to the Sierra Leone government. Soon after independence, the University Act of 1967 unified FBC and Njala, and the almost 100 years of affiliation with Durham came to an end. In 1977, about 300 students from other African countries attended the university because of its high standards and international reputation (Government of Sierra Leone, 1980, p. 145). Various students from the US also attended the University as exchange students in the 1980s.

By the start of the twentieth century, the CMS had overextended itself and its finances were in bad financial shape. The funds of the society were so depleted that it had to discontinue its activities in the hinterland. The society, which pioneered the establishment of Fourah Bay College, could no longer afford to maximize the operations of the college. Despite its reputable intellectual progress since May 16, 1876, the curricula of the college could not induce enough students to attend the college, which made the college an unviable self-supporting institution (Sumner, p. 141).

Other institutions of higher learning followed in short order. Milton Margai Training/Teachers College and Njala University College were established in 1963 and 1964, respectively. Milton Margai was originally intended to be a teacher's college, and Njala, a college of teaching and agrarian orientation. The orientation of Milton Margai has morphed over the years to accommodate changes in education and technology. The nomenclature of Milton Margai college has progressed from Milton Margai Teachers College to Milton Margai College of Education (MMCE) and Milton Margai College of Education and Technology (MMCET).

In the past, Milton Margai College was not affiliated with the university. It concentrated on the supply of teachers for secondary school education but is now currently affiliated with the University of Sierra Leone. It has been upgraded to a degree-awarding institution in selected subject areas. However, the college continues to award Higher Teacher Certificates in two years rather than three. The college now offers a B.Ed. degree. Those with HTC and two years of teaching experience (post-HTC graduation) could spend two years to obtain the B.Ed. degree.

Formal education in the hinterland gravely lagged behind that of the colony until the establishment of the Bo School in 1906. However, the first mention of Protectorate education (technical schools for carpentry and building) in official reports was in 1895 (Sumner, p. 133). In the nineteenth century, Christian missionaries made incursions into the tribal areas of Sierra Leone to spread Christianity and the Western form of education. They were able to infiltrate northern and southern frontiers though they met strong opposition in the north with strong Islamic influences (see Table 1.1). Nevertheless, the establishment of the Bo School expanded a nuanced form of education in the hinterland.

The establishment of the Bo School provided a major boost to the moral of formal education in the interior, but the Bo School was originally intended to be different from the schools of Colony. The educational philosophy at the time had shifted from Western orientation to traditional orientation because of the fierce opposition to colonial rule in the hinterland by the late 1890s. The curricula of

Table 1.1 Educational expansion into tribal areas

Ethnicity	*Year*	*Ethnicity*	*Year*
Creole	1787	Koranko	1897
Bullom (NW)	1812	Yalunka	1897
Susu	1817	Kono	1910
Temene	1840	Krim	1912
Sherbro	1842	Galinas	1923
Bullom (S)	1855	Gola	1923
Mende	1882	Kissi	1947
Loko	1891		

Source: Sumner, p. 268.

schools in the hinterland were localized to be compatible with the immediate cultural and environmental needs of the natives. Yet the hinterland was less competitive in enrolment.

Matsumoto (2014) finds that the level of educational enrolment was high in Freetown, the colony. In 1900, 7,000 students were enrolled in primary school out of an estimated 14,000 children of primary school age (Sumner, 1963). On the other hand, fewer than 900 children were enrolled out of estimated population of 1,500,000 in the hinterland, the protectorate. Moreover, within the hinterland, too, there was a great discrepancy between regions.

The pioneers of education in the Western region of the country were missionaries who had clearly defined purposes for their brand of religious orthodoxy and standardized education, generally intentional in the spread of denominational Christian beliefs, while also preparing the students to occupy vacant spaces of clergymen, doctors, lawyers, and teachers in the country – an opportunity for emancipated slaves and indigenes to become economically independent.

By the turn of the twentieth century, the colonial administration did not share the ambitious educational philosophy of the Christian missionaries. The Hut Tax War of 1898, which had fractured the relationship between officials of the colonial administration and the Creoles, and the Creoles and the indigenes, generated distaste for the proliferation of Western education in the hinterland. The repugnance of the proliferation was very palpable[4] and captured by the Bo School prospectus of 1906, an announcement of the bifurcated educational philosophy at the time:

> *From the beginning of the Institution, the pupils will be taught that Labour is as necessary a part of Education as a knowledge of Reading, Writing, and Arithmetic. The main and primary object of the teaching will be to train the sons of chiefs in such a manner as to make them good and useful rulers of the country in the future . . . . It is not the intention of the Government to employ any of the pupils after they shall have passed through the school . . . . Each pupil [was] expected to bring 1 Country Gown, 1 White Gown, 3 Kerchiefs, 1 Cap, 1 Hammock (optional), [and] 1 Mat (country).*
>
> (Fyfe, pp. 304–5)

The post-colonial format and structure of education in Sierra Leone did not deviate from the colonial paradigm to any significant extent, except for salaries of teachers. During the 1960s and 1970s, there were vigorous debates about territorial equity between the Western area and the hinterland, universal education, and the functionality of education in the hinterland. The United Nations Universal Declaration of Human Rights (1949) had already established that education is a fundamental right.[5] Targets were set to double the enrolment of children in the hinterland schools to bring enrolment in juxtaposition with the Western area. It was estimated that 80 percent of the children had access to schooling in the Western area while only 6 percent had access in the hinterland (Government of Sierra Leone, 1980, pp. 139–140). Not only was enrolment to be increased, but education was also expected to be responsive to the needs of the local communities (Sierra Leone Government, 1958, pp. 1–2).

Between 1976 and 1977, primary school enrolment increased by nearly 60 percent, with the lion's share going to the hinterland because of the drive to obtain inter-regional equity in education between the hinterland with that of the Western area. Enrolment at the secondary school level grew by 100 percent between 1968 and 1976/77 (State House, 1980, pp. 139–140). The capacity to continuously increase human capital came under stringent scrutiny because of the incapacity of the post-colonial countries to absorb increasing levels of human capital in the 1960s. A bifurcated debate ensued.

The theory of human capital and education as a universal human right merged to influence newly independent countries to institute mass education policies for social and economic development (Chabbott & Ramirez, 2000). Despite the broad consensus that schools should be a key component in the planning and growth of national economies, an opposing school of thought questioned the absorptive capacities of newly independent countries in the face of increasing levels of education; for example, Foster (1965) showed how the disparity between an increasing number of school-leavers in Ghana and the low rate of economic expansion led to mass unemployment among the educated. The uncertainties of the escalating levels of education surfaced in the "Conference of African States on the Development of Education in Africa" held in Addis Ababa in 1961. The notion that Western curriculum was not clearly relevant or useful to the lives of many Sierra Leonean students who were in rural areas was recurrent (Banya, 1991, 1993). The goal of achieving universal primary education within two decades was formally established at the meeting, but anxiety about an overproduction of educated people more than what "development" could accommodate also lay at the heart of conference discussions (Pai, 2014).[6]

The intensification of the debates about universal education and growth capacities (e.g., see the work of Abernethy (1969) and Coleman (1965)) led to the Bunumbu Project of the 1970s in Sierra Leone. Furthermore, while the 1960s emphasized the development of secondary and postsecondary education to meet the shortage of skilled manpower, the modern industrial sector began to stagnate in the 1970s. In the 1970s, school enrollment remained higher in the Western area (near Freetown) as was the quality of school conditions (Hawes, 1976, p. 3). However, the Sierra

Leonean government was confronted with the task of educating Sierra Leoneans as teachers to replace foreign expatriates. When the All People's Congress (APC) took power in 1968, about 40 percent of the secondary school teachers were foreigners; by 1977 over three-quarters were Sierra Leoneans (Government of Sierra Leone, 1980, p. 141).

To address the stubborn and menacing disparities, as well as retard the increases in enrollment rates, the Stevens administration called for a Sierra Leone Education Review – a comprehensive survey of the education system that brought together staff at the University of Sierra Leone, government administrators, and international consultants for a series of meetings in 1973 (Pai, 2014). A divergent composition of ideas culminated in the Bunumbu Project (1974–late 1980s). In 1974, the Government of Sierra Leone called upon the United Nations Special Fund and UNESCO to assist in implementing the Bunumbu Project – a program designed to make schools more relevant and central to rural communities (Pai, 2014).

Specifically, the project translated the National Development Plan of accelerating primary school expansion into the following strategic objectives: (i) development of a new primary curriculum with a rural bias; (ii) expansion of existing functions of the teacher training colleges, and (iii) development of a country-wide network of community educational centers providing both formal and non-formal education and training for young people and adults in the rural areas (UNESCO, 1983, p. 2). To achieve the larger goal of rural development, the Bunumbu Project attempted to redesign curricula and integrate schools into the "community." The program became a mixed success for a variety of reasons, including the absence of a clear definition of program targets and shifting goals.[7]

The Bunumbu model was well-intentioned but handicapped by misguided assumptions of the time. It assumed that human capital should be territorially immobile, and it failed to map out innovative sectors that could absorb the growth of human capital, mostly because of the incapacity of the social planners to plan beyond development that was circumscribed by the tripartite sectors of agriculture, manufacturing, and the civil service. Universal education could be more meaningful today if African social planners could properly target civil and mechanical engineering, digital technology, energy supply (especially solar and wind), teaching, insurance, infrastructure, conservation science, data science, law enforcement, health science and pharmacology, waste disposal and processing, water well technology, and the tertiary programs for developing rudimentary education.

The opportunities for employing functional human capital during the formative stages of the development of any country are just too extensive even when human capital is presumed to be territorially immobile. The central issue is whether social planners are willing to embrace broad-based economic growth and development to accommodate the expanding pool of newer talents for a given period, say 10 or 20 years. In fact, private companies (domestic and foreign) could always utilize a surfeit of competitive human capital at competitive cost. Hence, the public sector need not be the sole employer of expanding human capital though the public sector could play a dominant role in the employment of an expanding human capital. It is always helpful to attract long-term investments in areas of developmental need. Further, could the beneficiaries of expanding human capital be innovators and skilled entrepreneurs? It is hardly a good idea to stifle the innovative capacity of any country. Innovation is always waiting for the creativity of somebody.

The assumptions of capital immobility in the 1960s and 1970s, aversion of excess accumulation of human capital, occurrences of disinflation programs, and lack of innovative uses of human capital during a developmental phase did not augur well for the expansion of human capital after the 1980s. Literacy rates plunged to abysmal levels, public investment in education dwindled, and government spending as a percentage of GDP flatlined around 2.5 percent for nearly a decade by the turn of the twentieth century (see Figure 1.4). Teachers earned horrifying incomes, and the country was gripped by brain-drain syndrome. That is, education was insidiously collapsing.

The 2015 Population and Housing Census paints a very bleak picture of education in Sierra Leone – a stunning reversal of the once prosperous trajectory. Forty-nine percent of the population was illiterate in 2015, and the inequities in the territorial distribution of literacy remained unresolved. Thirty-seven percent of the rural population was literate compared to an urban proportion of 70 percent (Statistics Sierra Leone, SSL, p. 3). Educational achievements are marked by gender disparities (see Table 1.2).

Households with no female education exceed those of males with no education. In all, categories of education households with males have outperformed households with females. Notwithstanding, the gap between adult male and female literacy rates has been shrinking between 2004 and 2022 (see Figure 1.1). Yet the growth in adult literacy has not measured up with comparable cohort countries in the subregion (see Figure 1.2).

Between the 1985 and the 2015 censuses, the most notable improvement in access to education was observed in the northern region, especially among females. In 1985, only 10.6 percent were attending school. By 2015, the number increased to 31.1 percent (SSL, p. 210). It is very probable that discrepancies in adult literacy rates affect the performance of Sierra Leonean students in standardized examinations. Accordingly, the deficiency in literacy is not without poignant external effects.

Table 1.2 Highest level of education attained (Statistics Sierra Leone, 2017)

	Total	*Male*	*Female*
No education	56.7	51.6	69.8
Basic school	19.5	20.6	16.6
SSS	13.3	15.4	7.8
Vocational/Technical/Nursing/Teacher Training	4,6	5	3,5
University	3.7	4.4	1,8
Other	2.3	3	0.5

Source: Statistics Sierra Leone (2017, p. 125)

Note: University education includes Higher (First degree) and Tertiary (Post-graduate) and PhD.

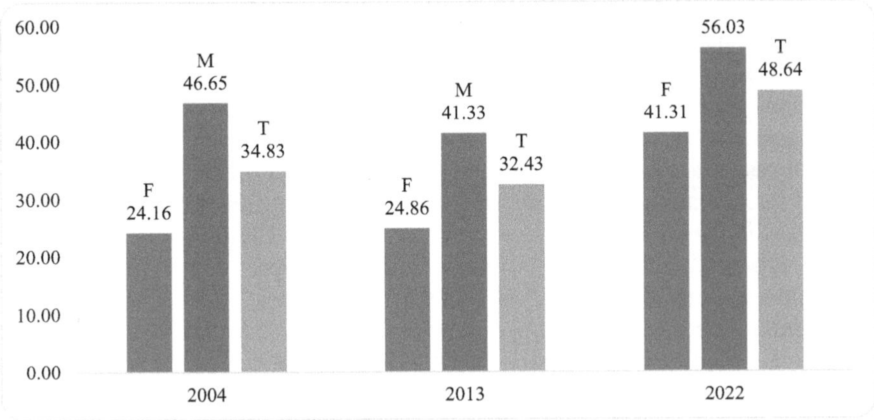

Figure 1.1 Adult literacy rate (2004–2022).

Data source: World Bank's World Development Indicators (WDI) 2023

Note: Adult literacy rate is the percentage of people ages 15 and above who can both read and write with understanding a short simple statement about their everyday life. F = females, M = males, and T = total.

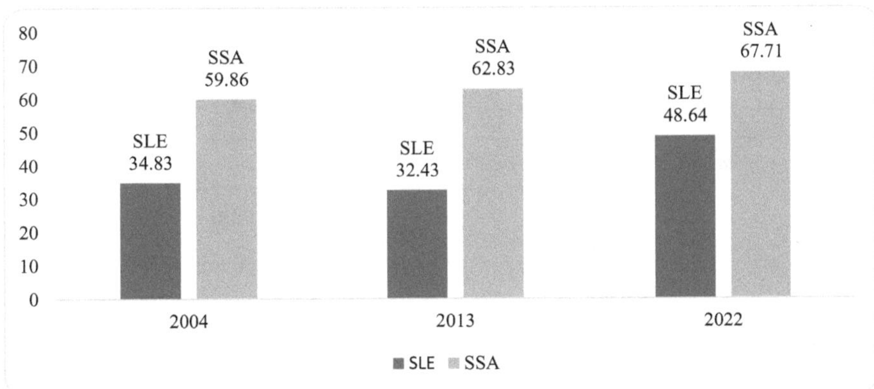

Figure 1.2 Adult literacy rate in Sierra Leone (SLE) and Sub-Saharan Africa (SSA).

Data source: World Bank's World Development Indicators (WDI) 2023

Note: Adult literacy rate is the percentage of people ages 15 and above who can both read and write with understanding a short simple statement about their everyday life. SSA excludes high-income countries. It is made up of countries with gross national income (GNI) per capita of less than 12,535 (at current US dollars) for 2020/21, which is consistent with the general data for this study. We must note that there are further intra-income variations in the sample – low income (<1,036), lower-middle income (1,037–4,045), and upper-middle income (4,046–12,535).[8]

Inadequate human capital has adverse implications for long-term capital flows, productivity, and regional competitiveness. Pointedly, a country with deficient human capital is not likely to attract foreign firms or businesses that require the use of the skills of its local population; long-term capital inflows are stymied. The 2015 census also reveals that most of the consumers (65.3 percent) had no formal education (SSL, p. 5). Consumer education has an impact on the competitive landscape of market structure. Competition thrives when consumers are educated and informed. Literacy also determines the consumption of capital goods, the magnitude of self-employment or job selection, and general productivity of a country; some of these issues will be dealt with in the next chapter.

In terms of occupation, 74.2 percent of the population with no education was engaged in agricultural and fishery activities and 13.4 percent were service workers. Similar percentages for persons with basic education were 47.0 percent and 24.7 percent; and for those with senior secondary education the proportions were 17.4 percent and 33.0 percent. Professional occupations prevail among those with vocational, technical, nursing, and teaching skills at 50.4 percent, first degree at 46.8 percent, and higher levels of education at 48.9 percent (SSL, p. 231).

High levels of educational attainment tend to be correlated with a high proportion of ownership of durable (capital) goods. For instance, household heads with tertiary and higher education topped the list of ownership of all durable goods, except boats (SSL, P. 4); see Table 1.3. Residents with tertiary qualifications outperformed others in all categories of the list of selected capital goods. Meanwhile, some of these goods are essential irrespective of the level of education. That is, the level of education confers inequitable privileges on those with upper tier education. Notably, access to computers and generators is important for increasing overall

Table 1.3 Human capital and ownership of capital goods (%)

Household capital goods	*Voc//Tech/Nursing/ Teacher training*	*Higher*	*Tertiary*
		(First Degree)	*(Post-graduate and PhD)*
No. of HH	58,085	33,487	13,063
Total	100	100	100
Generator	21.8	37.9	47.5
Fridge/Freezer	28.4	54.1	61.7
Television	48.3	73.3	75.4
Computer	19.6	46.4	53.3
Radio	88.5	89.8	90.6
Mobile Phone	92.5	96.2	95.9
Bicycle	12.8	15.5	18.7
Motorcycle	17.2	17.6	17.5
Car	8.6	26.9	39.2
Truck	1.1	2.8	4.2

Source: Statistics Sierra Leone (2017) Population and Housing Census, p. 351

Note: A truncated table.

productivity. Disparities in the ownership of mobile phones (useful for mobile banking inter alia) and radios are not unreasonably high.

Educational inequities are intimately related to deprivation, which is measured by years of schooling (attainment) and school attendance. In the 2015 census, a household is considered deprived if no member has completed at least six years of schooling (primary education).

> *Consequently, the educational attainment indicator is described as "primary school completion" since that is precisely what it seeks to measure. For the school attendance indicator, a household is deprived if at least one child of school going age is not in school. Thus, this indicator is aptly referred to as "child school attendance."*
>
> (SSL, p. 329)

For the country, 22.3 percent of households were deprived in 2015. This result is consistent with findings reported by SSL that in 2004, 29 percent of 6- to 11-year-olds had never attended school (Statistics Sierra Leone, 2017) and a decade later, that nearly half (48 percent) of all Sierra Leoneans had never had any formal education. One-third of these were children of school-going age (less than 18 years old) (Statistics Sierra Leone, 2017; SLE, p. 330).

Educational attainment is defined as the highest level of schooling each student attended and successfully completed (UN year). In the education sector, primary school completion is measured by the gross completion rate (GCR) for that level. It is the total number of pupils completing the final year of primary education, regardless of age, expressed as a percentage of the official primary school graduation age.

Quantitative indicators are not holistic representations of academic achievements. They target specific objectives that disclose nothing or implicit information about the quality of education, competence of teachers, and the motivation of teachers and students alike. However, quality education and equitable learning opportunities have not pointedly been obscure policy objectives of the government (Alghali et al., 2005).[9]

Comparatively recent result of standardized test (an objective measure of educational policy) indicates that the educational policies are not generating their intended results, and there is no quick fix to the substandard performance of Sierra Leonean students in competitive external exams (see Figure 1.3). The essential needs for student success are rather enormous – the intensity of poverty, appropriate physical infrastructure, training for teachers, competent staffing, availability of educational equipments, student finance, academic resources, access to digital technology, energy supply, targeted government spending (public investment), and appropriate placements (linkages) after graduation.

Figure 1.3 depicts an unspectacularly poor performance of Sierra Leonean students in the 2020 WASSCE, which raises consternation. Sierra Leone received a 4.5 percent pass rate in five subjects, relative to competing countries of comparable status – Ghana (68.5%), Nigeria (65.8%), and The Gambia (64.8%). Yet

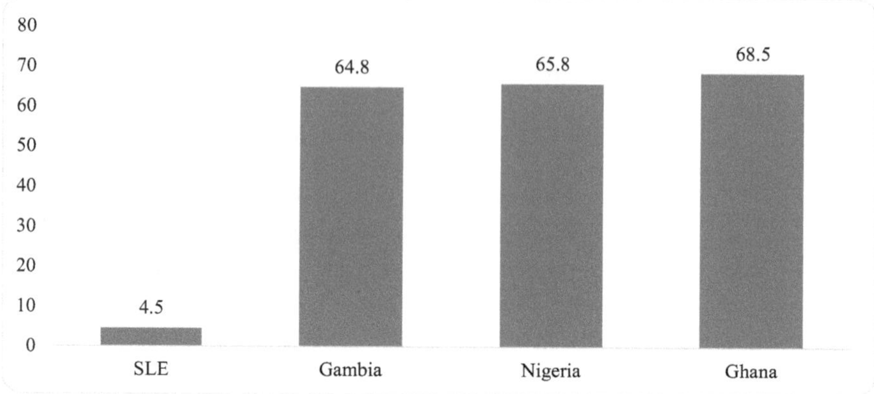

Figure 1.3 WASSCE pass rate in five subjects (2020).

Data sources: Feika (2019) and Mannah (2020)

the lackluster performance of the students in a standardized exam should not be entirely surprising.

> *While some students have succeeded in passing this examination, there has also been a mass failure of poor pupil performance, especially in Sierra Leone. According to the WAEC Statement on the 2017 examination results, published in The Standard Times newspaper, while senior secondary results are improving in Sierra Leone it remains behind other WAEC countries. Almost 40 per cent of students failed to obtain a single WASSCE credit (C6 or better) in 2017 and only 10 per cent received credits in four or more subjects, with just one in 20 per cent obtaining the five credits needed for university entry.*
>
> (Feika, 2019)

Naturally, a substantial number of policymakers do not spend a lot of time thinking about the effects of poverty on academic performance, and how they could go about reducing child poverty. However, there is a wealth of scientific evidence that shows a correlative relationship between academic achievement and socio-economic status. When students are poor and distracted, they tend to perform poorly in standardized and non-standardized academic assessments. Children raised in poverty usually experience emotional and social challenges, chronic stressors, and cognitive lags due to significant changes in brain structure in areas related to memory and emotion (Brito & Noble, 2014; Jensen, 2009). Of course, there are other mundane and banal impediments to learning when the economic wherewithal is lacking, prominent of which are lack of food, transportation (immobility), access to academic information, and financing the purchases of essential academic materials that are necessary for academic success. In 2016, UNICEF discovered that about

Table 1.4 Total schools in Sierra Leone (by ownership, School Census, 2019)

	Community	*Government*	*Mission*	*Other*	*Private*	*Total*
Pre-primary	256	151	721	5	625	**1,758**
Primary	881	1,163	4,412	7	691	**7,154**
J. Secondary	347	166	784	3	333	**1,633**
S. Secondary	95	61	305	1	161	**623**
Total	**1,579**	**1,541**	**6,222**	**16**	**1,810**	**11,168**

Source: Teacher Service Commission Sierra Leone

Note: *The Government owns little more than 16% of schools in Sierra Leone. The majority of schools are mission schools, and there are large numbers of community and private schools. Approximately 60% of schools are approved, meaning that they are government or government-assisted schools – either financially or in other ways. Not all teachers in approved schools are on the government payroll.*

80 percent of the children in Sierra Leone are poor (impoverished or deprived of basic human needs). Once upon a time, the colonial administration and Sierra Leonean government in the 1960s provided books, writing utensils, and food for primary school students.

Policymakers who are committed to closing the achievement gap between students raised in poverty and those raised in more affluent homes or countries need to use the most current research, alter classroom environments, empower students, promote the teaching of social skills, create inclusive classrooms, and recognize the signs of poverty (McKenzie, 2019). Too often, public spending on education is seen as an inconvenience, and education is usually an easy target for budgetary cuts in advanced and poorer economies alike. Such cuts dangerously stifle the prospects of generating competitive human capital and innovators in a highly competitive global economy. Private missionary and secular schools continue to play a dominant role in the provision of education (see Table 1.4).

Apart from the period between 2016 and 2021, government spending on education has hovered around 2.5 percent of GDP before the precipitous drop in government spending on education after 2021 (see Figure 1.4). The precipitous drop in government spending on education from 2021 to c. 2007 level in 2022 partly reflects the squelching effect of disinflationary adjustments on social programs when countries must deal with severe inflationary pressures. Governments are expected to cut expenditures as part of contractionary fiscal policies to achieve some measure of disinflation (reduction in the growth rate of the general level of prices); meaning that the subsidization of social programs will be adversely affected as collateral occurrences during the implementation of painful stabilization programs.

Painful cuts are not new to Sierra Leoneans. In the 1980s, farm subsidies took a hit under stabilization programs, and the cut in educational spending is a sordid reminder of the painful consequences of inflation. In effect, it should be expected that governments would renege on promises to fund social programs like free education during the implementation of punishing stabilization programs. The percentage of GDP that is spent on education is not necessarily a sufficient indicator of meaningful

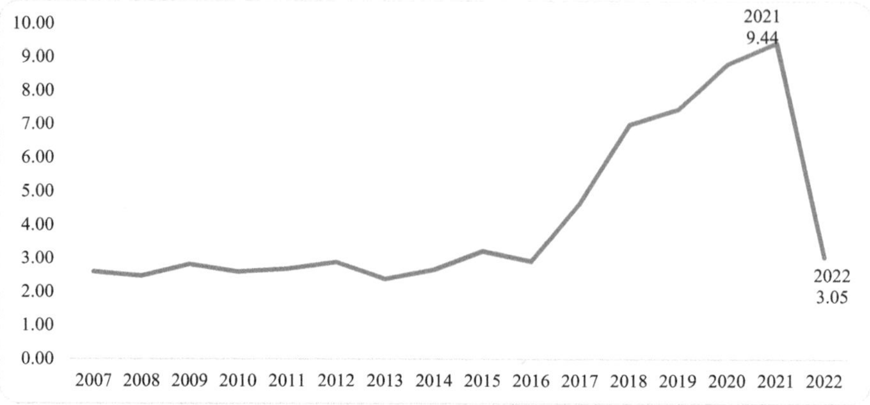

Figure 1.4 Government expenditure on education (total percentage of GDP, 2007–2022).

Data source: World Bank's World Development Indicators (WDI) 2023

Note: General government expenditure on education (current, capital, and transfers) is expressed as a percentage of GDP. It includes expenditure funded by transfers from international sources to government. General government usually refers to local, regional, and central governments.

intervention. The targets and accomplishments of public spending are just as important, if not more important. It is unclear how the spending cuts are going to affect the push for the government's free education policy at the basic (primary and junior secondary) level. Nishimuko (2007) finds that the introduction of a fine or a term of imprisonment (or both) for parents or guardians who do not send their children or wards to school has brought some positive outcomes in terms of increased access to primary education. But the main objectives are yet to be achieved. The fact that over 20 percent of households are deprived shows that a lot more needs to be done to ensure universal education for all children in Sierra Leone (SSL, p. 331).

The brain-drain syndrome, incidence of poverty, and paucity of qualified teachers could only elicit unreasonable demand on students to maximize their academic potential in standardized examinations. At a very critical stage in the educational rung (primary schools), nearly two out of every three teachers are unqualified (see Table 1.5), and nearly a third of all teachers are unqualified. Obviously, these teachers valiantly serve the country by responding to a very critical social need, filling a void as the second-best option when others are unavailable for meager salaries, compounded by the perception that investment in education is worthless. They deserve the much-needed support to transform their professional status for the benefit of students and the country. The inception of the brain-drain syndrome, which will be subsequently addressed, was the result of poor socio-economic conditions and inadequate compensation for teachers – a very important food for thought when pursuing restorative programs – which started in the 1980s.

Reasonable compensation of primary teachers as an incentive has a long history going all the way back to January 1, 1928, when the colonial government mandated the evaluation of teacher qualification for reasonable pay and promotion (Sumner,

Table 1.5 Government teaching staff, 1809–1816.

Year	*Teachers* Males	Females	Total	Salaries
1809	3	3	6	£300
1810	3	3	6	£300
1811	3	3	6	£450
1812	2	2	4	£370
1813	2	2	4	£370
1814	2	2	4	£370
1815	2	2	4	£500
1816	2	2	4	£500

Data source: Sumner, p. 26.

Note: This author (Warburton, C.E.S.) assumes that the salaries are cumulative annual values for the total number of teachers; for example, in 1816, a total of four teachers would have made a cumulative annual amount of £500, which translates to an annual rate of £125 per teacher or about £10.4s per month before decimalization; alternatively, about £1,200 per month in 2023 pounds.

p. 203). Surprisingly, at the time of this writing, twenty-first-century teacher pay in Sierra Leone is below the pay of teachers in 1816 (the nineteenth century). Consider Table 1.5 and the ensuing discussions.

Teachers in Sierra Leone, indeed in most countries of the world, do not get the benefits of cost-of-living adjustments (COLAs). Therefore, their nominal income depreciates rapidly without timely inflationary adjustments.

> *The value of £21,902 in 1816 is equivalent to about £2,632,913.14 in 2023, an increase of £2,611,011.14 over 207 years. The pound had an average inflation rate of 2.34% per year between 1816 and 2023, producing a cumulative price increase of 11,921.34%.*
>
> *This means that today's prices are 120.21 times as high as average prices since 1816, according to the Office for National Statistics composite price index. A pound today only buys 0.832% of what it could buy back then. The inflation rate in 1816 was –8.66%. The current inflation rate compared to last year is now 6.70%. If this number holds, £21,902 today will be equivalent in buying power to £23,369.43 in 2024.*
>
> (official data.org)[10]

The foregoing estimates provide sufficient information to estimate the expected real value of the salary of Sierra Leonean teachers in 2023, based on the 1816 pay structure and the relatively modest rate of inflation in Britain,

where the number of current pounds =

$$1816(\text{£}) * \frac{2023(\text{£})_{PL}}{1816(\text{£})_{PL}} \rightarrow \text{£}125 * 120.21 = \text{£}15{,}026.25.$$

In 2023, the average annual teacher salary in the UK was about £44k. A substantial number of teachers in Sierra Leone will gladly accept £15k annually or the equivalent of £1.252k in leones per month. People are more productive and efficient when they are paid an efficiency wage. Of course, it will be foolish to presume that a nineteenth-century pay structure should prevail 207 years (over two centuries) after the fact. For over two centuries, the governments of the UK have not entertained such a thought though the teachers of the UK will gladly accept a pay raise. The tragedy is that Sierra Leone is not even meeting the nineteenth-century threshold.

The estimated total pay for a Teacher at Ministry of Education in Sierra Leone is SLL 1,000,000 per month in 2023, which is about £40 a month (far less than the expected value (equivalent) of £1.252k a month over two centuries ago). SLL 1,000,000 represents the median, which is the midpoint of the ranges from our proprietary Total Pay Estimate model and based on salaries collected from Glassdoor users (Glassdoor).[11] This suggests that the teachers of Sierra Leone are being paid less than the teachers of 1816 (or the nineteenth century) after adjusting for inflation (see Table 1.6). It is noteworthy that teacher salary in Sierra Leone has wide variations – about 6,007 (standard deviation) in purchasing power parity terms (2011 dollars) for teachers with permanent contract (Evans et al., p. 11), which is insufficient to repudiate the generality of inadequate compensation of teachers in Sierra Leone.

Clearly, the preconditions for better-quality education need to be improved. There are just too many schools without approved status, partly because policymakers have outsourced the administration of education to the private sector (see Table 1.7). Inordinate privatization of education has inequitable consequences for those who cannot afford to purchase private education to become literate and productive citizens. The increasing cost of education makes private education much more expensive and unstable. It is worth recalling the threats and financial challenges that the missionary proprietors incurred by the turn of the twentieth century after overextending their ambitious operations.

Table 1.6 Teachers by qualification (School Census, 2019)

	Bachelor in Ed	*Masters, PhD + ED*	*HTC (Secondary)*	*HTC (Primary)*	*TC*	*Unqualified*	*Total*
Pre-primary	51	9	123	485	2,206	2,692	**5,566**
Primary	454	39	1,350	5,666	22,875	17,354	**47,738**
J. Secondary	2,615	239	8,679	954	1,841	5,560	**19,888**
S. Secondary	3,666	304	3,029	166	223	2,453	**9,841**
Total	**6,786**	**591**	**13,181**	**7,271**	**27,145**	**28,059**	**83,033**

Source: Teacher Service Commission Sierra Leone

Note: TC= Teacher Certificate and HTC = Higher Teacher Certificate. *The figures above refer to teachers across all schools, including government, community, Mission, and private. Nearly a third of all teachers are unqualified and should either be replaced or become qualified over the next couple of years. Teachers in secondary schools are generally well qualified with many degree holders, but there are still considerable numbers of unqualified teachers at this level.*

In primary schools, nearly two out of every three teachers are unqualified. Some teachers who are unqualified may be partially educated in teaching, have valuable teaching experience, or have an education that does not directly qualify them for teaching, but is useful.

Table 1.7 Total approved and unapproved schools

	Approved	*Unapproved*
Pre-primary	728	1,030
Primary	4,707	2,447
J. Secondary	1,125	508
S. Secondary	440	183
Total	**7,000**	**4,168**

Source: Teacher Service Commission Sierra Leone.

Note: For a school to be approved, it must meet certain criteria in terms of the number of qualified teachers, facilities, etc. While the approval of schools is a ministerial responsibility, the teaching service must ensure that the majority of teachers are qualified to deliver teaching of a high professional standard through its recruitment and deployment practices, school leadership, and through provision of professional development.

The relatively substandard academic performance of the Sierra Leonean students in the standardized test of 2020 should not be instantly baffling. The gap in adult literacy (15 years and above) rate between Sierra Leone and similarly situated countries of the subregion has been chasmic (see Figure 1.3). Sierra Leone has moved up from about 35 percent in 2004 to about 49 percent in 2022. Yet the adult literacy rate in the benchmark countries of the region has ranged from about 60 percent to 68 percent over the same period. Sierra Leone is slowly converging, but its adult literacy rate is rather disappointing for a country that was once highly regarded as the "Athens of West Africa."

1.4 Land tenure, agriculture, and mining

Sierra Leone has about 28,000 square miles (72.500 km^2) of land, of which an average of about 55 percent was used for agriculture between 2010 and 2021. A greater portion of the land area of the country (26,700 square miles of land) forest is under closed forest, including a large portion of secondary forest caused by shifting cultivation (Renner-Thomas, p. 3). The southern half of the country is within the heavy tropical forest belt while the northern interior, with relatively less rainfall, is made up of grassland mixed with mangrove swamps (open savannah woodland). In 2010, about 80 percent of the population depended on land for their living, with the majority engaged in subsistence farming. Accordingly, the land is not optimally utilized for commercial agriculture and national income.

All civilized laws are expected to have utilitarian effect. That is, civilized laws are made to attain the greatest good for the greatest number of people. I have deliberately decided not to use "developed countries" as a paradigm because not all "developed countries" obey customary laws, general principles of law, and equity (what is reasonable and just without explicit statements of law).

I should note that I allude to "rule utilitarianism" rather than "act utilitarianism." Act utilitarianism is a dangerous conception of utilitarianism because everyone maximizes utility in a self-serving manner without consideration of the common good. Rule utilitarianism necessitates the promulgation of laws and regulations that maximize the sum of utilities across any given population (even though some might be displeased or offended).

Evidently, Sierra Leone has conflicting principles of law within its dual system of laws, and the conflicting principles of laws are incapable of resolving themselves to reflect the quintessential utilitarian principle of law, general principles of law, and equity (fairness); for example, it is inequitable for land to be purchased in one area of the country but not in another. It is equally inequitable for a traditional law to prevent the food security of a nation. A more sensible national policy would be to have land reservations for commercial-scale agriculture, industrialization, mining, and energy generation. That is, there must be an underlying public policy or law to regulate the use of land for the common good.

The land tenure system touches on the principle of the common good to a limited (communal) spatial extent. It has no meaningful or significant national effect on the level of output that is required to sustain the twenty-first-century population of the country while also maintaining a reasonable trade balance with the rest of the world. Pointedly, the chiefs of the hinterland are no longer dealing with the Protectorate population of the 1880s and the British colonial officials (aliens) who needed land for agriculture and extractive purposes. The land tenure system that was extended to the colonial administration is a derivative of ancient Roman law, which treats strangers as outsiders with no inherent or vested interest in the use and safety of property (*usufruct*). The principle did not apply to members (nationals) with vested interest in the use and preservation of property, in this case, land. The laws of all serious nations evolve to meet contemporary challenges (circumstances and needs) for long-run prosperity.

Certainly, a compromise could be worked out with the chiefs for better annual compensation from large-scale farming and other forms of relevant agriculture. Volatile prices for agricultural goods in global markets, which coexist with nonproprietary ownership of land, are disincentives for private investment in commercial-scale farming or agriculture as broadly defined. As should be expected, advanced economies subsidize farming to ensure food security even with proprietary ownership of land. Of course, proprietary ownership of land in a small open economy like Sierra Leone is a double-edged sword. It could also lead to unproductive use of valuable land that endangers the country. Therefore, the issue of land reform is an unavoidable public policy if the country should have any semblance of trade balance, convertible currency in the near or distant future, and food security in the twenty-first century and beyond. Development starts with producing marketable goods and services for domestic and international consumption, investments in infrastructure, and the development of human capital.

For over half a century, traditional land law has proven to be inadequate for the national welfare of the country (assuming we are talking about one country). The land tenure system can no longer guarantee the food security of the country – given the current state of subsistence farming – and the country cannot possibly staunch the bleeding of foreign reserves by importing food and cereal at exorbitant costs. The percentage of people who engage in subsistence agriculture (about 80%

or more) in the country is lopsidedly low for a population that is very capable of growing exponentially; the issue of production and trade balance will be further explored in Chapter 4.

Countries repeal or amend laws when they fall into desuetude (become anachronistic) or become dysfunctional. This means that it is incumbent upon the policymakers of Sierra Leone to preserve what is good about traditional law and repeal or amend what is an impediment to the economic growth and prosperity of the country. Box 1.1(a) is indicative of the magnitude of the national problem, which has festered with increasing costs for more than half of a century. The Western area – with proprietary ownership of land – is spatially inadequate (just too small) to accommodate an overwhelming influx of migrants from the hinterland and out of the country.

Though there has been traditional usage of land in Sierra Leone and other areas of Africa, what is formally considered to be the land tenure system in contemporary Sierra Leone is a colonial construct of the twentieth century. The Protectorate Land Ordinance of 1927 was enacted to regulate the exercise of the former Tribal Authorities (subsequently, Chiefdom Councils) of their power to permit the use and occupation of Protectorate land by nonnatives [essentially, aliens] (Renner-Thomas, p. 22). The way Sierra Leoneans could be perceived as aliens after 1961 is lawfully inconceivable and counterintuitive. Of course, the Ordinance was a by-product of indirect rule that was belatedly instituted in Sierra Leone between 1901 and 1945 after a Crown Colony had been established on January 1, 1808.

Significantly, the Ordinance was issued about three years after a deliberate effort to unify the Colony and the Protectorate under the Slater Constitution of 1924. For the very first time, the colonial administration considered the prospect of unifying the Protectorate and the Colony as one country by enlarging the Legislative Council to accommodate Protectorate representation in the government of what had been the colony.[12] The post-colonial judiciary was equally incapable of reconciling the inconsistent principles of land law in Sierra Leone.

Though the English-type courts were established throughout Sierra Leone, their jurisdiction in matters of land tenure is significantly restricted. Section 21 of the Court Act of 1965 specifically excludes from the High Court's jurisdiction *any action or original proceeding to determine the title to land situated in the Provinces other than leasehold granted under the Provinces Land Act, Cap.122* (Renner-Thomas, p. 30). Specifically, the High Court of Sierra Leone does not have original jurisdiction in matters of land tenure. However, the Magistrate Courts of Sierra Leone were not prevented to exercise original jurisdiction by the law of 1965.

> *Jurisdiction to hear and determine matters involving a question of title to land arising in the Provinces is expressly vested in the Local Courts as part of their general jurisdiction to hear and determine all civil cases governed by customary law.*
>
> (Renner-Thomas, p. 33)

Naturally, the forays of the colonial administration into the hinterland, which accompanied political accommodations of Traditional Authorities, unequivocally showed that land and commercial-scale farming were very important to the pecuniary operations of the colonial administration. Unsurprisingly, by the time of independence in 1961, Sierra Leone was exporting rice that it is now importing at great peril (at great cost). Land was acquired for farming and mining, and the railway infrastructure (to be discussed in the next section) facilitated the transportation of agrarian and mineral products to Freetown for export and colonial income.

In the 1970s, agricultural development was granted some serious consideration and the government subsidized farming until it ran into current account problems after delinking the local currency from the British pound and floating the local currency in the 1980s. By the start of the 1970s, agriculture (broadly defined) was contributing about 40 percent of the country's export income. Livestock, fisheries, and forestry offered the greatest scope of export promotion and import substitution. Subsistence farmers were integrated into the money economy and the Integrated Agricultural Development Program (IADP) optimized agricultural production in various regions after feasibility studies.

Small-scale farmers were provided supervised credit for the purchase of seeds, fertilizers, and equipment in addition to expert advice on improved methods of cultivation. As early as 1923, scientific education and research were already set up to improve farm output. Njala University College was first established as Njala Agricultural Training Institution for training teachers at rural primary schools with a focus on agriculture in later years. The college eventually offered degree-level agricultural training.

In the 1970s, the government also established centers to educate and train farmers to improve techniques of crop production and pest control. A Rice Research Station in Rokupr helped to foster increases in the acreage of swap rice. Other initiatives spurred rice production, for example, the Rice Seed Multiplication Programme and the swap rice project under the auspices of the World Food Programme (WFP). Schools encouraged students to develop gardens to learn the basics of farming. Thus, farming had a strong foothold in the immediate post-colonial period before the 1980s when things started to unravel.

The climatic conditions of the country are favorable for a variety of products, including cassava, groundnuts, oil palm (that induced the construction of the railway in the 1890s), coffee (*robusta* and *liberica*), cocoa, piassava, ginger, sugar cane, and assorted categories of fruits. Invariably, some of these products have been produced for internal consumption as cash crops. The investment opportunities for large-scale production of some of these products are by no means trivial. Other categories of agriculture include forestry, livestock, and fishing. Land is equally useful for mining. After the discovery of diamonds in Kono District in 1930, the mining sector became an alternative to the agricultural sector for farmers who wanted to become richer. However, the colonial administration was rather disciplined in maintaining a balance between food production and mining. An extensive wave of illicit mining started in the 1950s.

The fortunes of the agricultural sector started to wane after the then government initiated a structural adjustment program in June 1986, agreed to float the leone (local currency), removed subsidies on rice and petroleum, liberalized trade, and increased producer prices. Further, the government had to make substantial payments to creditors. IMF stabilization in the 1980s was very stringent; some of the consequences will be discussed in Chapter 4. The first generation of stabilization programs of the 1980s, the orthodox programs, was much more stringent than the second-generation programs of the heterodox variety.[13] It is noteworthy that by the time the then government started to beg international institutions and creditors for money – that is binding on subsequent generations – the economy of the country had been badly mismanaged and plundered. It is rather puzzling that leaders of very rich countries could be indulged in the business of begging international institutions and creditors for money that will endanger the lives of subsequent generations (the syndrome of debtor profligacy and creditor overindulgence).

Organized mining began in the 1920s with bauxite first being recorded in 1920 along the Falaba to Waia road. Diamonds were found in the early 1930s; from 1934 to 1956, the Sierra Leone Selection Trust (SLST) held the monopoly for mining, prospecting for and marketing diamonds throughout Sierra Leone. The Consolidated African Selection Trust Ltd (CAST), which owned mining operation around West Africa, provided the initial capital for the SLST (Greenhalgh, p. 3).

Unlike diamond mining, mining for rutile started much later. It started during the waning years of colonial rule. In 1955, the British Titan Products Company was granted an exclusive prospecting license covering about 2,000 square miles of the Bonthe and Moyamba Districts (Fyle, p. 187). In 1964, the company teamed up with the Pittsburgh Plate and Glass Company of the United States to form the Sherbro Mineral Rutile Company (SMRC). The first shipment of rutile was made in May 1967. The SMRC ceased operations in 1971 but was replaced by Sierra Rutile Ltd. in 1972. In 1989, a new agreement between Sierra Rutile and the Sierra Leone government gave the government increased revenue from rutile mining. Instability in the hinterland caused the company to suspend operations in 1995, but a new agreement was signed in 2001.

Mining has been the mainstay of the economy since independence and subsequent governments have heavily relied on mining. In 2018, mining contributed 0.7 percent to GDP, constituted 65 percent of export earnings, and 3 percent of employment. Sierra Leone has been prominently associated with vast endowment in minerals which include diamonds, rutile, bauxite, gold, iron ore, limonite, platinum, chromite, coltan, tantalite, columbite, and zircon. The pioneers of the more than a decade-long civil war (1991–2002) were implicated in diamond smuggling and the violent ambition to control the diamond fields of Sierra Leone. Thus, there is abundant evidence that farming and mining were indispensable to economic growth during the early stages of post-colonial rule. A railway infrastructure was developed to facilitate large-scale production and transportation of agricultural and mining products from the hinterland to Freetown for international trade and income.

1.5 The railway infrastructure

Railways serve a useful purpose for the development of any nation. It is very common for railway infrastructure to be subsidized by governments because of the positive externalities that are associated with rail transportation and economic growth and development. Railways are naturally good for hauling products and efficiently transporting people to and from work. As such, railways constitute one of the most efficient systems for economic and social integration. Therefore, advanced economies efficiently use railways to transport goods and people across domestic and international territorial spaces. In fact, Britain, a former colonial power of Sierra Leone, has one of the most efficient, if not the most efficient systems of rail transportation in the world to ease congestion, haul products, and expeditiously take people to productive work. Further, rail transportation is also good for reducing the toxic emissions from cars, trucks, and other polluting systems of transportation.

The now-defunct railway system of Sierra Leone was established by Britain in 1906 during the period of colonial rule. It took slightly over a decade to construct the railway, which started in 1895. The railway provided a mechanism to transport iron ore from Lunsar, palm products from the eastern part of the country to Freetown (see Box 1.1(a)), and administrative officials to and from work from Hill Station to Freetown. The eastern part of the country was naturally propitious for a robust growth of palm product that could generate substantial national income.

The rail moved from Freetown to the eastern terminus at Pendembu, some 220 miles eastward. In 1916, a branch line was added that left Bunya and went northward to Makeni, covering 83 miles (Fyle, p. 184). Before mining could start under the auspices of the Sierra Leone Development Company (DELCO) in 1930, a 52-mile railway track had to be constructed to convey heavy iron ore from Lunsar.[14] The Lunsar rail project was divided into two sections, one from Sahr Maranak Bridge to Marampa (about 26 miles), and another in the opposite direction from Sahr Maranak Bridge to Pepel.

DELCO mined iron ore in Sierra Leone from 1930 to 1975 after the discovery of iron ore in Marampa (in the northern province) in 1926. Iron ore was Sierra Leone's second major export, but the company started to incur increasing cost of production by the early 1970s. The company closed its mining operations in November 1975 as export prices started to decline. To resuscitate the mining operations, the government of Sierra Leone, with limited success, tried to incentivize other companies. The ephemeral operations of Austromineral Gas (MBH), a successor company, ended in 1984.

In a memorandum of 1964, the Government of Sierra Leone reaffirmed the usefulness of the railway for economic growth and development and provided proposals to widen the narrower gauge from 2 ft 6 in to 3ft 6 in (Pratt, p. 145). A rough and tentative estimate was provided for the expansion of the gauge in British pounds is provided in Table 1.8.

Fyle (2006) reports that the railway revolutionized the transportation of agricultural and manufacturing goods to and from Freetown, and it became the most important conduit for the movement of Western goods and ideas from Freetown (the capital of Sierra Leone) to the protectorate. Railway workers became one of the largest groups of workers in Sierra Leone, and they attempted to unionize for better working conditions. Collective activities led to two major work stoppages in 1919 and 1926. The colonial government started to complain about operational losses in the 1940s, and such complaints continued into the post-colonial period.

Table 1.8 Cost of gauge expansion

Object	*Cost (£, thousand)*
Surveys	£600
Realignment and conversion to 3ft 6 in	£8,100
Bridge strengthening and reconstruction	£1,100
Land acquisition	£100
Locomotives and rolling stock	£5,400
New plant and services	£400
Stock spares	£50
Renewal of buildings	£100
Training and staff	£100
Total	**£16,000**

Source: Pratt, p. 145

The military government led by Andrew Terrence Juxon-Smith phased out the railway in 1968 (Fyle, p. 185).

At the time of this writing, the revitalization of the railway is highly improbable for a variety of reasons: (i) The once robust agricultural (farming) sector of the country, which necessitated the construction of the railway in the first place, is now a pale shadow of its former self; (ii) migration to the city from the uninhabitable sections of the hinterland now makes the restoration of the railway an unproductive proposition; and (iii) African leaders are less tolerant of disruptive collective action. Unless the policymakers of Sierra Leone are strongly invested in balanced regional developments and the resuscitation (revitalization) of the agricultural and mining sectors, the restoration of the railway is an untenable proposition. In fact, there is no reason why the development of newer or innovative products could not necessitate rail transportation, for example, the development of manufacturing products or parts in abandoned areas of the country, assembly of cars, and transportation of people to and from work in manufacturing or productive areas. Sierra Leone, a former exporter of rice, now imports rice and cereal at exorbitant costs that cause problematic trade imbalances and inflation; I fully address this issue in Chapter 4. The post-colonial destruction of the agricultural sector was precipitous and unfortunate.

Self-indulgent corruption plagued the agricultural sector of Sierra Leone at the outset of post-colonial rule. Farmers were robbed and discouraged from engaging in productive farming. Farmers were underpaid and the effacement of the railway caused precious exportable products to rot in the hinterland. Many farmers had to abandon farming in favor of mining or migration to Freetown. There was no sustainable program to grow crops for national self-sufficiency or food security and linkages to industrialization.

In 1949, the Sierra Leone Produce Marketing Board (SLPMB) was set up by the colonial administration to take control of the marketing of agricultural products. It was essentially a buying agent to ensure market access and price stability for the agricultural products of farmers. Prices of agricultural products are naturally volatile in international markets. But in the 1940s, prices for agricultural products were relatively higher, which made it profitable to engage in farming. The farmers made profits that were not properly distributed but invested abroad. The profits were not repatriated after independence, which would not have meant much anyway because of the corruption propensities that infested the post-colonial governments.

Much to the chagrin of the farmers in Sierra Leone, the SLPMB continued its operations as a mechanism of self-enrichment and underpayment of farmers after colonial rule. Farmers sometimes resisted low offers (bids) in favor of much more lucrative outlets in neighboring countries. Unsurprisingly, there were allegations of corruption among board members who enriched themselves on the backs of impoverished farmers. On August 1, 2013, the Sierra Leone Produce Marketing Act dissolved the SLPMB, which was replaced by the Sierra Leone Produce Marketing Company.

1.6 Rural–Urban migration

The concept of rural–urban migration could be discussed without loss of generality. There are invariable reasons why people move from rural areas to urban areas in advanced economies as well as underdeveloped economies. The Harris-Todaro (H-T) model affirms some fundamental premises of the inclination to migrate from rural to urban areas:

- (i) Migration is stimulated primarily by rational economic calculations incorporating cost–benefit analysis.
- (ii) The decision to migrate is contingent on expected rather than actual urban–rural real-wage differentials, where the expected differential is a function of the actual urban–rural real-wage differential and the probability of obtaining work in a city (center of attraction).
- (iii) The probability of obtaining work in a city is directly related to the city's urban employment rate (or inversely related to the city's urban unemployment rate).
- (iv) Migration rates that exceed the urban opportunity growth rates should be anticipated when the expected urban–rural income differentials are expansive (wide). High rates of urban unemployment are directly related to serious imbalance of economic opportunities between urban and rural areas in most underdeveloped economies (Todaro and Smith, p. 362).

The fundamental assumptions of the H-T model follow hereafter.

Intra-country migration from rural to urban areas is virtually always based on a rational migrant's cost–benefit analysis of economic gains. A migrant evaluates the urban–rural differences in expected income rather than actual earnings and weighs all his/her options in rural and urban labor markets to choose the one that maximizes his/her expected gains from migration. That is, actual and potential members of the labor force in a country compare expected incomes in the urban sector (W_U) for a given period with prevailing average rural incomes (W_R). A rational decision maker will migrate from the rural to the urban area if W_U is significantly greater than W_R. It is noteworthy that this inequality is also important for reverse migration.

Many of the rural workers in underdeveloped countries like Sierra Leone who migrate to the urban area, say Freetown, are usually not very well educated for the white-collar jobs that may be unavailable in Freetown. They end up being hawkers and peddlers, vendors, repairmen, itinerant day workers, casual employees, or outrightly unemployed. Entries into low-skilled work and small-scale operations are usually relatively more competitive. Migrants with more sophisticated levels of education like secondary and university education (abysmally few in numbers) are more likely to be employed for higher rates relatively quickly. Analysis of literacy levels (implicitly by English language standards) indicates that 51.4 percent of Sierra Leoneans were literate in 2015, with the majority in the urban areas where 69.7 percent were literate and 37.3 percent of the rural population were literate (Statistics Sierra Leone, 2017, p. 232).

Accordingly, in debating whether to migrate from a sector in the rural area to the urban area within a country, migrants must consider the probabilities of being unemployed (or underemployed) for a considerable amount of time against the positive urban–rural real income differential. Therefore, probabilities are built into the calculus of migrants; low probabilities of landing a job in the urban sector discourage migration, but high probabilities encourage migration. Yet probabilities may be miscalculated. Further, potential migrants may well add adverse living conditions in rural areas into their risk calculus.

The country may be losing able-bodied workers to unemployment in the urban area, because younger migrants are less risk averse and could patiently wait for longer periods as part of their risk calculus. The dominant ages of urban population in Sierra Leone range from 5 to 29 years (see Statistics Sierra Leone, p. 39). The median age for the urban population (20.1 years) was higher than that for the rural population (17.6 years). The higher median age for the urban population is partly attributed to rural–urban migration of population in the middle brackets (Statistics Sierra Leone, p. 78). Incidentally, there is not that much discrepancy in ages between the Western Area Urban district and the Western Area Rural district. The Western Area Urban district had the highest median age of 22.0 years, while Western Area Rural district had a median age of 20 years (Statistics Sierra Leone, p. 81). Figure 1.5 summarizes the main arguments of the H-T model.

The labor demand curves for workers in the rural and urban sectors are given by *RR* and *UU*, respectively.[15] The curves reflect the hiring decisions of employers in the two regions or sectors in the regions, assuming that the rural area is preoccupied with farming, and the urban area is preoccupied with white-collar jobs. The curves show the value of marginal product of labor (VMP_L) – a firm's revenue that is associated with the marginal product of labor. The wage rate (W, cost of labor) would fall as the marginal product of labor falls. In explicit terms, they show the profit-maximizing input usage. Rational employers will be willing to employ workers only to the point where $VMP_L = W$, and preferably when VMP L > W.

What is the unemployment equilibrium between urban expected wages and average rural income? The total labor force (employed and unemployed) in the country is defined by the range of O_R and O_U. In the neoclassical (flexible-wage model) or full employment model that is associated with advanced economies, the labor market for any combination of two sectors clears at $L_R^* L_U^*$ and $W_R^* W_U^*$.

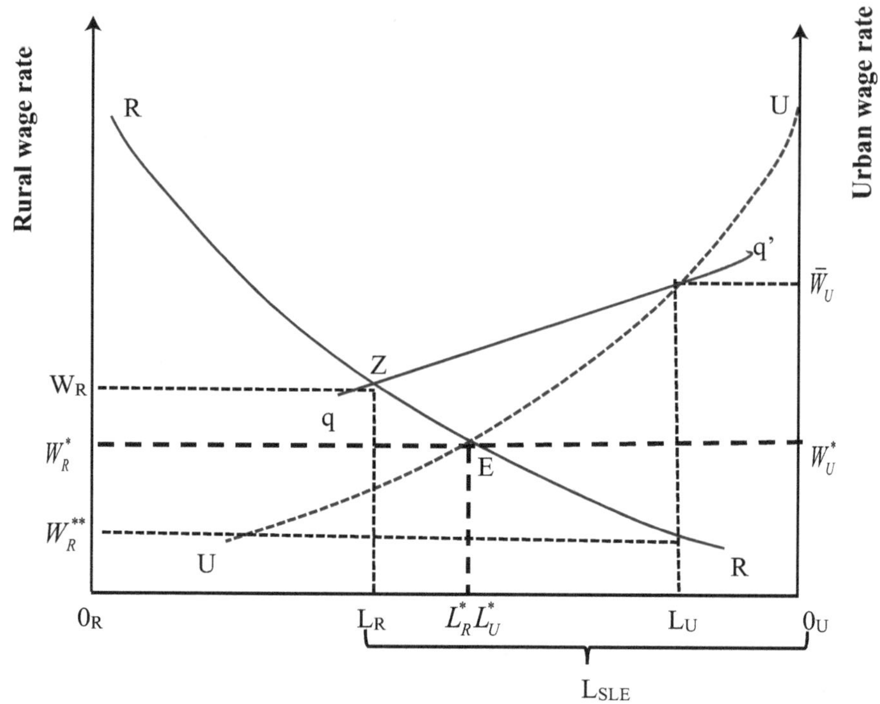

Figure 1.5 The Harris-Todaro migration model.

Source: Todaro and Smith, p. 361

However, when urban wages are institutionally determined (contractual and inflexible downward), there is a discrepancy in wage rates and the number of workers that could be employed in the urban and rural areas. Contractual urban workers will be paid an average of $\bar{W}_U$, which considerably exceeds the neoclassical projection of W_R^*, and only L_U workers will be employed for that wage. Assuming that all those who are looking for a job can get a job, the urban sector will absorb $O_U L_U$, with the residual employment being $O_R L_U$ for a rural employment wage of W_R^*; the urban–rural wage gap becomes $\bar{W}_U - W_R^{**}$. So, even when $O_U L_U$ jobs might be available in Freetown, some migrants will be willing to unproductively tough it out in Freetown. To encourage any form of reverse migration, the wage rate in the rural area (hinterland) must rise above W_R^*. At W_R migrants become indifferent:

$$W_R = \left(\frac{L_U}{L_{SLE}}\right)\bar{W}_U, \qquad 1.1$$

where the LU-to-LSLE ratio is for the labor in the urban sector relative to the employable urban pool of urban workers. Equation 1.1 is indicative of the probability of successfully getting a job in Freetown that equates with the average wage rate in the hinterland; the right-hand side of Equation 1.1 gives the expected urban income. The locus of indifference to job locations is given by qq', with the new unemployment equilibrium at *Z*, which narrows the wage gap to $\bar{W}_U - W_R$ (see Todaro and Smith, pp. 358–362).

The H-T model modestly presents the migration issue as an intra-state migration dichotomy. Realistically, an influx of foreigners has exacerbated the migration problem in Sierra Leone. Since the 1980s and even earlier, a large percentage of migrants in Sierra Leone came from other African countries, 87 percent in 1963, and 85 percent in 1974 (Okoye, 1980). Since most of the migrants were uneducated, their chief motive for relocation was economics (Jarrett, 1990). In 2015, foreigners were mainly enumerated in urban areas, accounting for 72.4 percent (Statistics Sierra Leone, p. 87).

Apart from the African migrants of the twentieth and twenty-first centuries in Sierra Leone, the Lebanese started to move into Freetown (colony) from Guinea and Dakar in Senegal by the end of the nineteenth century.[16] Between 1921 and 1923, the number of "Syrian" migrants in Sierra Leone rose from 184 to 804, and by 1926, there were about 1,077 "Syrians" on the Aliens Register in the colony. It has also been alleged that they played a significant role in the mismanagement of the country's macroeconomy in the 1980s (Fyle, p. 104). Notwithstanding, internal rural–urban migration has been the most dominant form of migration in the country.

The 2004 census estimates the internal migration rate to be 21.6 percent. However, in the 2015 population census, the resident population born outside their districts of residence has risen to 24.8 percent, with the Western area accounting for 54.5 percent of lifetime in-migration (Statistics Sierra Leone, 2017). In the 2015 census, it was reported that the "Western region" received the most migrants from all other regions, with 57.9 percent of the total immigrant population, increasing the movement from the hinterland to Freetown (see Box 1.1 (a) for perspective of movements). It is projected that there will be some amount of reverse discrimination because of public investments in agriculture and mining.

The 2015 urban growth rate of 4.2 percent indicated a faster growth rate than the corresponding value for the rural areas (2.6 percent) (Statistics Sierra Leone, p. 3), which necessitates competition for limited jobs and puts a considerable strain on the limited educational and health facilities in the urban area of Freetown. The Western Area Urban district (Freetown City) was the most populous district in the country in 2015, with a population of 1.1 million persons, contributing 14.9 percent of the total population (Statistics Sierra Leone, p. 68).[17] In the 1970s, multiple authors, including Byerlee (1974) and Todaro (1971), attributed rural–urban migration to price distortions such as high urban wage rates and low agricultural prices, particularly for export crops (see also Figure 1.1(a)).

The burden that migration exerted on the urban labor market of Freetown in the 1970s was estimated to be growing at a rate of 5.5 percent annually, which exceeded employment in large-scale (formal) sectors by about 3.5 percent annually. Given that about half of the urban labor force was employed in large-scale sectors, the implied growth rate of the labor force which must be absorbed in small-scale (informal) sectors or become unemployed was estimated to be about 10 percent (Byerlee et al., p. 2). Demographically, the rural–urban migrants of the 1970s were relatively younger and more educated than the residents who were left behind. The age disparities show that the younger migrants adjust their risk calculus to prolong their stay in cities without a competing indifference to rural wage (see Figure 1.1 for the persistence of friction in the labor markets and the suboptimal rural wage rate).

The festering problems of rural–urban migration in Sierra Leone, induced by geographically (spatially) skewed economic opportunities, is a challenging phenomenon that could only be ignored at the great peril of economic deterioration. Of course, if the social planners of Sierra Leone would like to preserve the traditional policy that was blessed by the colonial administration, then the planners must surely find a way to compensate the chiefs to promote commercial-grade agriculture for food security and trade equilibrium. Significantly, it is counterintuitive for an independent country to have bifurcated laws that are detrimental to its national welfare.

Box 1.1(a) is instantly revealing of the national problem at hand. It strains credulity to understand why people without the sophisticated skill sets required for white-collar and professional jobs in Freetown will move away from free (communal) land in the hinterland to costly capitalist land in the Western area that requires relatively sophisticated skills for employment and survival. Apart from fleeing persecution and oppression – as noted earlier – people migrate for economic reasons after calculating risk calculus. They generally do not have jobs, access to education, affordable health care, essential energy supply, or affordable means of communication. Pointedly, to reverse the trend of migration, people must be given incentives to stay in their local communities. Alternatively, social planners must target the "indifference wage" in the rural areas (see Figure 1.1) via regional development programs and socio-economic opportunities, realizing that three-quarters of the paid employed population are in urban areas (Statistics Sierra Leone, p. 4).

Unproductive and underproductive lands that are incapable of attracting private investments could be revitalized and reoriented toward national purposes, for example, commercial-scale agriculture, industrialization, infrastructure, hospitals (or health centers), and energy production inter alia. Meaningful reconstruction could create thousands of high-paying jobs, eagerly sought incomes by idle residents in Freetown, tax revenue for the government, "balanced trade," increase in the value of the local currency, and the provision of food security for the country. The purposeful implementation of growth options will reduce idleness, vagabondary, trade deficits (associated with the importation of rice and cereal), loss of reserves, and depreciation or devaluation of the local currency. Balanced regional development is indispensable to the reversal of rural–urban migration and economic growth and development.

Box 1.1(a) Land ownership and net migration

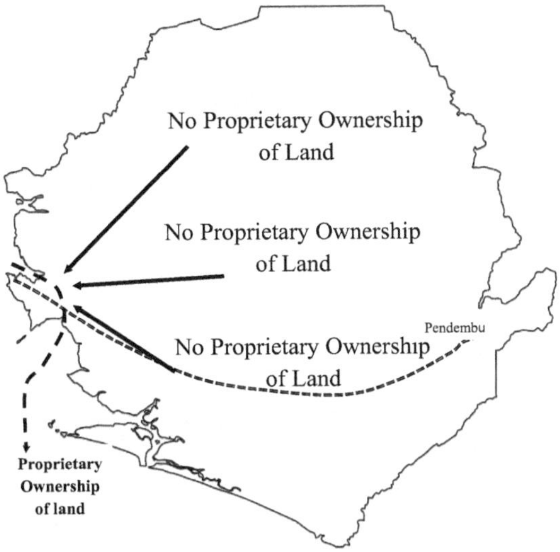

Source: All inserts are by the author. A rail track from Freetown to Pendembu has been superimposed; see Sumner, p. 161, for feeder roads from the track to towns in 1910.

Box 1.1(b) Major cities and towns of Sierra Leone

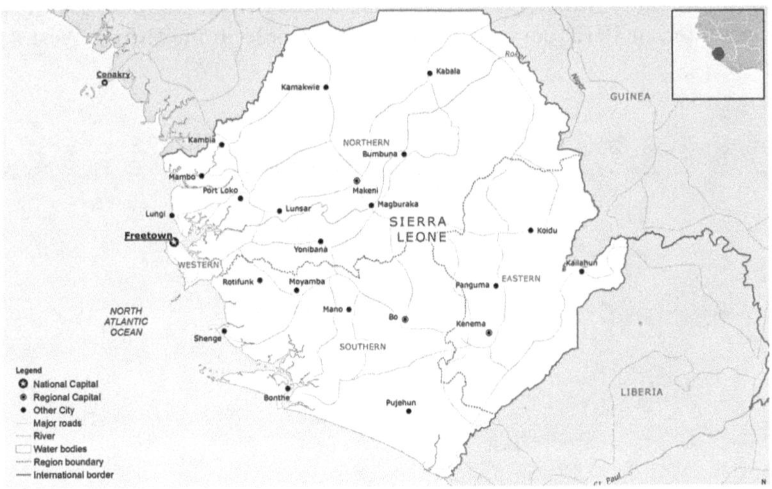

Source: JRC, European Commission, CC BY 4.0, via Wikimedia Commons

1.7 Monetary policy and the general price level

The Bank of Sierra Leone (BSL) was established by the Bank of Sierra Leone Act of 1963. The statutory functions of the bank as prescribed under Section 5 of the Act are not any different from those of most central banks in the world: (i) to issue the legal tender (currency) of the nation (see Box 1.2), (ii) to maintain external reserves to safeguard the value of the currency, (iii) to bank for the government and provide public policy advise, and (iv) to provide monetary stability and a sound financial structure. However, the 1963 Act did not give the bank any mandate to target full employment.

The 1963 Act was amended in 1970 to tie credit and exchange conditions to the balanced growth of the economy. Additionally, the bank was expected to maintain reserves that would cover three months' worth of imports, based on the value of the three preceding years. The bank issued its own notes and coins for the first time on August 4, 1964. The bank has reasonably met its mandate of maintaining stable economic growth (see Figure 1.6). The targeted band of fluctuation is imprecise, and it is unclear whether a monetary policy rule or discretion is used for price stability. Notwithstanding, real GDP growth seems to tightly hover around ±2 percent.

The 1991–2002 civil war adversely affected the performance of economic activity. The economy exceeded its long-run equilibrium to a peak of about 26 percent GDP growth after recovering from the war, loss of human lives, and destruction of capital. The Ebola breakout (2014–16) also negatively impacted the economic performance of the country. In many ways, the Ebola outbreak seemed to have prepared the country to properly react to the COVID-19 pandemic. Unlike the millions of deaths that were reported elsewhere in the world, the World Health Organization (WHO) reports that from January 3, 2020, to November 30, 2023, there were 7,766 COVID-19 cases, resulting in 125 deaths.

Prior to the Bank Act of 1963, the British West African Currency Board, which was constituted in 1912, controlled the money supply in the British West African

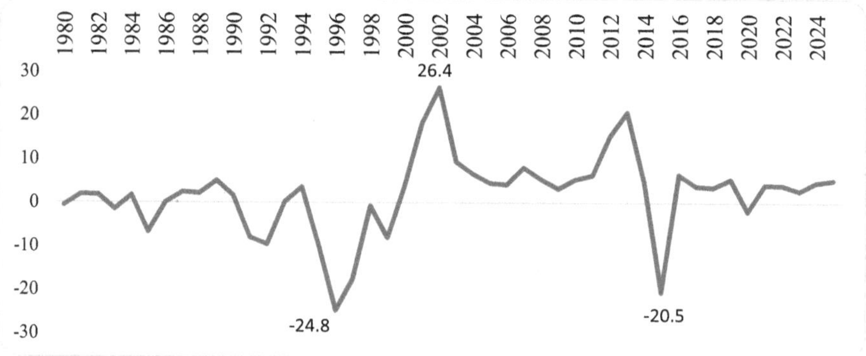

Figure 1.6 Real GDP growth (1980–2025).

Data source: IMF (World Economic Outlook, October 2023)

Colonies. The West African Currency Board currencies circulated in the British colonies of Nigeria, Ghana, the Gambia, and Sierra Leone. The linking of the leone to the British pound guaranteed convertibility of the leone and put less pressure on the central bank to a maintain reserves. That is, the leone was instantly a reserve currency. Indeed, in the immediate post-colonial period, a US dollar could fetch about 75 Sierra Leonean cents. The delinking of the leone in 1980s created impracticalities to maintain price stability and balanced growth for a country that was not competitive in international markets to boost its reserves.

The bank has been trying to bring down the rate of broad money growth on an annual basis (see Figure 1.7). However, it might be a challenging proposition to attain the targeted objective if the bank is not autonomous and capable of controlling the money supply of depository institutions of the country. Tightening could also increase unemployment and raise the cost of financing long term or investments.

In the 1970s, the bank was highly regarded as one of the best clearing houses in West Africa. Though the bank had its charter in 1963, banking was first introduced to the country in 1898 by the then Bank of West Africa, which subsequently became the Standard Bank of Sierra Leone. After the delinking of the local currency, the leone was subsequently linked to the synthetic reserve, special drawing rights (SDRs) before it was permitted to float in June 1986. The delinking of the leone from the pound during the teething period of development was one of the most fatal and unforgivable errors in the macroeconomic policy of the country. Of course, with hindsight we now know the motive for the movement to the so-called monetary independence – the desire to squander money from the national coffers without any foundation for sustainable development and long-term capital flows that are guaranteed by convertible currencies.

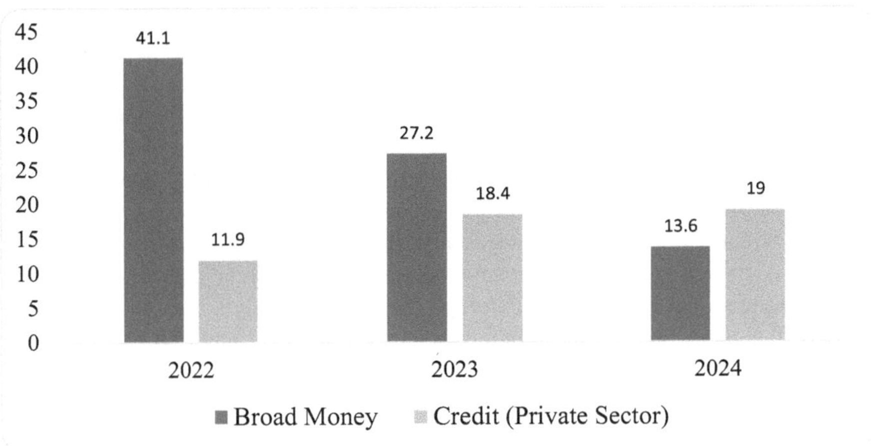

Figure 1.7 Broad money (M2) and credit to the private sector (annual percentage change).
Data source: IMF (World Economic Outlook, October 2023)

The country's first indigenous commercial bank, the Sierra Leone Commercial Bank Ltd., was opened in 1973 as a government-owned depository institution. The government directed its attention to financing agriculture and development in the 1970s, and monetary policy was oriented toward the objective of development. A premium bond scheme was launched in 1978 toward that end. Also playing a vital role in the country's growth and development was the National Development Bank, which was founded in 1968. Aforesaid, the delinking of the leone created intractable balance-of-trade problems, which resulted in the implementation of structural adjustment programs of the International Monetary Fund (IMF) in the 1980s; programs that mandated conditionalities of the "irreducible core" – devaluation, liberalization, and reduction of government spending and subsidies. The stabilization programs circumscribed the ability of the government to provide social spending and public investments, thereby setting the country on the path to backwardness. Clearly, the monetary and fiscal policies of the country were inconsistent with the short-term mandate of the IMF's Articles of Agreement.

> *To give confidence to members by making the general resources of the Fund temporarily available to them under adequate safeguards, thus providing them with opportunity to correct maladjustments in their balance of payments without resorting to measures destructive of national or international prosperity.*
>
> (Art.1,§v)[18]

The country has been saddled with creeping inflation since the global oil crises of the 1970s, but it has episodically and foolishly financed its national debt by *seigniorage*. Some policymakers fail to understand that an inevitable (predictable) outcome of *seigniorage* is inflation and, probably, hyperinflation (inflation spells exceeding 40 percent per month). All policymakers in Africa must quickly understand that inflation is imminent whenever they finance national debts by monetizing them (*seigniorage*). The literature on inertial inflation is abundant, including Warburton (2018, pp. 33–59). Of course, nations with exorbitant privileges (with dominant convertible currencies in international markets) can afford to monetize their debt to a limited extent because of the commanding presence of their currencies in international markets and as reserve currencies in the global economy.

Countries without convertible currencies or without links to reserve currencies (countries with floating regimes) can least afford to monetize their debts as a financing mechanism when they are not adequately increasing real national income or competitiveness in the global economy. *Seigniorage* (SE) is essentially the purchasing power of money that is put in circulation for any given period (Sachs and Larrain, p. 340):

$$SE = \frac{M - M_{-1}}{P} \rightarrow \left[\frac{M - M_{-1}}{M}\right]\left(\frac{M}{P}\right), \qquad 1.2$$

where M is for the stock of money for a given period over the stock of money in a previous period (M_{-1}), P is for the general price level, and M/P is for real money balances, the value of the money stock that is adjusted for inflation, or the real value of money that is in the possession of Sierra Leoneans and foreigners who are inclined to hold the local currency. The latter part of Equation 1.2 shows the product of the change in the stock of money and the real value of the stock of money. The quantity theory of money (Equation 1.3) should clearly help us to see the effects of money growth on the general price level:

$$M\bar{V} = P\bar{Q}, \qquad \log M = \log P, \tag{1.3}$$

where V is for the velocity of money (the number of times a unit of currency is used to purchase output, Q). The regularity with which purchases are made within an economy affirms a theoretical assumption that velocity is relatively constant (does not change much). National output does not change in the market or immediate period, and it could be presumed to be invariable. The two regularity conditions permit us to link money growth directly to the general price level when velocity and output do not change in significant or disturbing ways. The theory might have some resonance in a country that has not been significantly increasing net exports (foreign sales minus domestic absorption). Significantly, the imbalance has been enlarged over the years.

Given the definitions and regularity conditions of Equations 1.2 and 1.3, we can now rewrite Equation 1.2 to reflect changes in the general price level and the inflation tax (IT) (Equations 1.4 and 1.5):

$$\frac{M - M_{-1}}{M} = \frac{P - P_{-1}}{P}, \tag{1.4}$$

$$IT = \left[\frac{(P - P_{-1})}{P}\right]\left(\frac{M}{P}\right). \tag{1.5}$$

IT is indicative of the capital losses of those holding domestic currencies during inflationary periods. Printing and redenominating money are very easy and virtually costless, but the consequences of *seigniorage* are not. The looming question is always whether people will be willing to accept and hold money that is rapidly losing value. History has shown that people are unlikely to hold money that is rapidly losing value. Precipitous loss of a currency's value could lead to *de facto* dollarization if not *de jure* dollarization. The equality of Equation 1.4 must be viewed with some amount of precaution. The equation says nothing about exchange rates and changes in relative interest rates. Therefore, the validity of the inflation tax, as derived from Equation 1.2, is contingent on exchange rate (ε) and the movement of relative interest rates (r*/r) (omitted variables).[19]

Nations with inconvertible currencies and a *seigniorage* capture usually make the mistake of thinking that they could increase interest rate (tighten monetary policy) to prosperity when they come under inflationary pressures. Yet it is important to understand the causes of inflation. What is causing the persistent increase in the general price level to begin with? What are the effects of continuous increases in the policy rate (contractionary monetary policy)? Naturally, inflation could be caused by cheap money (excessive liquidity) and absorption (demand-pull inflation) just as it could also be caused by the cost of production (cost-push inflation) or the paucity of goods for consumption in domestic and foreign markets. Therefore, accurately diagnosing the inflationary problem is essential to providing the appropriate remedies for inflationary pressures. Realistically, apart from cocoa, diamonds, and iron ore, Sierra Leone must start producing goods and services that are attractive to the rest of the world while maintaining a reasonable amount of surplus food security. That is, the country must move to large-scale agriculture (broadly defined) to reduce unnecessary imports (goods that could be produced cheaply at home, based on the country's comparative advantage) and target competitiveness in global markets to increase its export capacity.

By increasing output and revenue – without taxing consumers and businesses to oblivion – the country could also attain price stability by resolving the fundamental friction that is causing loss of foreign reserves (assuming the neutrality of corruption). A lot of Sierra Leoneans are already just too poor to pay higher prices for unavailable food and energy supply. Evidently, the original transgression was *seigniorage*. Governments in the past have been unable to pay for absorption (imports and government expenditures), and they abysmally failed to staunch the bleeding of foreign reserves. To be clear, inflation, which is a sustained increase in the general price level, is just "*too much money* chasing *too few goods*." That is, excess money and the unavailability of goods are indispensable prerequisites for aggregate price increases. Consider Figures 1.8(a) and (b) for a supply-side disruption and correction.

The shortfall in domestic production (or revenue) and foreign absorption pushes the aggregate supply curve to the left, triggering a loss of reserves that puts an upward pressure on the domestic price index (PI). Importantly, the magnitude of the national debt and negative trade imbalances are not going to uneventfully disappear. Alternatively, the country could be staring down the abyss of hyperinflation if it does not quickly correct a deviant trajectory of unsustainable absorption, dwindling productive capacities, and loss of reserves.

A reduction in aggregate supply (or production), loss of competitiveness (or productivity), and plummeting foreign absorption in an open economy cause the aggregate supply (AS) curve to shift to the left from AS_1 to AS_2 (Figure 1.8 (a)), thereby putting an upward pressure on the domestic price index (PI) and causing the index to rise from PI_1 to PI_2. Consumers reduce consumption from NI_1 to NI_2 at a higher price level (PI_2) and the local currency loses value. It is instantly revealing, without loss of generality, that by increasing domestic production via the productivity, international competitiveness, and the foreign absorption channels, the price level (PI_2) could move downward (PI_3) on the path to its original or natural equilibrium. Figure 1.8 (b) shows, as an example, that when the residents of the UK increase their demand for Sierra Leonean goods, the UK will supply more pounds, for leones the Sierra Leonean government will increase its reserves, and the leone

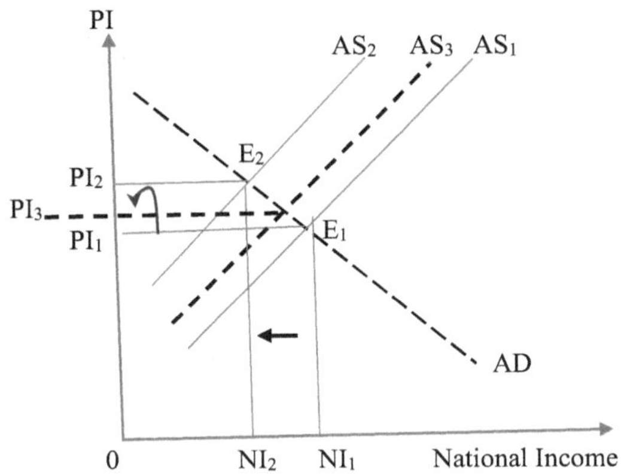

Figure 1.8a Loss of reserves and price instability.

Source: (in a small open economy)

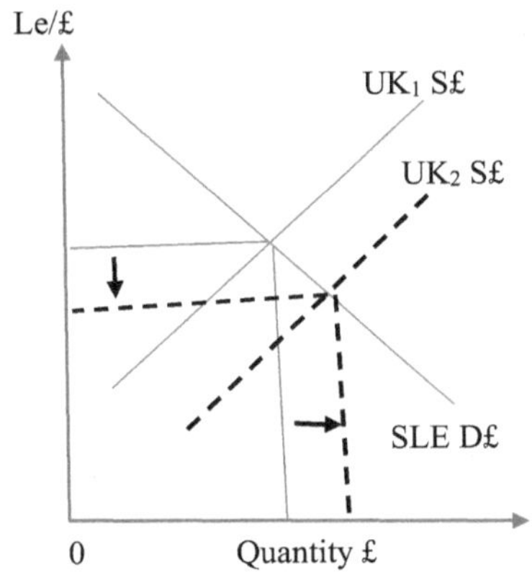

Figure 1.8b Appreciation of the leone.

Source: (in a small open economy)

will gain value in international markets. Notice that less leones will now fetch British pounds. Alternatively, we now have an increase in the supply of British pounds relative to leones. When nations increase the relative supply of their currencies, the value of their currencies will depreciate and appreciate otherwise.

The purchase of Sierra Leonean goods by the residents of the UK is not automatic. Sierra Leoneans must give the residents of the UK (and foreign countries for that matter) reasons to purchase the goods and services that originate from Sierra Leone. The policymakers of Sierra Leone must quickly understand that they cannot penetrate the agricultural markets of the advanced economies of the world. The agrarian markets of advanced economies are subsidized (probably heavily) and heavily protected. This does not mean that Sierra Leone should not produce agricultural products for domestic consumption (food security) and limited exports to regional trading partners. Import substitution limits the loss of precious reserves emanating from the importation of costly rice and grains that could be competitively produced in Sierra Leone, given the comparative advantage of the country. Product diversification is an indispensable requirement for robust international trade, disinflation (slower increases in prices), and economic growth and prosperity. Issues of trade and market penetration will be further developed in Chapters 4 and 5.

Without increases in the depleted reserves of the country, no amount of interest rate hikes, loss of *seigniorage*, and contractionary fiscal policy (increases in taxes and reduction in government spending) could cure the fundamental disequilibrium of the small open economy. While the convenient options are very capable of remediating the problem, they provide no assurances of durable solutions to the country's fundamental disequilibrium and loss of global competitiveness – they paper over the cracks.

Over the years, Sierra Leoneans have become too impoverished to simultaneously provide for their subsistence and national capital accumulation through the saving channel (interest rate hikes). Further, in contradistinction to countries with convertible currencies and stable political systems, interest rate hikes seldom attract long-term capital inflows from stable countries with convertible currencies to unstable countries with inconvertible currencies in a balanced manner. Accordingly, contractionary monetary and fiscal policies are necessary but insufficient preconditions for price stability in a *seigniorage* captured economy with inconvertible currency. The mechanisms for stabilization cannot possibly exclude productivity (cost-reducing measures of production), incentives for long-term investment to prevent capital reversibility, competitiveness, increases in real national output, and acquisition of foreign reserves. Politics and macroeconomics are highly interrelated or interdependent (they have a dual-causal relationship), and they mirror each other in a predetermined manner. When macroeconomics is bad, politics is bad; when macroeconomics is good, politics is also good, and human welfare improves exponentially.

1.8 Corruption and political instability

It did not take long for the Sierra Leonean political elites to start fighting among themselves for the spoils of political power after the British departed the country. Rather than developing a coherent plan for sustainable regional and national development of the country, the Sierra Leonean political elites immediately started to fight among themselves for political power after the pretentious pronouncement that they could govern themselves and the country. The rallying cry was "one country, one people" though the notion of shared national values was patently false.

The basis for the new form of nationalism was abrupt and surprisingly bold for a country that had been ruled as two separate geographical entities (Colony and Protectorate) with arguably irreconcilable cultural sensitivities or animosities. It may well be that the first breed of nationalists was very sincere. Yet the sincerity was hardly estranged from latent opportunism. Like Singapore in the 1960s, it was essential to unify the country around a common purpose for economic development and national prosperity. That sense of urgency was largely lacking in Sierra Leone, and it never filtered through the minds of the political elites who jockeyed for the "independence" of Sierra Leone (this thought of awareness and the lack thereof will be further developed in Chapter 4).

The leaders of Sierra Leone were impulsively determined to kick the British colonial administration out of the country to gain political and economic autonomy (independence) that was wrapped up in a cocoon of selfish ambitions. In the absence of a clear plan for national development (involving all regions of the country) and economic prosperity, Sierra Leoneans were doomed from the very outset of the ill-fated political "independence." Atavistic tribal tensions for personal gain – a cultural proclivity of separateness that the British colonial administration was incapable of eliminating or managing – ravaged the bourgeoning political autonomy without any chance of economic development for the country.

Upon the independence of the country in 1961, Milton Margai became prime minister, and the SLPP became the ruling party. The SLPP and almost all the political parties of Sierra Leone at the time signed the new constitution for independence at the London Constitutional Conference; the APC had reservations and did not fully participate in the conference. The concept of unity was rather estranged, and it certainly had nothing to do with the governance of the country.

In 1964, after succeeding his brother, Sir Milton Margai, Sir Albert Margai became leader of the SLPP and Prime Minister of the country. Albert immediately started to construct new forms of civil–military relations to safeguard his political destiny. Further, plans for a single-party system of government – a thought that was later perfected by the APC under Siaka Stevens in 1978 – started to seep into the political discourse of the nascent country (about three years after political independence).

> *During Sir Albrt Margai's period of rule a fusion of senior army officers and Leading members of the civilian elite became the order of the day. Thus, of the nine most senior officers in the army, seven belonged to "extended families" whose membership played a prominent role in Sierra Leone political life.*
>
> *In some instances, the civilian relatives held political office directly, either as an ordinary member of parliament but more usually as a minister in the government . . . .*
>
> *On the most elementary level, a common ethnic identity helped forged bonds between military officers and civilian "big men" [Brigadier] Lansana and Sir Albert, of course, both belong to the Mende tribe [see Box 1.2] and as Gershon Collier expressed it, "the Force Commander, Brigadier Lansana, was completely loyal to Sir Albert Margai, his tribesman."*
>
> (Cox, p. 65)

Box 1.2 The distribution of major ethnic groups in Sierra Leone

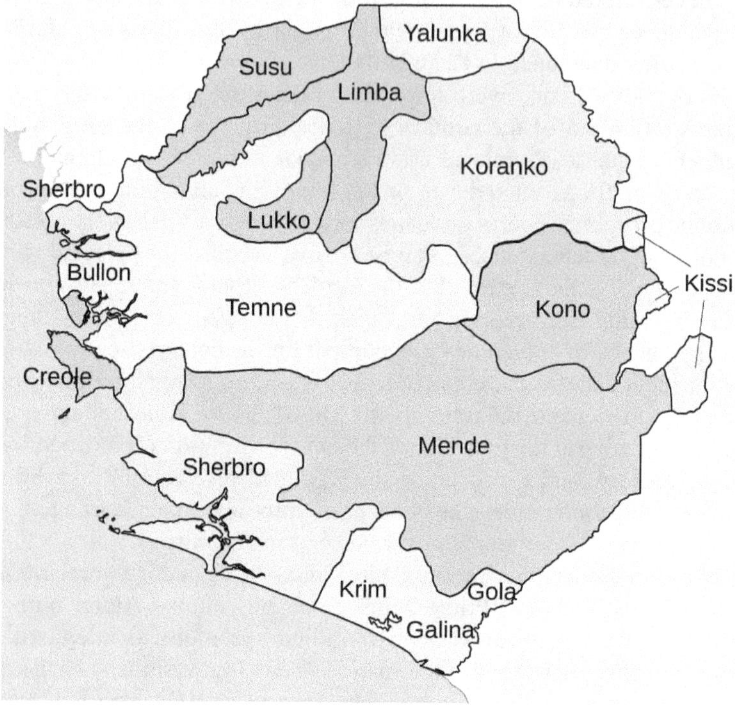

Source: Wikipedia.

By the time the first shot of political catastrophe was literarily fired in 1967, discipline and morality in the military had deteriorated badly.

> Between January 1966 *and* February 1967*, the officer corps of the Royal Sierra Leone Military Forces experienced a breakdown of those disciplinary and command patterns that the British had longed hoped would be established in the fabric of the African armies.*
>
> *During that fourteen-month period, an unrelenting spate of bickering Among members of the senior command became the order of the day.*
>
> (Cox, p. 79)

Military intrigue, corruption, and coup plots prefaced the dawn of the republic. Essentially, Sierra Leoneans never had a chance to take off for economic development and national prosperity. Rather, the country was preoccupied with ethnic rivalry of men with self-serving ambitions during the teething phase of post-colonial rule. By March 23, 1967, Sir Albert possessed assets worth £250,000, based on an annual salary of £4,000. Between 1961 and the end of 1966, Sierra Leone's net foreign exchange reserves declined from Le 29m to Le11.4m (slightly less than two months' worth of exports). The decline was directly attributed to diversion of funds belonging to the SLPMB (Cox, p. 93).[20]

In the 1960s, Sierra Leoneans, indeed Africans, were hardly acquainted with the regularities of the adversarial parliamentary system of government or the Western principles of civilized democratic government. In fact, one could argue that the concept of a civil and adversarial system of government is still a challenging proposition today. Intolerant leaders consider opposition (constructive criticisms) to be repugnant and destructive to their political ambitions, and they are virtually always distrustful of replacement governments (their successors). Notwithstanding, Sierra Leone braced for a prototypical model of a peaceful transfer of political power in Africa, the persistence of which was an alien concept to Africans at the time. Surely, the country had handled the 1957 and 1962 elections reasonably well, and optimism about a peaceful transfer of political power could not have been far-fetched.

The complaints of the APC to the Sierra Leonean electorate about the conduct of the SLPP were concrete and specific – SLPP officials had been engaged in self-enrichment, they had seriously mismanaged the country's fragile economy, and they had favored Mendes over northern tribes (see Box 1.2) in the dispensation of political rewards or apportionment of revenues. With hindsight, the complaints would have been serious if the APC government did not spend more than 18 years replicating the objectionable and obscene behaviors that it had complained about except, of course, that the APC government did a lot to suppress the manifest and arrogant symptoms of distasteful tribalism that preceded its ascension to power. The APC provided a unifying force (a new lease of life) while its leaders incrementally mismanaged and plundered the economy of the country for over 18 years of projection. Yet the suspended animation of tribalism seems to be a recurring episode in the political annals of the country. It rears its proverbial ugly head ever so often.

After the election on March 17, 1967, and tally of the votes, it became apparent that Siaka Stevens of the APC had won the election. The APC had won a plurality of the parliamentary seats. Accordingly, the Governor General (representing the British Monarch) Henry Josiah Lightfoot Boston declared Siaka Stevens, the APC leader, the new Prime Minister. Sir Albert neither conceded defeat nor facilitated a peaceful transfer of political power for the continuity of governance. Within a few hours, Stevens and Lightfoot Boston were placed under house arrest by Brigadier David Lansana, the Commander of the RSLMF on grounds that the election was indeterminate, and that the determination of leadership must await the election of the tribal representatives to the house. The first shot of political catastrophe was literarily fired in 1967, just six years after the colonial administration expeditiously vacated the country and turned over the reins of government over to the political elites of Sierra Leone who had pledged to govern the country as one country for one people; but the rookie elites neither had a perspective of civilized parliamentary procedures nor were they willing to embrace the principles of parliamentary procedures for the good and prosperity of the country.

Unsurprisingly, Brigadier Lansana (1922–1975), a Mende by tribe who had been groomed and assimilated into the vagaries of tribal civilian politics, was the first to declare martial law (suspending the civil constitution) in the country on March 21, 1967. Not even the RSLMF was proficiently accustomed to the requirements for executing a successful coup détat (a "benevolent" and long-lasting coup). The officers of the RSLMF clumsily staged coups in a planned but ad hoc or awkward manner to govern the country with very little knowledge of the principles of civilian government.

Significantly, Lansana had alienated a significant proportion of the senior officer corps, and the *esprit de corps* of the RSLMF had badly deteriorated to an unprofessional level. Sir Albert and Brigadier Lansana were eventually arrested and detained at Pademba Road prison for conspiring to impose an illegitimate government on the people of Sierra Leone and failing to facilitate a compromise government. Yet the concept of compromise (coalition) government was a superficially inequitable construct that was inconsistent with the declared will of the people. It was a reconciliatory measure to sympathetically accommodate the raw and unsettling emotions of southerners who had lost the election because of the corrupt and polarizing leadership preference of the SLPP.

After the arrest of the Brigadier and the former Prime Minister, Major Augustine Blake informed the country about the formation of a military government. Major Blake and other officers had wrested power from Lansana and the former Prime Minister. The upper echelon of the military had been contaminated by civilian politics, and even the coup plotters were torn in the polluted situation. They equivocated between the thought of preserving Mende hegemony and replacing the leader of the party, Albert Margai. Colonel Juxon-Smith provided the perfect compromise for internal equanimity and external validity. Accordingly, he was invited from England to head the newly formed National Reformation Council (NRC).

The council was supposed to work collaboratively and rather seamlessly. However, the disciplinary principles of Colonel Juxon-Smith, his predilection for unilateralism, and intolerance of corruption created dissent and fissures within the council and the country. Internal contradictions within the council, like elsewhere in the country, unspectacularly ended the reign of the council. In April 1968, the NRC was overthrown by a group of military officers who formed the Anti-Corruption Revolutionary Movement (ACRM), led by Brigadier John Amadu Bangura. The ACRM imprisoned senior NRC members, restored the constitution, and reinstated Siaka Stevens as Prime Minister.

The greater tragedy of the untoward conflicts was that the experiment of democracy in Sierra Leone had disastrously and woefully failed to achieve the intended effects of political independence, at least in the minds of rational people. Between 1967 and 1968 there had been three coups d'état. The democratic experiment was ruined by unpatriotic introverts who had unleashed and injected the worst instincts of political leadership – corruption and tribalism (or separateness) – into the body politic of the country.

Though there were military skirmishes elsewhere in Africa, the Sierra Leonean experiment was exceptional but laden with a subterranean reality of the suspended animation of tribal frictions that coexisted with colonial rule.

> *[I]n the Sierra Leone experience of the 1960s, there seemed little reason for the army to exchange barrack duties for the more serious game of political intrigue. In short, Sierra Leone society manifested few of those early warning indicators of future military praetorianism, such as bourgeoning ethnic divisions, elite corruption, flirtation with foreign ideologies and single-party systems with reduced tolerance for the rights of minorities. On the contrary, both the ruling [Sierra Leone People's Party] (SLPP) and the opposition All People's Congress (APC) displayed a rather notable regard for the democratic process and a willingness to avoid simplistic or militant solution to the problem of nation building.*
>
> (Cox, p. 48)

Post-independent party politics was parochially perfunctory with no discernible national agenda. Cox captures the lackluster performance of the SLPP in the 1960s:

> *Rarely did the SLPP enumerate a carefully considered party position on the so-called national issues. In short, it would have been hard to determine with any degree of precision SLPP position on such issues as economic development, or Pan-Africanism, Government ministers rarely conducted their business in light of "what the party is thinking or would think" under such circumstances.*
>
> (Cox, p. 50)

Two competing aspirations introduced tension into civil–military relations in the 1960s – the Africanization of the military and the balanced ethnic composition of the military. Pointedly, the military was seen as the protector of civilian administration at the outset of the post-colonial rule, a rather intriguing aberration of the civil–military relations that the British had expected. This anomaly was unequivocally responsible for a series of coups in Africa during the 1960s and 1970s when most of the African countries had no serious debate about economic development and national prosperity. Yet in Sierra Leone, neither the Africanization nor the "tribal composition" of the military seemed to have seriously affected civil–military relations (Cox, p. 51).

The RSLMF lost a rare opportunity to define its role within the structure of the state and civilian politics. It had failed to become the custodian of democracy in Sierra Leone at a critical moment when a political ballast was needed to maintain political stability for economic growth and sustainable development. Clearly, the praetorian (excessive and abusive) use of the military in civilian politics was inconsistent with the expected functions of the military within a modern state. It is rather surprising that the British monarch did not intervene to streamline the role of its military (RSLMF) at a time of critical need, even when the Governor General (representing the British monarch), Henry Josiah Lightfoot Boston, was arrested.

Understandably, the call for independence by the political elites of Sierra Leone was acrimonious and politically distasteful, and its antagonizing effects could only have angered the British monarch. The political elites of Sierra Leone had given the colonial administration assurances, with elevated national puffery, that they were very capable of governing themselves and the country. Had the military appropriately separated itself from the vagaries of civilian politics and performed a custodial role during the formative stage of democracy in Sierra Leone, the military would have been in the precedential and admirable position of escorting recalcitrant and rogue politicians out of office when they were disrespectful of the will of the people. The RSLMF had failed to protect the country from the ensuing anarchy and socio-economic backwardness that awaited the country. Unfortunately, the civil–military model in the 1960s became the paradigm for civil–military relations of the country for the rest of the twentieth century.

The APC came into power in 1968 with a lot of well wishes and socio-economic optimism. It was supposed to be a breath of fresh air. However, the APC was beset with antagonisms and coup plots by dissentious opponents of its rule from the very beginning. An unsuccessful coup was attempted in 1971 (within three years of the administration of the APC), and an aborted plot was uncovered in 1974 (see Table 1.2). The leaders of the coup plots were tried and executed. In 1977, massive student demonstrations against the government almost ended the legitimacy of the regime. Notwithstanding, under a republican constitution of April 1971, the Sierra Leonean Parliament appointed Siaka Stevens to be President of the Republic in March 1976 for a second term of five years.

Following the May 1977 national parliamentary elections in which the APC won 74 seats and the opposition, SLPP, won 15 seats, Stevens consolidated political power by facilitating the enactment of the one-party constitution of 1978. In effect, Stevens perfected the implementation of authoritarian rule that the SLPP had flirted with. It is apparent that the body politic of the country had been contaminated by unhealthy distrust and a phobia of retaliatory politics, despite the efforts of the APC to placate its political opponents.

The first election under the new one-party constitution took place on May 1, 1982, but elections in about two-thirds of the constituencies were contested. Claims of irregularities forced the government to cancel elections in 13 constituencies and by-elections were held on June 4, 1982. The new cabinet that was appointed after the election tried to reconcile ethnic tensions by maintaining a balance between Temnes and Mendes (see Box 1.3). The cabinet included the new Finance Minister Salia Jusu-Sheriff, a former leader of the SLPP (who returned to that party in late 1981). Siaka Stevens ruled Sierra Leone for 18 years and retired from that position in November 1985.[21] In August 1985, the APC named military commander Maj. Gen. Joseph Saidu Momoh – Steven's own choice – as the party's candidate for succession. Momoh was elected President in a one-party referendum on October 1, 1985, and a formal inauguration was held in January 1986. New Parliamentary elections were subsequently held in May 1986.

The APC had the greatest opportunity to set the country on the path for economic growth and development because of the longevity of its rule and the global economic conditions that coexisted with its rule of more than two decades. On its part, the SLPP made prospects of political stability and economic growth impossible at a time when they mattered most. Accordingly, the APC squandered opportunities though it worked to obtain a sense of national awareness and cohesion, something that was badly missing in the country after a contentious period of colonial rule. Like the SLPP, the APC was beset with accusations of corruption and mismanagement of the national economy. Though the APC made some gains in bringing about awareness of national cohesion, the primitive feeling of tribal superiority or preference has always been in suspended animation. Indeed, the perception of tribalism, rightly or wrongly, is a discomfiture that has episodically characterized the operations of the SLPP. Thus, the party has routinely struggled to build convincing and successful national coalitions.

It is inconceivable that an individual or political party could rule a country for 18 years while also badly mismanaging the country with impunity and international support. Of course, the notion that African leaders are the state (*L'éat c'est moi*) is nothing new. Apparently, some African leaders have exorbitantly squandered extravagant tenure of leadership – Haile Selassie of Ethiopia (1892–1975, c.83 years), Mobutu Sese Seko of Zaire (1965–1997, c.32 years), Mugabe of Zimbabwe (1987–2017, c.30 years), William Tubman of Liberia (1944–1971, c.27 years), Sékou Touré of Guinea (1958–1984, c.26 years), Julius Nyerere of Tanzania (1962–1985, c.23 years), Siaka Stevens of Sierra Leone (1967–1985, c.18 years), and Jean-Bédel Bokassa of the Central African Republic (1966–1979, c.13 years) – political longevities that are unimaginable in developed or advanced countries with accountable systems of government. The leaders virtually took ownership of the countries as their personal assets or properties.

Despite the constitutional provisions for the restoration of multiparty rule in Sierra Leone, which was ratified on October 1, 1991, the incidence of political instability was hardly subdued. A rebel war, led by Capt. Foday Sankoh and his Revolutionary United Front (RUF), broke out in the eastern part of the county, causing considerable loss of blood and treasure. The unparalleled brutality and savagery of the war invited foreign capital and military assistance for resolution. It took more than a decade of hostilities to resolve the conflict after the destruction of physical and residual human capital (Sierra Leone suffers from a brain-drain syndrome). It is estimated that about 30 percent of educated Sierra Leoneans left the country as part of a third wave of emigration between 1991 and 2002.[22] The likelihood of an incremental movement of this cohort of emigrants predated the wave of 1991 and thereafter.

On April 29, 1992, a group of military officers, led by Capt. Valentine Strasser, launched a military coup, which ousted the APC government of Momoh and sent him into exile in Guinea the National Provisional Ruling Council (NPRC) of the military became the ruling authority in Sierra Leone. Aversion of military rule and international pressure led to presidential and parliamentary elections in April 1996. Out of 13 candidates who contested, Ahmad Tejan Kabbah (SLPP) won the presidential elections.[23]

The praetorian tradition of militarism that had started in the 1960s continued into the turn of the twenty-first century. The Armed Forces Revolutionary

Table 1.9 Coups and countercoups (1967–1999)

Coups and countercoups	*Dates*
Brigadier Lansana	March 21, 1967
Major Blake/Colonel Juxon-Smith (National	March 22, 1967
Reformation Council (NRC))	March 25, 1967–8
Colonel John Bangura	April 18–22, 1968
Brig. John Bangura (abortive\failed)	March 23, 1971
Mohamed Sorie Fornah et al. (alleged)	1974
Capt. Valentine Strasser	April 29, 1992
Maj. Johnny Paul Koroma	May 25, 1997
ECOMOG	March 10, 1998
RUF (abortive attempt)	January 6, 1999

Note: Lieutenant-Colonel Ambrose Genda was previously favored to head the NRC. Indications that he wanted to hand power to the winning party, APC, destroyed his chances and Colonel Juxon-Smith was favored as a compromise candidate because of his ethnicity (creole, see Box 1.3) inter alia. Brig. John Bangura was surveiled by the President and stopped by Lieut. Col. Sam King. Note that the Economic Community of West African States Monitoring Group (ECOMOG) had sufficiently reduced hostilities before the return of President Kabbah to power on March 10, 1998. Also, there was civil war in Sierra Leone from 1999 to 2001.

Council (AFRC), led by Maj. Johnny Paul Koroma, overthrew President Kabbah on May 25, 1997, and invited the RUF to join the government. The junta was ousted by the Nigerian-led ECOMOG forces ten months later, and the democratically elected government of President Kabbah was reinstated in March 1998. On January 6, 1999, another abortive attempt to overthrow the government by the RUF resulted in massive destruction of physical capital and loss of lives in Freetown and its immediate environments. Political hegemony and control of diamond fields were central to the thrust of the insurgency. Table 1.9 provides a synopsis of the evolution of political instability in the country, including the fateful years of the 1960s that brought horror and destruction to the country and set the country on the trajectory of economic backwardness and underdevelopment (ruin).

Notes

1 In 1807, as the trade in slaves increasingly became obscene and odious, the British Parliament declared participation in the trade by British citizens and subjects to be illegal, but the termination of the trade was not immediate. Even though English law did not formerly recognize slavery, the slave trade continued till its abolition in 1833 and thereafter (see Warburton, 2021, pp. 1–9, for a complete history of the abolitionist movement and normalization of trading relations). By 1772, there were about 14,000 domestic slaves under the ownership of British farmers who were on leave or retirement in the West Indies (Omer-Cooper et al.:131). Chief Justice Mansfield's pronouncement that English law did not recognize slavery in the Somerset case implicitly meant that at least 14,000 slaves were immediately freed. London became a magnet as slaves who desired their freedom feverishly found ways to make it to London so that they could be emancipated (see Warburton, 2021, p. 2fn for a discussion of the Somerset case).

2 *The Recaptives, a later group of settlers, built huts in mountainous villages, possibly as a protective and defensive mechanism against external aggression. Cabenda (later named*

as "Wilberforce" by Sir Charles MacCarthy in 1816*) was established by an Acting Governor, Lt. R. Bones, as the new home for 42 Recaptives from an estuary of the Congo, Cabenda.* In 1827*, some Recaptives settled in Pa Sandi Village (later renamed "Lumley" after the acting Governor, Lt-Col Lumley who resettled them there in 1827). With the aid of Governor MacCarthy, others were settled in Hogbrook (renamed "Regent") and 10 more villages in the* Colony in 1820 *(Foray:126). The villages had to be serviced by educational resources and the missionaries filled that void. Though some have characterized the missionaries as the ideological wing of Western capitalism, there is every reason to believe that some of the missionaries must have genuinely felt the need to disseminate Christian education with theological emotion and religious fervor* (Warburton, 2021, p. 7).

3 See Warburton (2021) for a comprehensive historical analysis of the WAM Collegiate School.

4 By the late 1890s, the colonial administration needed money to finance its operations in Sierra Leone. The Governor, Cardew, levied taxes on huts (houses) to raise revenue, but the very Western concept of property taxes was alien to the indigenes who felt that they no longer owned their huts or had proprietary control over their property. A massive and violent rebellion broke out in the hinterland in protest of the tax. The indigenes wrongly blamed the Creoles who had advised against the imposition of the taxes on huts for the taxes, just as the colonial officials blamed the Creoles for inciting the rebellion. Thousands of Creoles who had ventured into the hinterland as teachers, clergymen, traders, and doctors to improve the lives of the indigenes were brutally hacked and maimed. The incident engendered distrust and raw animosities that existed at the time of independence and beyond.

5 A General Assembly resolution that is intended to have a widespread (general) normative effect with the force of international law.

6 To mitigate frictions in the education and labor markets conference attendees argued that agricultural productivity and rural employment must be increased. It was hoped that agricultural productivity and rural employment would reduce rural–urban migration. "Adapting educational programmes to rural conditions" was conceptualized as the mechanism to stimulate rural development (UNESCO, 1961, p. 6).

7 See the work of Pai (2014) for a comprehensive assessment of the program.

8 According to the World Bank 2021/22 country income group classification, LMI Africa has 23 member states: Algeria, Angola, Benin, Cameroon, Cape Verde, Comoros, the Republic of the Congo, Côte d'Ivoire, Djibouti, Egypt, Ghana, Kenya, Lesotho, Mauritania, Morocco, Nigeria, São Tomé and Príncipe, Senegal, Eswatini, Tanzania, Tunisia, Zambia, and Zimbabwe. Membership is based on the World Bank classification of income ranging from US$1,046 to US$4,095 based on 2020 gross national income (GNI) per capita.

9 Indeed, this is a succinct summary of the various national legislations (Education Act 2004, the Child Rights Act 2007), policies (The Sierra Leone Education Sector Plan 2014–2018, The Sierra Leone Sector Capacity Development Strategy 2012–2016 and the Sierra Leone Education Sector Plan 2007–2015), and international goals to which Sierra Leone is a signatory (Education For All, and Millennium Development Goal (MDG) of primary school completion rate of 100 percent by 2015). The Government of Sierra Leone introduced a fee-free primary education policy in the 2002/03 academic year (UNESCO, 2013). The country also had a national and MDG target of a primary school completion rate of 100 percent by 2015 (SSL, 2004). In 2007, Nishimuko reported that the completion rate of primary education in Sierra Leone is still below 60 percent nationally, but this increased to 74 percent by 2011 (UNESCO, 2012; SSL, p. 329).

10 See *www.officialdata.org/uk/inflation/1816?amount=21902*

11 The estimated base pay is SLL 1,000,000 per month. The "Most Likely Range" represents values that exist within the 25th and 75th percentiles of all pay data available for this role; *www.glassdoor.com/*.

12 Certainly, the perception of colonial governance changed after educated Africans challenged the authority of the colonial administration to provide better working conditions and recognize the African-educated elites as competent political partners of government. The railway strike of April 20, 1926, had also rattled the governor, Slater, who lamented in uncompromising terms that "deplorable exhibition of political perversity" was deflecting the attention of the colonial administration from educating public opinion (Foray, p. 202).
13 Orthodox programs entailed a reduction in government spending (fiscal restraint) that affected employment, subsidies, and reduction in the money supply to bring down inflation. Subsidies, which were seen as mechanisms to increase consumption, adversely affected food production. Orthodox programs also required the devaluation of local currencies to increase exports and reduce imports. The problem is that incapacity to increase exports and trade restrictions abroad adversely affected the successful implementation of orthodox programs in some cases. Affected governments were also expected to liberalize economic transactions (remove price controls), some of which protected poorer consumers. The stringency of the orthodox programs led to widespread riots in some countries that were dubbed "IMF riots." Heterodox programs relied on government management of disputes between workers and firms over the relative shares of national income. That is, targeting aggregate demand was an insufficient mechanism for price stability (see Cardoso and Helwege, pp. 172–188).
14 DELCO was a subsidiary of a British company, the African and Eastern Trading Company Ltd. The company obtained a lease for 99 years at an annual rent of £250, payable to the tribal authority in the Marampa Chiefdom (Fyle, 181).
15 The H-T model uses the agricultural sector for the rural area, and the manufacturing sector for the urban area. I have eliminated some of the original arguments and notions without loss of generality for parsimony. Readers may imaginatively choose sectors for rural and urban production.
16 The Lebanese were first identified as Syrians because Lebanon was part of Syria till the end of WWI.
17 The population of Sierra Leone increased from 2,180,355 in 1963 to 2,735,159 in 1974 and 3,515,812 in 1985. Between 2004 and 2015, the population increased by about 2.1 million persons from 4,976,871 to 7,092,113, representing an inter-censal percentage increase of 42.5 percent.
18 A very good discussion of the Articles of Agreement can be found in the work of Viterbo (2019). The use of the Fund's resources is expected to be temporary and not forever. However, there have been irreconcilable differences over the availability of the Fund's resources and the prosperity of national economies while also counterbalancing the availability of the pool of resources for international stability and prosperity. Most of the criticisms of the Fund have unfairly discounted the severity of kleptocracy, profligacy, and mismanagement – without consultations – of national economies before the implementation of conditionalities (see also the work of Vines and Gilbert (eds.)).
19 Under normal circumstances, external reduction of interest rate that causes a decline in domestic interest rate causes an increase in real money balances. Foreign assets become less attractive, and domestic residents will try to dispose of them for local currency. That is, changes in relative interest rates can cause real money balances to change. Changes in the general price level are also contingent on assumptions about the exchange rate regime; for example, if inflation is zero, the inflation tax will be zero only when the exchange rate is fixed; see Sachs and Larrain (p. 340) for further discussion.
20 *The SLPMB, which had committed its liquid assets to long-term payments, was unable to meet current liabilities to the buying agents of approximately Le3m and did not have the financial resources needed to purchase for export* (Cox, p. 96).
21 Stevens continued his role as chairman of the ruling APC party after retirement.
22 The emigration of Sierra Leoneans has been categorized into three distinct waves. The first wave is presumed to have preceded the independence of Sierra Leone in 1961. A small number of Sierra Leoneans emigrated in search of better education and training opportunities and ended up constituting a fraction of the diaspora constituents that

struggled for independence. The second wave occurred after independence when young Sierra Leoneans migrated to China, Libya, Russia, the United Kingdom, etc. to acquire education that was necessary to fill vacancies in the public sector after independence. The third wave of emigrants constitutes approximately 30 percent of the educated nationals who emigrated for security and economic opportunities in the face of falling living standards and civil war (1991–2002) (see the National Migration Policy of Sierra Leone, p. 17); *https://slid.gov.sl/wp-content/uploads/2022/02/20220114-Final-Draft-National-Migration-Policy-4.pdf.*

23 As a result of the then prevailing war conditions, parliamentary elections were conducted under the system of proportional representation (percentage of votes cast in relation to the number of available seats). Thirteen political parties participated, with the SLPP winning 27 seats, UNPP 17, PDP 12, APC 5, and DCP 3.

Further reading

Abernethy, D. (1969). *The political dilemma of popular education: An African case.* Stanford University Press.

Alghali A.M., Edward D.A., Turay E.D.A., Thompson E.J.D., & Kandeh J.B.A. (2005). *Environmental scan on education in Sierra Leone with particular reference to open and distance learning and information and communication technologies*. The Commonwealth of Learning.

Banya, K. (1991). Economic decline and the education system: The case of Sierra Leone. *Compare*, 21(2), 127–143.

Banya, K. (1993). Illiteracy, colonial legacy and education: The case of modern Sierra Leone. *Comparative Education*, 29(2), 159–170.

Brito, N.H. & Noble, K.G. (2014). Socioeconomic status and structural brain development. *Frontiers in Neuroscience,* 8(276), 1–12. doi:10.3389/fnins.2014.00276

Byerlee, D. (1974). Rural-urban migration in Africa: Theory, policy and research implications. *International Migration Review*, 8, 543–566.

Byerlee, D., Tommy, J.L. & Fatoo, H. (1976). *Rural-urban migration in Sierra Leone: Determinants and policy implications,* African Rural Economy Paper No.13. Michigan State University. https://catalog.lib.msu.edu/Record/folio.in00004962740

Cardoso, E. & Helwege, A. (1992). *Latin America's economy*. The MIT Press.

Chabbott, C. & Ramirez, F. O. (2000). Development and education. In *Handbook of the sociology of education* (pp. 163–187). Springer.

Coleman, J.A. (1965). *Education and political development.* Princeton University Press.

Coupland, R. (1964 [1933]) *The British antislavery movement.* Frank Cass.

Cox, S.T. (1976). *Civil-military relations in Sierra Leone: A case study of African soldiers in politics*. Harvard University Press.

Evans, D.K., Yuan, F. & Filmer, D. (2022). Teacher pay in Africa: Evidence from 15 countries. *World Development.* 155, 1–29.

Feika, M.S.M. (2019, August). Sierra Leone's declining education results in the WAEC. https://blogs.lse.ac.uk/africaatlse/2019/08/03/sierra-leones-declining-education-results-in-the-waec/

Foray, C.P. (1977). *Historical dictionary of Sierra Leone.* The Scarecrow Press.

Foster, P.J. (1965). *Education and social change in Ghana*. The University of Chicago Press.

Fyfe, C. (1964). *Sierra Leone inheritance.* Oxford University Press.

Fyle, C.M. (2006). *Historical dictionary of Sierra Leone*. The Scarecrow Press.

Government of Sierra Leone (1980). *Background to Sierra Leone*. Office of the President.

Greenhalgh, P.A.L. (1985). *West African diamonds*, 1919–1983: *A*n economic history. Manchester University Press.

Hawes, H.W.R. (1976). *Curriculum and curriculum development in Sierra Leone*.Department of Education in Developing Countries, University of London Institute of Education.

International Monetary Fund. (2023, October). *World Economic Outlook*. IMF.

Jarrett, A.A (1990). The encouragement of rural urban migration in Sierra Leone. *International Social Work*, 33(1), 49–72.
Jensen, E. (2009). *Teaching with poverty in mind.*ASCD.
Mannah, J. (2020, November). Sierra Leone's dismal performance in the WAEC school exams needs fixing fast. Sierra Leone Telegraph. www.thesierraleonetelegraph.com/
Mathieson, W. (1926). *British slavery and its abolition* 1823–1838. Longmans.
Mathieson, W. (1929). *Great Britain and the slave trade.* Longmans.
Matsumoto, M. (2014). Young people, education, and the 'new' wars: The case of Sierra Leone. *Infaancia Contemporanea,* 6, 1–17.
McKenzie, K. (2019). The effects of poverty on academic achievement. *BU Journal of Graduate Studies in Education*, 11(2), 21–26.
Mellor, G.R. (1951). *British imperial trusteeship.* Faber & Faber.
Nishimuko, M. (2007). Problems behind education for All (EFA): The case of Sierra Leone. Research paper, *Educate*, 7(2), 19–29. www.educatejournal.org/19.
Okoye, C.S. (1980). Migration in Sierra Leone. In K.C. Zachariah (ed.) *Demographic Aspects of Migration in West Africa, I* (pp. 1–40). World Bank.
Omer-Cooper, J.D., Ayandele, E.A., Afigbo, A.E. & Gavin, R.J. (1972). *The growth of African civilization: The making of modern Africa to the partition*. New Art Printing.
Pai, G. (2014). Particularizing universal education in postcolonial Sierra Leone. *Current Issues in Comparative Education*, 16(1), 62–73.
Porter, A. (1963). *Creoledom*. Oxford University Press.
Pratt, S.A.J. (2010). *Jolliboy: From Street Starch Hawker to United Nations Debate Champion.* Lulu.
Renner-Thomas, A. (2010). *Land tenure in Sierra Leone: The law, dualism, and the making of a land policy*. Author-House.
Sachs, J. & Larrain, B.F. (1993). *Macroeconomics in the global economy*. Prentice Hall.
Sierra Leone Government. (1958). *White Paper on Educational Development.* Government Printing Department.
State House. (1980). *Background to Sierra Leone*. Office of the President.
Statistics Sierra Leone. (2017). *Sierra Leone 2015 Population and Housing Census:* national analytical report. Statistics Sierra Leone.
Sumner, D.L. (1963). *Education in Sierra Leone*. Jarrold & Sons.
Todaro, M.P. (1971). Income expectations, rural-urban migration and employment in Africa. *International Labor Review*, 104, 387–414.
Todaro, M.P. & Smith, S.C. (2015). *Economic development* (12th ed.). Pearson.
UN. (1949). *Universal declaration of human rights*. United Nations.
UNESCO. (1961). *Final report: Conference of African states on the development of education in Africa,* Addis Ababa, 15–25 May 1961. UNESCO. http://unesdoc.unesco.org/images/0007/000774/077416e.pdf
UNESCO. (1983). *Sierra Leone: Primary school teachers for rural areas*. Project Findings and Recommendations. UNDP. UNDP/SIL/73/009. http://unesdoc.unesco.org/images/0005/000560/056049eb.pdf
Vines, D. & Gilbert, C.L. (eds.). (2004). *The IMF and its critics: Reform of global financial architecture*. Cambridge University Press.
Viterbo, A. (2019). *International monetary fund* (3rd ed.). Wolters Kluwer.
Warburton, C.E.S. (2018). *The development of international monetary policy*. Routledge.
Warburton, C.E.S. (2021). *The West African Methodist Collegiate School, 1911–2021: A byproduct of missionary work in West Africa*. Wipf & Stock.
Williams, E. (1994). *Capitalism and slavery*. University of North Carolina.

2 Contexts for business strategies and rivalry in an underdeveloped economy

2.1 Theories of market structure

Firms operate within a structure that is defined by the number of firms (competitors), the degree of market power (control over prices), entry restrictions or absence, the types of products or services that they can produce, and the tax structure which is beyond their control. Of course, governments can subsidize the operations of businesses/firms to make them more competitive or gain strategic advantage in global markets. Often, notions of competitiveness discount the intelligence of consumers or the unimpeded flow of information to consumers that results in information asymmetry and market inefficiencies. Markets are not competitive when consumers or uninformed about the products or services that they are consuming. Invariably, consumers are generally uninformed about a lot of things when they are not educated consumers. A collusive form of market organization with few producers is oligopolistic and dissembles information. Obviously, consumers need not have sophisticated education, but they need to have sufficient information about the products or services that they wish to consume to determine their consumption options.

The competitive market structure is usually a good starting point to evaluate efficient production and improved consumer welfare. It considers societal resource allocation, the cost of production, and improvements in consumer welfare. Consider Figures 2:1(a) and 2.1(b). Figure 2.1(a) reveals some attractive properties of competitive markets. Per unit cost of production (average total cost, ATC_1) is comparatively lower relative to ATC_2. There is considerable freedom to enter the market and compete. A prime mover makes profit equivalent to rectangle C_1-A-E-P* for producing output, Q*; where P* is the profit-maximizing price, C_1 is for the cost of producing Q*, and E is for the point of intersection between marginal cost (MC) and marginal revenue (MR), which is also the average revenue (AR) in competitive markets in which prices are invariable for a given period of time.

In the long run, firms produce at a point where the MC is equivalent to the minimum ATC, suggesting that consumers will eventually pay a price that is equivalent to productive efficiency (minimum ATC) and allocative efficiency (MC) in the long run; alternatively, a price that approximates the opportunity cost of using societal resources. In 2020, the government of Sierra Leone performed reasonably well in

DOI: 10.4324/9781003518464-3

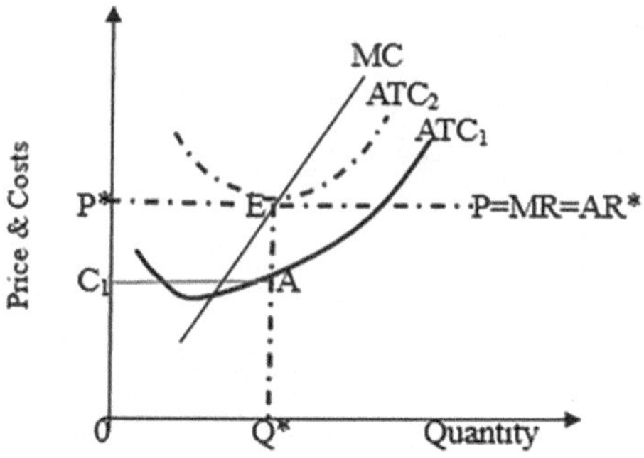

Figure 2.1a Competition and efficiency.

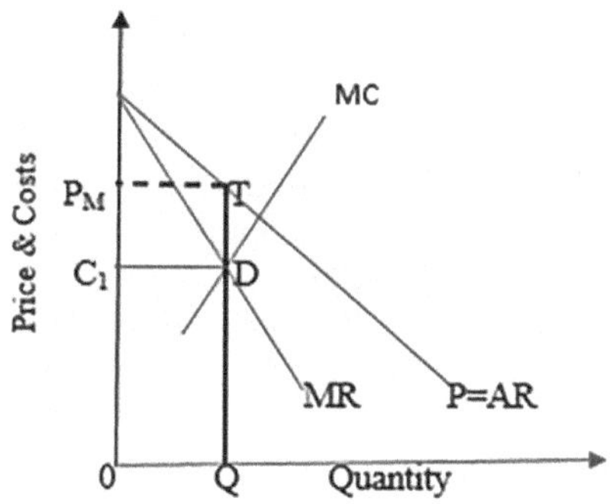

Figure 2.1b Monopoly and inefficiency.

Note: Monopolies are not always inefficient.

terms of removing restrictions from doing business in the country. With a 91.3 percent score for starting a business, the country ranked 58 out of 190 countries (see Table 2.1).

The data in Table 2.1 are consistent with the cost of doing business in the subregion (see Figure 2.2). Cost of business start-up procedures as a percentage of GNI per capita consistently fell below that of other countries in Sub-Saharan Africa. Hence, rational social planners will generally prefer the competitive structure unless the costs and incentives for producing socially valuable goods and services are too prohibitive to be left in the hands of the private sector. In fact, uncompetitive practices have also impinged on the ability of the National Revenue Authority (NRA) to collect equitable and optimal amount of revenue (NRA, 2007, p. 11).

For diverse reasons, the monopolistic market structure is not generally efficient as the competitive market structure. Unlike the competitor, the monopolist has

Table 2.1 Indicators of competitive structure in Sierra Leone (2020)

Starting a Business (rank)	*58*
Score of starting a business (0–100)	*91.3*
Procedures (number)	5
Time (days)	8
Cost (number)	7.6
Paid-in min. capital (% of income per capita)	0

Source: World Bank's *Doing Business* . . . (2020, p. 4).

Note: *To make the data comparable across 190 economies, uses a standardized business that is 100% domestically owned, has start-up capital equivalent to 10 times the income per capita, engages in general industrial or commercial activities, and employs between 10 and 50 people one month after the commencement of operations, all of whom are domestic nationals. Starting a Business considers two types of local limited liability companies that are identical in all aspects, except that one company is owned by five married women and the other by five married men. The ranking of economies on the ease of starting a business is determined by sorting their scores for starting a business. These scores are the simple average of the scores for each of the component indicators* (World Bank, 2020, p. 5).

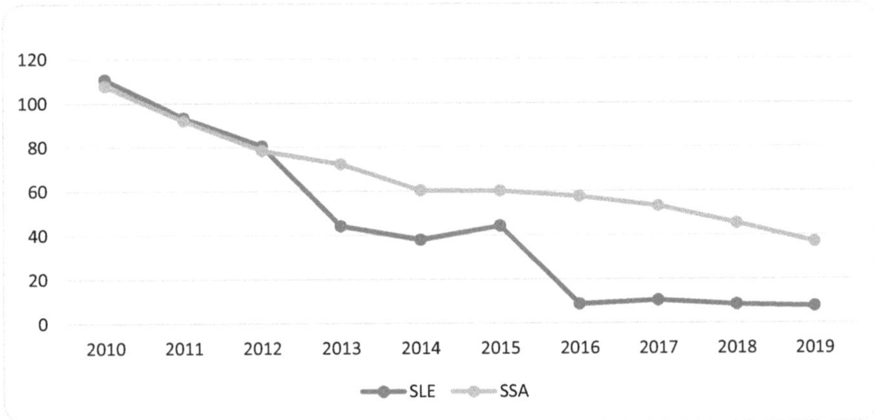

Figure 2.2 Cost of business start-up procedure in Sierra Leone and SSA (% of GNI per capita).

Data source: World Bank's WDI (2023)

Note: SSA = Sub-Saharan Africa.

market power (he/she could set prices) and he/she is not seriously threatened by competition or the introduction of substitute products; possibly because of protection, natural advantages (control over inputs), or initial outlays for producing similarly related goods and services. Therefore, a monopolist is a price maker with a downward sloping price line (P = AR) unlike the competitor who is a price taker (see Figures 2.1(a) and 2.1(b)).

The monopolist is in a unique position. He/she must lower prices to increase the amount of output to be sold for an increase in total revenue. However, price reductions have floors. Prices are reduced until total revenue is maximized. In effect, a monopolist is in a unique situation where the market price is greater than the marginal revenue but for the very first output – because the marginal revenue of the first unit sold must be equal to the price (see Figure 2.1(b)) but not thereafter. The distinction is usually not very apparent, but price theory and a mathematical formulation should help.

The downward sloping curve of the monopolist shows an inverse relationship between price and quantity. As price falls, consumers tend to buy more of a good or service when other significant variables remain unchanged. Accordingly, the change in price (ΔP) relative to the change in quantity (ΔQ) must be negative – (-) (ΔP/ΔQ).[1] Hence, MR is just:

$$MR = P + \left(\frac{\Delta P}{\Delta Q = 1}\right) * Q, \quad P > MR. \text{ (Goolsbee et al. p. 307)} \qquad 2.1$$

The monopolist makes a profit equivalent to box C_1-D-T-P_M, where P_M is for the price of the monopolist. The monopolistic structure is not always a reassuring structure for good consumer welfare. Monopolists could increase prices and reduce quantities or provide substandard quality goods and services for exorbitant prices. Realistically, monopolies are not always profitable, and monopolies can be beneficial to society if they can produce a considerable amount of output at lower per unit cost – a scale of production that is known as economies of scale. It is noteworthy that even with government regulation there could be no allocative and productive efficiency within the monopolistic market structure.

Unsurprisingly, it makes a lot of sense for governments to produce goods and services that will improve the welfare of their citizens when the private sector is incapable or unwilling to provide such goods and services. In the previous chapter, I discussed the railway infrastructure and the role of the colonial government (Great Britain) to pioneer its existence. No private entity could have willingly undertaken to absorb the overhead cost of constructing the railway without assurances of more than normal profit to operate the railway, not even on behalf of the government of the UK. In fact, given the utility that is provided by public goods and services, it is hardly the case that public forms of transportation are not subsidized by local and central governments. The UK continues to subsidize rail transportation (see Figure 2.3), albeit at levels that may be less than that of Belgium, Germany, or France. Remarkably, the rail system of the UK is probably the most efficient system (if not the best) in the world at the time of this writing.

Similarly, other European countries like Belgium, Germany, France, Italy, and Austria provide subsidies for their rail system. While the government of Sierra Leone mismanaged the funds of farmers, effaced the railway, and sold the parts and steel tracks in the 1970s, the UK and other countries have assiduously subsidized rail transportation for cargo and human transportation. Monopolies could also provide valuable social services.

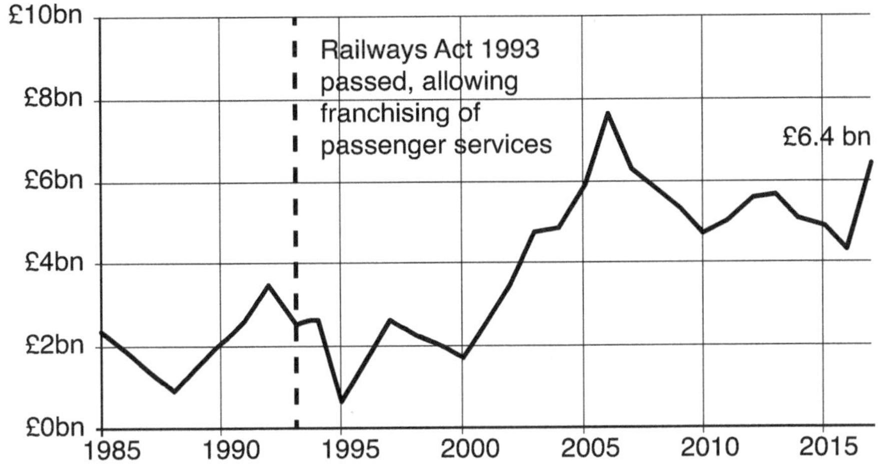

Figure 2.3 Government subsidy for railways in the UK (1985–2017).

Source: Office of Rail and Road, Rail Finance, 2017–18 Annual Statistical Release, Government support to the rail industry – Table 1.6 (see also https://fullfact.org/economy/how-much-does-government-subsidise-railways/)

Note: Annual government subsidy – not including loans to Network Rail – to the rail industry in Great Britain (2017/18 prices).

2.2 Business classifications and operations

Firms could be organized in a variety of ways. The most prominent forms of business organizations are sole proprietorships, partnerships, and public corporations. The most dominant form of business organizations in Sierra Leone is sole proprietorship. Many Sierra Leoneans operate their own businesses, which could also be a manifestation of underemployment that skews the unemployment data.

A sole proprietorship is a form of business organization that is owned by an individual. The longevity of the business is usually transient and contingent on the fortunes and life span of the owner of the business. There is no external ownership interest to be transferred, and therefore the business ceases to exist when the owner is no longer capable of operating the business.

Sole proprietorships are relatively easy to initiate, and they constitute the least expensive form of business organization to initiate. The sole proprietor must merely adhere to the laws of local and central governments. Registration does not necessarily mean that the proprietor could raise a considerable amount of money. The proprietor cannot raise any equity capital to finance his/her business like a corporation, and therefore the capital structure of the business is limited to the owner's wealth. This makes it very difficult for the sole proprietors of Sierra Leone to be competitive and innovative. This limitation deserves considerable attention when navigating Porter's Diamond model in the next section,

Transferring ownership rights is problematic because the net assets of the proprietor must be disposed of directly rather than indirectly. For example, partial ownership rights of corporations enable shareholders to sell shares of a public company to divest themselves of ownership of a public company. The sole proprietor does not have such an option.

The management and investment decisions of the sole proprietor are consolidated in a single individual, meaning that there is no separation of ownership and control. The most fatal threat to the viability of the business is probably the unlimited liability of the sole proprietor. The proprietor's assets are tied to business decisions, and personal assets cannot be separated from business assets when the sole proprietor becomes legally liable for a business decision. Partnerships are just a tier above sole proprietorship.

Two or more people may legally agree to manage a business known as "partnership." The partnership agreement stipulates the amount of capital that each partner must invest in the business, what their management roles will be, how the profits of the business will be distributed, the transfer of ownership, and the distribution of liabilities. This means that responsibilities for a partnership are not monolithic.

All partners actively own and manage a *general partnership. Limited partnerships* have owners who are not managers. Partnerships impose legal costs and responsibilities on the owners who must seek the services of attorneys to construct partnership agreements, delineating the rights and obligations of the partners. A partnership agreement could ensure continuity of the partnership when a partner decides to leave, thereby increasing or maintaining the prospects of liquidity.

Liabilities in partnerships could be bifurcated. A general partner could be liable for the liabilities of a partnership irrespective of his investment. Limited partners could insulate their personal wealth by limiting their liabilities only to the amount of capital invested in the business. Unlike sole proprietors and partnerships with unlimited liabilities, corporations have limited liabilities.

A corporation is a legal entity that is authorized to operate under a charter (license) or certificate of incorporation. "Legal entity" means that corporations have juridical personalities and that they can sue or be sued. Corporations may be private or public, a distinction that elicits different responsibilities from corporate entities. Public corporations raise capital from the public, and, in advanced economies, corporations are obligated to provide truthful and accurate information to their domestic and international investors. Public corporations do so by producing periodic financial statements to disclose their income (even on an accrual basis), assets, liabilities, equity, and directions of cash flows. Private corporations do not have such a responsibility because they do not raise capital from the public.

It is very costly to establish corporations because of the initial outlays and the costs of adherence to legal procedures. Public corporations initially raise funds in primary markets through initial public offerings (IPOs) that are usually financed by institutional investors. The stocks of public companies are eventually sold in secondary markets like the New York Stock Exchange or Nasdaq to common and preferred stockholders. Preferred stockholders have preferential dividend payments that may be rolled over unlike the common stockholders. However, the common stockholders have primal voting rights than the preferred stockholders. In all cases, bondholders are expected to have seniority rights when the capital structure of public corporations consists of bonds and equity.

Table 2.2 Protection of minority interest

Indicator	*SLE*	*SSA*	*OECDH*	*Best Regulatory Performance*
Extent of disclosure index (0–10)	6	5.5	6.5	10 (13 Economies)
Extent of director liability index (0–10)	8	3.5	5.3	10 (3 Economies)
Ease of shareholder suits index (0–10)	6	5.5	7.3	10 (Djibouti)
Extent of shareholder rights index (0–6)	0	1.8	4.7	6 (19 Economies)
Extent of ownership and control index (0–7)	0	1.4	4.5	7 (9 Economies)
Extent of corporate transparency index (0–7)	0	1.5	5.7	7 (13 Economies)

Source: World Bank, 2020 . . . p. 31

Note: SLE= Sierra Leone, SSA= Sub-Saharan Africa, and OECDH= OECD high income.

Shareholders establish the bylaws of a public corporation during their initial meeting. The bylaws establish the governance structure of a public corporation and the voting rights of the stockholders. The stockholders elect a board of directors that elects a firm's management in return. A major problem that continuously threatens the operations of public corporations is the principal–agent problem – the conflict between the owners (shareholders) of a public corporation and the managers (agents) of a corporation. The principal–agent problem occurs when managers make decisions that are in their own interest and not in the best interest of a public company. It is usually very time-consuming and costly to resolve corporate disputes in courts of law.[2]

It is easier to review the performance of corporations than other forms of business organizations. A World Bank study of the performance of corporations in Sierra Leone could be found in Table 2.2. Corporations have the greatest potential of penetrating international markets, investing in research and development (R&D), and fostering innovation.

The country did better relative to other Sub-Saharan African countries in matters relating to accountability of management but not in terms of shareholders' rights and the resolution of disputes between shareholders and management. The strength of minority shareholder protections against misuse of corporate assets by directors for their personal gain as well as shareholder rights, governance safeguards, and corporate transparency requirements that reduce the risk of abuse were considered by a round of data collection that was completed in May 2019 (World Bank, 2020, p. 30).[3]

The study considered various aspects of public business operations, for example, whether:

(i) A publicly traded corporation is listed on the economy's most important stock exchange;
(ii) A corporation adopted bylaws or articles of association that go beyond the minimum requirements; and
(iii) A company does not follow codes, principles, recommendations, or guidelines that are not mandatory.

Other salient aspects of the study included: the ability of minority shareholders to sue and hold interested directors liable for prejudicial related-party transactions, available legal remedies (damages, disgorgement of profits, disqualification from managerial position(s) for one year or more, rescission of the transaction), access to internal corporate documents, shareholders' rights and role in major corporate decisions, governance safeguards protecting shareholders from undue board control and entrenchment, and corporate transparency on ownership stakes, compensation, audits and financial prospects.

Is there business profit to be made in Sierra Leone? Can businesses profitably operate in the country? Data suggest that public corporations or limited liability companies could profitably operate in the country. From 2006 to 2018, the number of new businesses in the country increased or trended upward from 333 to 1,980 (see Figure 2.4). It is also true that the prospect of business attrition is a real threat to business registration and continuity. The issue of business attrition will be subsequently dealt with in this chapter.

> *Formal sector firms represent a relatively small fraction of employment in Sierra Leone (91% of the labor force is self-employed) but a much higher proportion of taxes and exports (corporate tax alone makes up 11% of tax revenues). Firms may also suffer indirect effects if consumers or small firms respond to uncertainty and disruption by increasing savings, reducing investment, and/or cutting back on discretionary purchases.*
>
> (Casey et al., p. 1)

Local disruptions could be local contexts in which business competitiveness and innovation could be discouraged. Porter's model of competition, rivalry, local conditions, and innovation will be discussed fully in the next section.

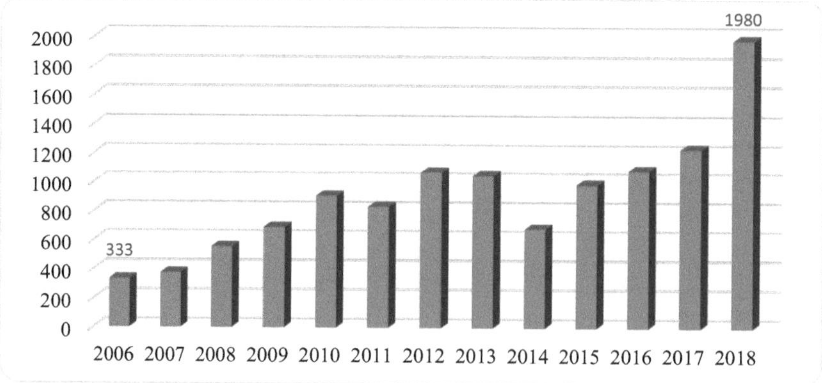

Figure 2.4 Registration of new business with limited liability (2006–2018).

Data source: World Bank's WDI (2023)

Note: New businesses registered are the number of new limited liability corporations (or its equivalent) registered in the calendar year.

Firms operate within various sectors in Sierra Leone; prominent of which are agribusiness consisting of agricultural sectors (food crops, cash crops, and horticultural crops), livestock production, and fisheries production,[4] marine operations, including fisheries, and processing facilities, assorted forms of tourism, and manufacturing. Manufacturing industries/factories are capital-intensive industries that rely on two major sources of energy supply, electricity, and water. Manufacturing industries incur higher costs of production whenever the sources of energy become dysfunctional. Higher costs of production adversely affect profit margins and tax liabilities (NRA, 2006, p. 15). The enormous potential of business operations in the country and the latent capacities raise issues about the competitiveness and innovative propensities of businesses in the country. I use Porter's diamond model to evaluate the possibilities of competitiveness and innovation in the country.

2.3 Porter's diamond model

Porter's diamond model provides the perfect segue to expand on market structure, a competitive business environment, and opportunities for growth and development (see Figure 2.5). Apart from providing a framework for analyzing the effects of competition and innovations, and the factors that are most responsible for innovation and global competitiveness, the model does not resonate too well for an underdeveloped economy like Sierra Leone. That is, the factors for innovation and international competitiveness are nonexistent in the underdeveloped economy.

The model stresses the significance of both internal and external sources that could help create competitive advantages for firms (Porter, 1990). How can a country gain competitive advantage? A truncated discussion of some of the most relevant factors follows. Notably, the author is not interested in parameterizing the variables of the external factors. Public policies create an environment for businesses to proper or perish. These policies go beyond the invitation of businesses to operate in a country. In the ecosystem of interconnected relationships, public policies also affect demand conditions and the quality of factor inputs.

Businesses need input and demand to create and maintain competitive advantage. Therefore, business competitiveness starts with preconditions in a home country. This section will focus on the external environment rather than firm creativity or innovation and internal controls (internal factors). Invariably, most foreign firms or investors are adept and imaginative. Creativity and innovation are enhanced by both internal and external factors, in addition to fortuitous circumstances public policies – both fortuitous circumstances and public policies have limitations.

Porter (1990) maintains that access to specialized and advanced factor conditions (such as highly skilled human resources or scientific and technological infrastructure) leads to competitive advantage for home countries. However, these production (external) factors are scarce, expensive, and more difficult for domestic and foreign rivals to achieve. Therefore, factor deficiencies or disadvantages in basic factors exert unreasonable pressure on firms to be innovative and competitive

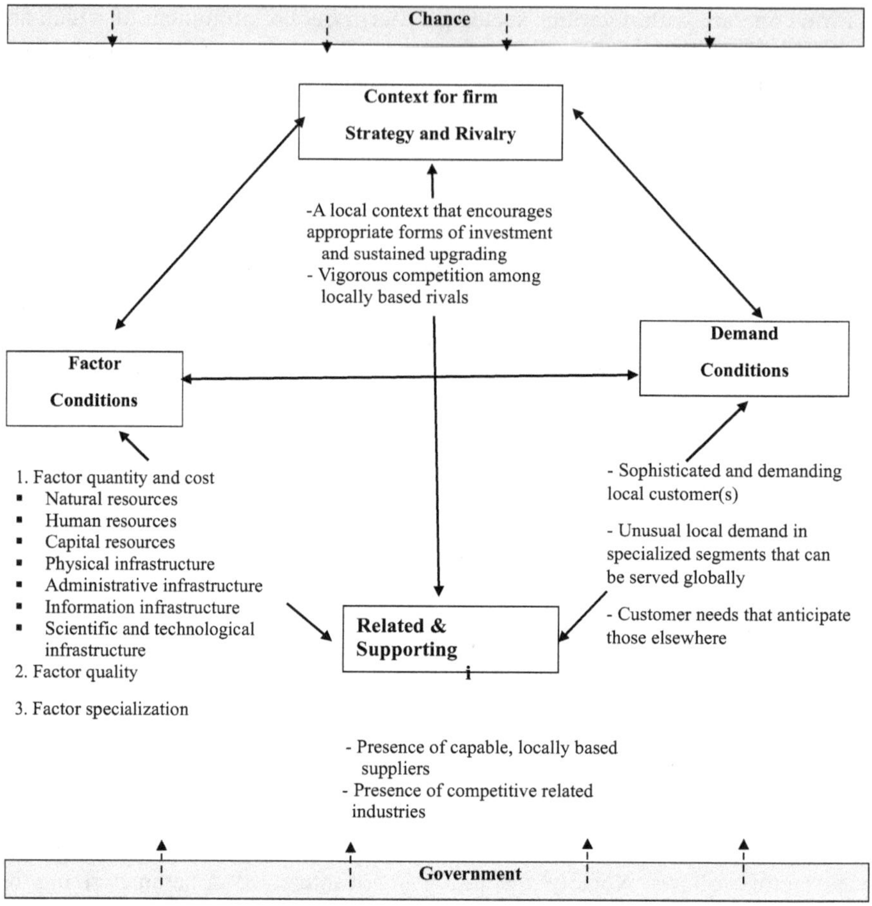

Figure 2.5 Porter's diamond model.

Source: Porter (2000)

in the global economy. Firms would have to make intentional choices and estimate their cost–benefit analyses in terms of resource (factor) abundance and scarcity (review the availability of natural resources, human capital, and public policy in Chapter 1).

Unfortunately, as was demonstrated in the previous chapter, the education and skills of the labor force in Sierra Leone are insufficient to meet the requirements of domestic and foreign demand. Some foreign firms have made efforts to mitigate the problem of inadequate human capital through training programs. For example, the mobile telecommunications company Zain has attempted to boost its human resource capital through its Celtel Academy, a school focused on business administration. The mining firms that have been in the country for several years also provide training to their employees. For the most part, however, companies rely on expatriates to fill highly skilled and salaried positions (UNCTAD, 2010, p. 21) in the context of decrepit infrastructure.

Sierra Leone made some progress to rebuild its moribund infrastructure after 11 years of an internecine civil war. Yet the infrastructural needs of the country have lingered. At the end of the conflict in 2002, the country was left with virtually no infrastructure but the reignition of mining activity resulted in resuscitation of the infrastructural reconstruction (International Monetary Fund, 2021, p. 6).

> *Some districts still have no paved roads, no electricity, and no water systems, almost 20 years after the war. Sierra Leone's public investments has been volatile, mirroring the huge swings in the economy and the fragile fiscal conditions. In anticipation of high growth, the government launched several major projects in the late 2000s. This led to a spike of public investments in 2009 and 2010. . . .*
>
> *The quality of infrastructure is also deteriorating. In the road sector, uneven surfaces of unpaved trunk roads cause huge shocks to vehicles equivalent of those of roller coasters. Because funds for routine maintenance are often neglected, government buildings and school facilities are in dilapidated conditions. This translates into large "efficiency gaps" in Sierra Leone's public investments, which are 48 percent, bigger than the average of Sub-Saharan African countries (41 percent).*
>
> (International Monetary Fund, 2021, pp. 6–7)

Energy problems, which will be fully discussed in the next chapter, are nothing new:

> *The lack of supply of electricity, water, roads and telecommunications is a considerable impediment to future development and investment in the country.*
>
> *The limited existing infrastructure deteriorated significantly during the war and The country is particularly challenged by electricity generation and distribution.*
>
> *This poses a serious constraint to attracting FDI [box 1.1 or 2.1 infra]. Electricity generation, estimated at just under 40 megawatts (MW), falls drastically short of the estimated power requirements, which range from 300 MW to 500 MW for the country. Transmission poses a further challenge in the sense that the network can only bear 46 MW. This is a critical issue that must be addressed rapidly as plans to increase production capacity move forward (e.g. the Bumbuna hydropower plant currently under construction and expected to begin generating power in 2009).*
>
> *Under these capacity constraints, only 2 per cent of households or 40,000 customers (mostly in or near Freetown) have access to electricity.*
>
> (UNCTAD, 2010, p. 10, and World Bank, 2007)

Box 2.1 The cost of power shortages for investors

Approximately 70 percent of power consumption in Sierra Leone is industrial or commercial, yet the lack and cost of electricity is one of the most frequently cited challenges facing investors. Typically, investors have chosen to operate their own generators rather than face frequent power interruptions. One example is Leocem, a cement manufacturer, which has built its own 5 MW powerhouse. Another example is Sierra Rutile, a mining company, which built a new powerhouse containing four 7.5 MW caterpillar generators at a cost of $29 million. Celtel, a mobile phone operator, uses a generator to run the main switch 24 hours a day and places two generators for every tower site in order to maintain 24-hour service. The company also pays for security guards to protect against the theft of the fuel in the generators. Implementing these measures has made Sierra Leone a very expensive place to do business.

Source: UNCTAD fact-finding mission, June 2008, and UNCTAD (2010, p. 11).

UNCTAD (2010). *Investment policy review*. United Nations.

World Bank. (2007). *Sierra Leone emergency power – meeting the challenge of turning on the lights*. World Bank.

Unlike the favorable score to initiate a business in Sierra Leone (see Table 2.1), the score for energy supply is discouraging (see Table 2.3). The cost of energy supply increases the variable cost of doing businesses – since energy usage is expected to increase with output – and therefore the overall total cost of doing business in the country. The country obtained a 31.6 percentile rank in the World Bank's study of the provision of energy supply, suggesting that about 69 percent of the subjects of inquiry (190 countries) performed better. Data for the study were collected since 2019, but detailed discussions of productivity and efficiency will be spared for the next chapter. To score on the energy index, the frequency of power outages must be between 0 and 100. If the minimum outage time considered for system average interruption duration index (SAIDI) or system average interruption frequency index (SAIFI) is over 5 minutes, a country was not eligible to score on the index.

Table 2.3 Energy supply

Getting Electricity (rank)	*181*
Score of getting electricity (0–100)	*31.6*
Procedures (number)	8
Time (days)	82
Cost (% of income per capita)	5,057.20
Reliability of supply and transparency of tariff index (0–8)	0

Source: World Bank's *Doing Business . . .* (2020, p. 4)

Box 2.2 Energy reliability

Mechanisms for monitoring outages (0–1) 0
Does the distribution utility use automated tools to monitor outages? No
Mechanisms for restoring service (0–1) 0
Does the distribution utility use automated tools to restore service? No
Regulatory monitoring (0–1) 0
Does a regulator – that is, an entity separate from the utility – monitor the utility's performance on reliability of supply? No
Financial deterrents aimed at limiting outages (0–1) 0
Does the utility either pay compensation to customers or face fines by the regulator (or both) if outages exceed a certain cap? No
Communication of tariffs and tariff changes (0–1) 0
Are effective tariffs available online? No
Link to the website, if available online
Are customers notified of a change in tariff ahead of the billing cycle? Yes

Source: World Bank (2020, p. 9).

Box 2.2 provides some substantive indicators of the inefficiency of energy supply in Sierra Leone, including financial deterrents for limiting power outages, mechanisms for monitoring outages, mechanisms for restoring service, and communication of "tariff" changes. The scores are not very encouraging. The modernization of telecommunications and the availability of foreign providers have relieved the government of the heavy cost of demoded forms of telecommunications infrastructure. Essentially, innovations have flowed into the country rather than out of the country.

The factor conditions espouse inherent challenges in the areas of human resources, capital resources, physical infrastructure, information infrastructure, and scientific and technological infrastructure. Some of the factors will be subsequently discussed in the context of foreign direct investment (FDI); see the previous chapter for human capital (resources). The factor deficiencies do not robustly complement the favorable subset of natural resources, and the demand conditions are too weak to compensate for the shortfall in factor conditions, leading to a systemic breakdown of innovative capacities in the country.

Are there related and supporting industries in the country?

> *There seems to be some level of activity by local firms providing services such as transport or printing to foreign firms, but such connections remain at best tenuous. While there is willingness on the part of foreign firms to engage local businesses, the characteristics of local firms make this option less attractive than outsourcing to firms outside the country. One of the most cited problems preventing linkages is supply capacity. Many of the local firms are*

> *small and do not have the capacity either in terms of manpower or equipment to supply foreign firms. Another issue is the informality of the local business sector. In the current tax and business registration environment, many firms operate without formal registration, making them both unattractive to foreign firms from a legal aspect and difficult to identify as potential suppliers from a practical perspective.*
>
> (UNCTAD, 2010, pp. 21–22)

The sparse and varied local industries do not have clearly defined vertical (supply chain) relationships, and foreign investors continue to face challenges in the areas of a coordinated skilled workforce and infrastructural support. Some investors have opted to train their employees to bridge the skill gap and increase the efficiency and productivity of their employees. However, these relationships do not guarantee consequential internal absorption or consumption in an environment of extensive poverty and inaccessible liquidity.

Demand conditions are contingent on the nature of the domestic demand for an industry's product or service (1990). Domestic demand is what is expected to generate pressures to catapult domestic industries into high-pressured rivalry, competition, and innovation. Of course, the domestic consumers must be well informed, financially well resourced, and dynamically demanding for industries to engage in high-stakes business competition. The consumption preferences of domestic consumers must not only be dynamic but also mirror the subsequent expectations of wants in the global economy. The economy of the country is not well structured for domestic consumers to manifest dynamic and pioneering choices.

> *To innovate, companies must have access to people with appropriate skills and have home-demand conditions that send the right signals.*
>
> *They must also have active domestic rivals who create pressure to innovate.*
>
> *Another precondition is company goals that lead to sustained commitment to the industry. Without such a commitment and the presence of active rivalry, a company may take an easy way around a disadvantage rather than using it as a spur to innovation . . . .*
>
> *[W]here the home demand gives their companies a clearer or earlier picture of emerging buyer needs, and where demanding buyers pressure companies to innovate faster and achieve more sophisticated competitive advantage than their foreign rivals. The size of home demand proves far less significant than the character of home demand.*[5]
>
> (Porter, 1990, p. 82)

Rivalry is less intense when firms do not have a substantial market to compete for. Fierce struggle to obtain competitive advantage in a market and dominate a market by price competition, product differentiation, marketing, and advertising (rivalry) requires the prospect of profitable feedback (returns). There must be a

Table 2.4 Financial infrastructure and creditor security

Getting Credit (rank)	*165*
Score of getting credit (0–100)	*25*
Strength of legal rights index (0–12)	5
Depth of credit information index (0–8)	0
Credit registry coverage (% of adults)	2.1
Credit bureau coverage (% of adults)	0

Source: World Bank's *Doing Business* (2020, p. 4)

financial infrastructure and a regulatory environment to configure meaningful, equitable, and consequential rivalry. The absence of these preconditions stifles competition and innovation in the context of a domestic or international economy.

The financial infrastructure for liquidity or expansion of credit is not very well developed to reach a preponderant amount of consumers in Sierra Leone. Unlike advanced economies with a relatively superior amount of human capital and significant presence of liquidity, unskilled, poorer, and impoverished people do not have access to credit (see the previous chapter for human capital and consumption). The skewed access to liquidity and financial resources dampens the prospects of robust consumption that is required to elevate the competitive and innovative postures of an underdeveloped economy in the global economy. The chain of production and consumption is somewhat broken or delinked in an irreparable way.

Table 2.4 provides a summary of the financial infrastructure for business credit. Information asymmetry and adverse selection are inherent financial risks within the system. The country obtains a 25-percentile rank on financial infrastructure for business credit and creditor security, suggesting that the foundations for institutional credit, competition, and consumption are very weak.

The annual growth of final consumption in Sierra Leone is highly volatile (see Figure 2.6) – with some unusual swings – while that of the UK and the US are rather stable and virtually predictable for investment and innovation. It is not unusual for aggregate consumption to overshoot its long-run equilibrium after periods of national adversity like wars and pandemics.

The average annual growth rates of final consumption in the UK, the US, and Sierra Leone from 1980 to 2020 are 2.3, 2.7, and 4.2 percent, respectively. It is noteworthy that the size of home demand could prove to be far less significant than the character of home demand (Porter, 1990, p. 82). Significantly, in the case of Sierra Leone, it is highly probable and plausible that final consumption is heavily skewed in favor of imported goods and services rather than the consumption of domestic goods and services, thereby giving foreign producers a significant competitive advantage. The excessive trade imbalance of Sierra Leone will be examined in Chapter 4 of this book.

Ironically, apart from the growth in final aggregate consumption, the growth of consumer inflation has been very high in Sierra Leone relative to the UK and the US (see Figure 2.7). Invariably, inflation devalues the purchasing power of

Figure 2.6 Annual growth of final consumption expenditure in the US, the UK, and Sierra Leone (1980–2020).

Data source: World Bank's WDI (2023)

Note: Final consumption expenditure (formerly total consumption) is the sum of household final consumption expenditure (private consumption) and general government final consumption expenditure (general government consumption). This estimate includes any statistical discrepancy in the use of resources relative to the supply of resources.

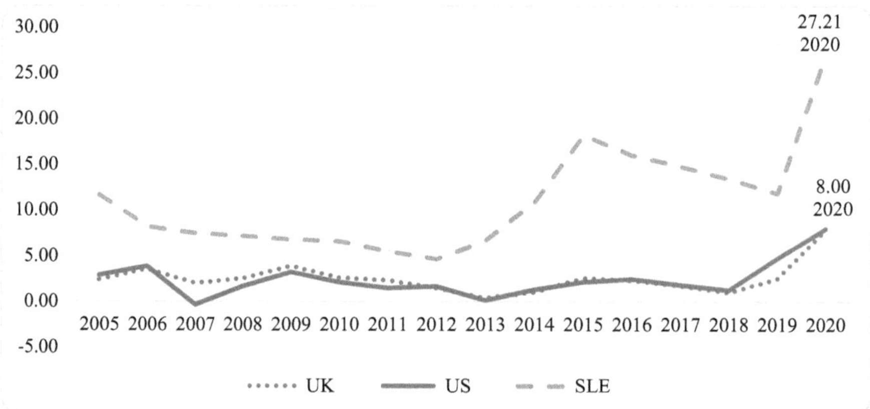

Figure 2.7 Growth of consumer inflation in the US, the UK, and Sierra Leone (2005–2020).

Data source: World Bank's WDI (2024)

Note: Inflation as measured by the consumer price index reflects the annual percentage change in the cost to the average consumer of acquiring a basket of goods and services that may be fixed or changed at specified intervals, such as yearly. The Laspeyres formula is generally used.

Figure 2.8 Household debt, loans, and debt securities in the US, the UK, and Sierra Leone (percent of GDP).

Sources: IMF (2023) and Global Debt Database (September 2023)

Note: Total stock of household debt, loans, and debt securities (percent of GDP).

nominal income and makes consumers poorer. Intuitively, a reduction in aggregate purchasing power is not usually expected to increase consumption of finished goods and services, except of course if consumers have access to credit. Access to credit in the underdeveloped economy of Sierra Leone is a challenging proposition. The inequity of access to human capital and unfavorable income distribution further complicates the analyses of liquidity or access to credit for consumption of goods and services. It is possible to have some amount of micro-prudential (micro) credit, but such an opportunity is inadequate to spur industrial-scale competition and innovation.

Clearly, residents of the underdeveloped economy of Sierra Leone do not have access to liquidity as their counterparts in the UK and the US (see Figure 2.8). Advanced economies with well-developed financial systems thrive on the expansion of credit for purchases of final goods and services. That is, they are consumer-oriented economies that propel competition and innovation.

Low-income residents of poorer economies with underdeveloped financial systems virtually always must depend on micro-prudential credit and family (noninstitutional) loans (or friendly ties) to make purchases of goods and services. Those with substantial amounts of human capital and relatively superior job placements usually have access to depository institutions and financial intermediaries. That is, people with sufficient or adequate human capital could afford to utilize depository institutions and other financial intermediaries to access credits and purchase capital goods (see Chapter 1 of this book for the relationship between human capital and consumption of durable goods). Accordingly, advanced, and emerging economies are better situated to exploit demand conditions for business competition and innovation.

Beyond demand conditions, there are legislative and regulatory challenges to industrial competition and innovation in an underdeveloped economy like Sierra Leone. Governance, the rule of law, business and human rights, dispute resolution, and finance and banking regulations help shape the competitive landscape of a country and the framework for firm productivity. Some of these issues will be addressed in the foreign investments section of this chapter.

2.4 (a) The regulatory environment

The country has tried to ensure that there could be no ignorance of its laws by promoting regulatory transparency. The Right to Access Information Commission was established in 2014 to make government records available to the public with punitive provisions for violations of business law. The country joined the Open Government Partnership (OGP) in 2014 to promote transparent and accountable governance and enable the discouragement of corruption in business operations.

The cumulative strength of legal rights as indexed by the World Bank is marginally below average (5/12) (see Box 2.3). The obtainable and unobtainable business rights have been recorded in affirmative and negative responses. Businesses could grant non-possessory (third-party-owned collateral) securities, enjoy flexibility of extended rights, all types of debts could be secured by the contracting parties, and alternative dispute resolutions (ADRs) are recognized. However, secured (debt holders) creditors do not have primacy. Legal framework that extends the creation publicity and enforcement of functional equivalents of secured transactions do not have recognition in the economy. Further, there are some ancillary legal issues with traditionally recognized senior creditors. There is not much difference in the performances of Ghana, Guinea, and the Sub-Saharan African countries. Of the African subjects of inquiry, only Kenya registered an impressive score (see Figure 2.9).

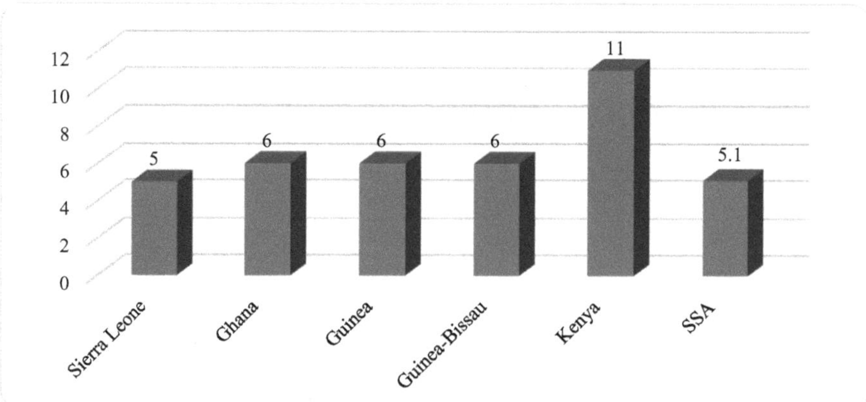

Figure 2.9 Legal rights for transacting business (2020).

Source: World Bank (2020, p. 28)

Box 2.3 Legal rights and business transactions

- Strength of legal rights index (0–12) 5
- Does an integrated or unified legal framework for secured transactions that extends to the creation, publicity, and enforcement of functional equivalents to security interests in movable assets exist in the economy? **No**
- Does the law allow businesses to grant a non-possessory security right in a single category of movable assets, without requiring a specific description of collateral? **Yes**
- Does the law allow businesses to grant a non-possessory security right in substantially all its assets, without requiring a specific description of collateral? **Yes**
- May a security right extend to future or after-acquired assets, and does it extend automatically to the products, proceeds, and replacements of the original assets? **Yes**
- Is a general description of debts and obligations permitted in collateral agreements; can all types of debts and obligations be secured between parties; and can the collateral agreement include a maximum amount for which the assets are encumbered? **Yes**
- Is a collateral registry in operation for both incorporated and non-incorporated entities, that is, unified geographically and by asset type, with an electronic database indexed by debtor's name? **No**
- Does a notice-based collateral registry exist in which all functional equivalents can be registered? **No**
- Does a modern collateral registry exist in which registrations, amendments, cancelations, and searches can be performed online by any interested third party? **No**
- Are secured creditors paid first (i.e., before tax claims and employee claims) when a debtor defaults outside an insolvency procedure? **No**
- Are secured creditors paid first (i.e., before tax claims and employee claims) when a business is liquidated? **No**
- Are secured creditors subject to an automatic stay on enforcement when a debtor enters a court-supervised reorganization procedure? Does the law protect secured creditors' rights by providing clear grounds for relief from the stay and sets a time limit for it? **No**
- Does the law allow parties to agree on out-of-court enforcement at the time a security interest is created? Does the law allow the secured creditor to sell the collateral through public auction or private tender, as well as, for the secured creditor to keep the asset in satisfaction of the debt? **Yes**

Source: World Bank (2020, p. 29)

Real land ownership is bifurcated. Since this issue was extensively discussed in the previous chapter, its replication will be redundant. However, it is important to recall that the Western Area the former British colony of Sierra Leone operates under a freehold system while land in the provincial areas outside the Western Area is governed under a leasehold system. Foreigners cannot own land under either system but can lease land for terms of up to 99 years (US DoS).

> *The [Sierra Leonean] Constitution protects property rights, but the rule of law is fragile and uneven across the country. In the absence of an effectively functioning legal framework, property rights and contracts are not adequately secure. Mortgages and liens are possible but rare and generally involve high-interest rates and short loan periods. There is no land titling system, and traditional tribal justice systems still supplement the national government's judiciary, especially in rural areas. In 2020, the World Bank Doing Business Report ranked Sierra Leone 169 in the World Bank ease of registering property.*
>
> *The process takes approximately 56 days with seven procedures and costs about 11 percent of the property's value.*
>
> (US DoS)

In 2020, the US Department of State finds that Sierra Leone's municipal law of intellectual property needs to be updated for consistency with contemporary international law.

> *Sierra Leone has been a member of the World Intellectual Property Organization (WIPO) since 1986 and a member of the African Regional Intellectual Property Organization (ARIPO), the common intellectual property body for English-speaking African countries, since 1980. As a member of the WTO, Sierra Leone is bound by the Agreement on Trade-Related Aspects of Intellectual Property Rights (TRIPS). Sierra Leone has not ratified the WIPO Copyright Treaty or the Berne Convention to protect Literary and Artistic Rights.*
>
> (US DoS)

Despite its recognition of international standards, Sierra Leone's intellectual property protection is limited. Laws pre-dating the colonial era have allowed patents and trademarks registered in the United Kingdom to be extended to Sierra Leone (US DoS). Yet the capacity of Sierra Leoneans to significantly recreate marks and patents in Sierra Leone is highly constrained. There have been efforts to update the country's legal framework, including the Copyright Act 2011, the Patents and Industrial Design Act 2012, and the Trademark Act 2014.

Inadequate resources and capacity limitations make it difficult to enforce legal protections of intellectual property rights. The pecuniary cost of the expropriation of intellectual property right is colossal; see Warburton (pp. 159–190) for the international law of intellectual property rights, consequences of innovation, and cost of expropriation. Invariably, there is an urgent need to modernize anachronistic laws of the country to facilitate innovation, economic growth, and sustainable development. The next section examines the issue of tax liabilities of businesses and public revenue.

2.4 (b) Taxes and business attrition

Taxes constitute the most readily available mechanism for governments to raise revenue. Yet taxes must be used sparingly as a mechanism for governments to raise revenue because of the detrimental societal effects of excessive taxation. Accordingly, increases in taxes must not be an alternative to production and revenue acquisition from production. Governments in underdeveloped economies are prone to impose and increase taxes on assorted categories of goods and services emanating from international and domestic sources. While a developed economy like the US does not necessarily tax exports, some income strapped underdeveloped economies tax exports and imports to obtain revenue.

The governments of Sierra Leone have historically derived revenue from multiple sources. The government collects a value-added tax (VAT) or goods and services tax (GST), which is designed to provide a broad-based system that will positively correlate the receipt of revenue to growth in all sectors of the economy. According to the National Revenue Authority (NRA), a variety of taxes all under the VAT/GST system: (i) Import Sales Tax, (ii) Domestic Sales Tax, (iii) Restaurant Tax, (iv) Message Tax, and (v) Entertainment Tax. Direct taxes (Corporate, PAYE, etc.) and Other Indirect taxes (i.e., Import duty, excise, and export duties) are distinct from the VAT (NRA, 2007, p. 36).[6]

As should be expected, taxes (tariffs) are imposed on international articles of trade. However, for over five decades, there have been movements to liberalize international trade. This issue will be comprehensively dealt with in Chapter 4. Bilateral and multilateral trade agreements have provisions to reduce barriers to trade and extend indiscriminate terms of trade to the member countries of a trade treaty. Sierra Leone has bilateral investment treaties with Germany, which has been in force since 1966, the United Kingdom (in 1981 and revised in 2001), China (in 2001), and United Arab Emirates (UAE) (2019).[7] Other bilateral agreements and regional trade agreements have provided tax concessions. These treaties will be discussed in Chapter 4.

Policymakers in underdeveloped economies easily make the mistake of increasing taxes on goods and services to compensate for shortfalls and inability to increase domestic production for revenue. Excessive taxes increase the deadweight loss to society and encourage tax evasion, avoidance, and corruption. The tax triangle (Figure 2.10) shows that consumers make taxed purchases from businesses that are contingent on disposable income. Businesses pay taxes to the government, and the government is expected to plough back revenue to society in the form of services and employment for economic growth and development. When a government fails to plough back revenue because of unseemly reasons and misguided policies, the macroeconomic system becomes dysfunctional and decrepit.

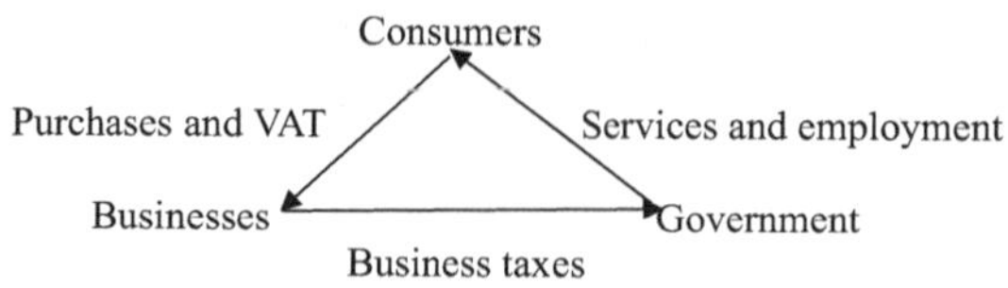

Figure 2.10 The tax triangle.

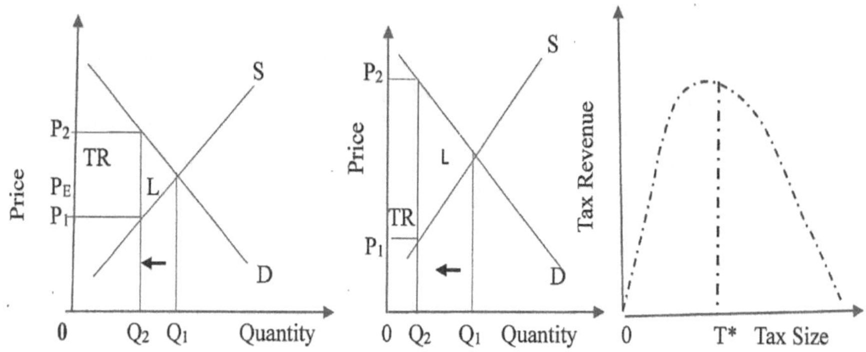

Figure 2.11a, 11b, 11c Relatively small tax (b) Large tax (c) Laffer Curve.

The goods and services taxes (GST) and value-added taxes (VAT) have limitations. Consider the effects of VAT or GST in a small open economy with a high unemployment rate and stagnant or insufficient production. Further, assume that consumers are indifferent to the consumption of a good (elasticity of demand = 1), as depicted in Figures 2.11(a), and (b) (see also Mankiw, p. 160, and Goolsbee et al., pp. 77–82). Larger tax sizes (inequitable taxes) could easily reduce the welfare of a country.

The sizes of taxes have implications for the welfare of a country when welfare is defined in terms of the societal net loss of surpluses that could otherwise accrue to consumers and traders alike (denoted as L in Figures 2.11 (a) and (b)). Consumers gain surplus when they pay less than what they are willing to pay for a good or service (think of the area underneath the demand curve and evaluated at the equilibrium price. P_E). Traders (sellers) gain surplus when they sell their goods above the inducement cost (think about the area above the supply curve that is evaluated at the equilibrium price P_E). Therefore, the combination of surpluses is largest at the market clearing equilibrium price. Any distortion of a market price, say P_2 (due to taxation), generates a loss of surplus to a country known as a deadweight loss. Figure 2.11(b) shows that societal loss increases *in tandem* with larger tax sizes. As such, policymakers must also think about optimal tax sizes when taxes become the preferred method of raising public revenue. A government cannot excessively rely on increasing taxes in lieu of income that is generated by cost-effective production. The thought of optimal taxation becomes unavoidable as a sound public policy, especially when higher taxes adversely affect the poor and low-income earners.

The theoretical proposition of Arthur Laffer's optimal tax is conceptually useful albeit arduously estimable.[8] Policymakers must be able to determine or estimate the tax size that results in the maximum amount of revenue without intolerable costs to consumers, retailers, and investors who are prone to evade (violate tax laws) and avoid (exploit loopholes in tax law) paying taxes.[9] That is, Figure 2.11(c) is conceptually useful to know that there exists a tax size that could maximize the tax revenue of policymakers (see Figure 2.11(c)). It turns out that such a tax size coincides with the plateau of the Laffer curve. Measuring the optimal tax poses some logistical problems (a dissonance between expectations and reality) because pinning down the marginal tax rate that is optimal is a rather challenging proposition. The curve does not illustrate anything about the sensitivities (elasticities) of consumers, retailers, and investors to incremental changes in tax sizes. Notably, the concept of the optimal tax rate is very much unlike that of an optimal tariff (t^*), which maximizes the net benefit resulting from the improvement in a nation's terms of trade relative to the negative effect associated with a reduction in the volume of trade:

$$t^* = \frac{1}{e-1}, \qquad 2.2$$

where e is the price elasticity of supply of a foreign nation evaluated at world prices.[10]

Notwithstanding, the Laffer Curve has some attractive properties. It certainly shows that it is impracticable for policymakers to continuously increase taxes and expect to simultaneously increase tax revenue at the same time. For example, a tax size of 100 percent, which is rather unrealistic, will generate zero revenue because nobody will be willing to work for zero income. Additionally, it will no longer be profitable for sellers to retail their goods and services, or for investors to invest. Analogously, as noted earlier, excessive taxes will cause people to evade and avoid the payment of taxes – this may well account for attrition rates and loss of tax revenue. Realistically, a tax size on the negative segment of the curve that approaches 100 percent is unlikely to generate more public revenue.

To be quantitatively useful, the optimal tax rate must be meaningfully estimated. Of course, such an estimation will be confounded or complicated by the variations of the tax structure of the country. Unsurprisingly, wide variations in collection activity should be expected in an underdeveloped economy. Figure 2.11(c) is more intuitive than estimable. Can the policymakers of Sierra Leone become over-reliant on taxes in lieu of production for public revenue? No. Tax policies must be augmented by the productive capacities of a country to generate public revenue and increase general welfare. Significantly, there are positive externalities accruing to the increase in value-added output, the principal of which is the better management of foreign reserves.

The 2008 NRA data show that there were attrition problems or factory failures, which impinged on the revenue base of the country. There were 56 registered factories, of which 29 were active and above threshold, 11 were active but below threshold, and 16 became extinct (NRA, 2008, p. 12). The uncertainty of business continuity poses revenue risk and forecasting challenges for the government. The empirical value of the aged data is naturally problematic, and researchers and consultants alike with a predilection for frequentists estimates have stumbled over the inadequacy of data to conduct frequentist analyses in underdeveloped countries. I approach the data problem differently by using Bayesian probability analysis to derive useful analytical information. The goal is to derive a relatively useful parameter estimate of attrition without tax liabilities and public revenue in Figure 2.12. Consider the posterior Bayesian probability estimate rather than a point estimate without adequate data:

$$p(\theta \mid \xi) = \frac{p(\theta) * p(\xi \mid \theta)}{p(\xi)}, \qquad 2.3$$

where the left-hand side defines the posterior distribution, the probability of observing a parameter (theta) given that the probability that the data, $p(\xi)$, nest all the possible values of the parameter estimate. The numerator of Equation 2.3 consists of the distribution of a prior belief of a distribution of the parameter ($p(\theta)$), which could be binomial or normal but binomial in this case, and a probable likelihood that the data contain the true value of the parameter. The likelihood is not as complicated as it might seem because the data already contain 40 successes (active factories with tax liabilities of different thresholds and a sample size of 56). The probability distribution of the parameter (successes) limits the range of possible values within the probability density function.

The available data provide information for the construction of a posterior distribution with a credible interval of factory retention based on current circumstances. The sample size of 56 cases indicates that the current chance of success (retention of factories for revenue) is 65 percent (36 cases). Figure 2.12 depicts the uncertainties associated with tax revenue (or going concerns), based on current circumstances. With the use of R-programming language, two credible intervals of opportunities can be evaluated or constructed: (i) the high-density interval (HDI), which contains the required mass such that all estimates (the outer boundaries of Figure 2.12), and (ii) the equaled tailed interval (ETI) of posterior distributions, which computes quantiles of possibilities (the inner bounds). The probability of being below the interval is equal to the probability of being above it (see the density function of Figure 2.12). Tax evasion, avoidance, and failures of businesses are unavoidable occurrences in an underdeveloped economy – to a greater extent than in advanced economies.

Given the effects of available data, the ETI shows that factory retention could be as low as 55 percent and as high as 78 percent with a 95 percent credible interval (CI) – where the CI is the posterior mean +/– the relevant z multiple times the posterior standard deviation – depending on policy initiatives and economic circumstances. Hence, there must be some public policy implications for unfavorable business attrition rates and loss of public revenue. Although the country has made some improvements in the perception and margins of corruption, could evaders and

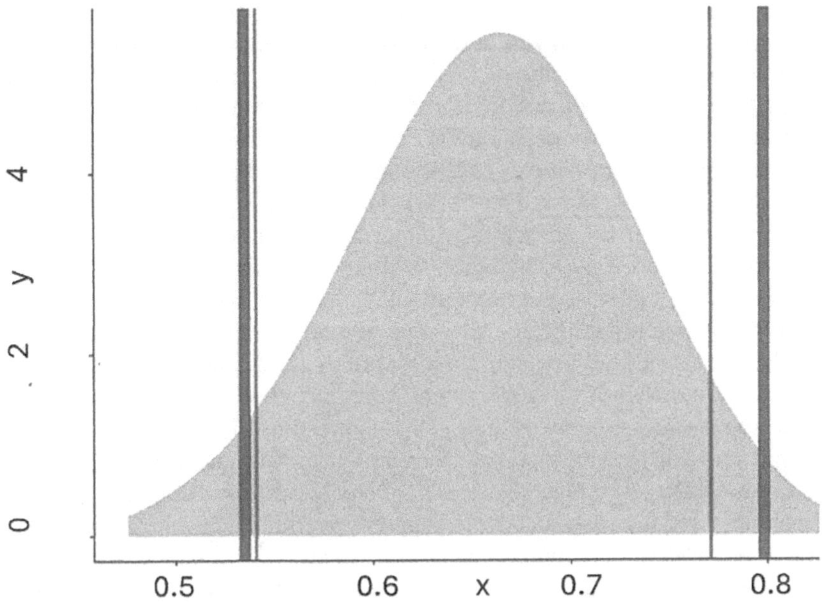

Figure 2.12 A Bayesian HDI and ETI credible intervals of factory retention.

avoiders exploit corruption and loopholes in the tax system?[11] Are Porter's external factors conducive to the retention and continuity (going concern) of businesses in the country? Is there insufficient internal demand for products? Are external shocks (sudden but temporary disruptions) overpowering? What could be done by policy-makers to considerably reduce attrition rates of businesses in the country?

Exogenous shocks are uncontrollable incidents beyond the control of policy-makers in developing countries. However, the policymakers must seriously consider policies and interventions that could attenuate or blunt the effects of inevitable external threats. For example, the 2008 global crisis impacted domestic revenue collection, non-tax revenue, and international trade taxes – mainly because of the decline in imports (including high-end ostentatious goods), drop in the supply of crude oil and increases in energy cost, and reduction in remittances from abroad.

The multiplier effects of exogenous shocks are palpable. The shocks affect the operations of businesses on impact. In 2008, most businesses revised their profit estimates downward due to increases in marginal cost, high production costs induced by increases in electricity tax, which went up by 50 percent, and anticipated demand for wage increases (indexation) (NRA, 2009, p. 18).

Diamond exports dropped by (30.2%) from US$141.566 million in 2007 to US$98.801 million in 2008. Drop in the world market price of diamonds among other things, coupled with the drop in export volume from 603.6 thousand carats in 2007 to 371.3 thousand carats in 2008 (i.e., by 38.5%) partly explains the drop in foreign exchange earnings from diamond exports (NRA, 2009, p. 20).

In 2008, Sierra Leone's revenue effort, at just over 10.0 percent of GDP, was estimated to be among the lowest in the world, which necessitated a revision of the tax code to include the GST, harmonized Customs laws, Customs Tariff Act 2009, Customs Regulations 2009, and Customs Act 2009 (NRA, 2010, p. 8). It is noteworthy that even active businesses could fall short of revenue expectations, making revenue receipts susceptible to volatility. More individual businesses paid their taxes in 2009 (3217) compared to 2811 businesses in 2008 (NRA, 2010, p. 23). Company (corporate) tax fell short of target due to the low returns of tax documents for proper verifications and the low return of business profits as most businesses such as the financial and telecommunication industries continued to plough back their profits in order to capture a larger market share (NRA, 2010, p. 26).[12]

The NRA continues to maintain its mandate to assess and collect tax and non-tax revenues on behalf of the government, administer and enforce laws relating to the national revenue, and make consequential amendments to certain laws relating to revenue and other relating matters. The authority was also established to minimize revenue leakages, protect the importation of harmful and contraband products in the country, and increase tax base to support government development programs in an investment-friendly environment (NRA, 2011, p. 2).

The macroeconomic tax environment of Sierra Leone is admittedly complex, with more than 80 percent of the registered business units considered to be small and micro enterprises. The small businesses contribute about 20 percent of the revenue collected by the Income Tax Department. Apart from a large shadow (underground) economy that contributes about 45 percent to GDP, there are several parallel regulations hindering the effective administration of tax laws. Put simply, the environment of tax administration in the country is anything but straightforward (NRA, 2011/2012, p. 2). The next section examines foreign direct investment (FDI) and frictions.

2.5 Foreign direct investments

Foreign direct investment is the sum of equity capital, reinvestment of earnings, and long-term capital with an ownership of 10 percent or more voting shares that flows into a foreign country. This means that foreign owners of a company have substantial or significant control of the management of a business that resides abroad or in a foreign country. The direct investors or foreign investors acquire long-lasting interest in a company by owning 10 percent of equity or voting rights of a company.

Although the empirical inquiry into the effects of FDI flows may be controversial, FDI has the potential of making significant contributions to the economic growth of a country, especially in underdeveloped economies with a paucity of national saving – FDI augments inadequate national saving and facilitates technological transfers. However, the flow of FDI is highly contingent on the internal conditions of destination countries. The internal pull factors are multifarious, including the quality of human capital, political conditions (stability), the quality of infrastructure, energy availability, rule of law, protections of private property against expropriation, regulation of the use of foreign property, and macroeconomic conditions inter alia.

Data on FDI inflows into Sierra Leone are not readily available, but extrapolation of data on FDI has been possible. The Central Bank's balance of payments questionnaire for foreign investors has provided a reliable proxy to gain insights into the operations of a large proportion of foreign firms that operate in the country together with the general characteristics of FDI in Sierra Leone. Notwithstanding, the contributions of FDI to economic growth are much more noticeable (see Figure 2.15).[13] Historically, FDI flows into Sierra Leone have not been significant (UNCTAD, 2010, p. 14) though it contributes to national income, but mining and telecommunications provided the mainstay in the 1930s and 1990s. Between 2004 and 2007, FDI flows recovered after wartime disruptions and suspensions.[14]

The Central Bank's data (2007) reveal that among the larger foreign investors, most firms were concentrated in services, primarily banking and telecommunications, but there are also accounting, airline, and shipping firms (see Figure 2.13). In the next chapter, I use the Markov Chain process to examine the long-run potential of the service sector. Foreign firms in the industrial sector are primarily in light manufacturing and mining along with two oil and gas firms (UNCTAD, 2010, p. 16).

The FDI inflows are also indicative of not only local skill sets that foreign investors would require to employ the residents of Sierra Leone but also the skills that Sierra Leoneans will need abroad to fulfill the investment requirements of reciprocity, especially in the banking sector. Evidently, a skilled workforce with adequate human capital is required to sustain the inflow of FDI and recruitment of Sierra Leoneans (even though some FDI inflows would naturally require less intensive

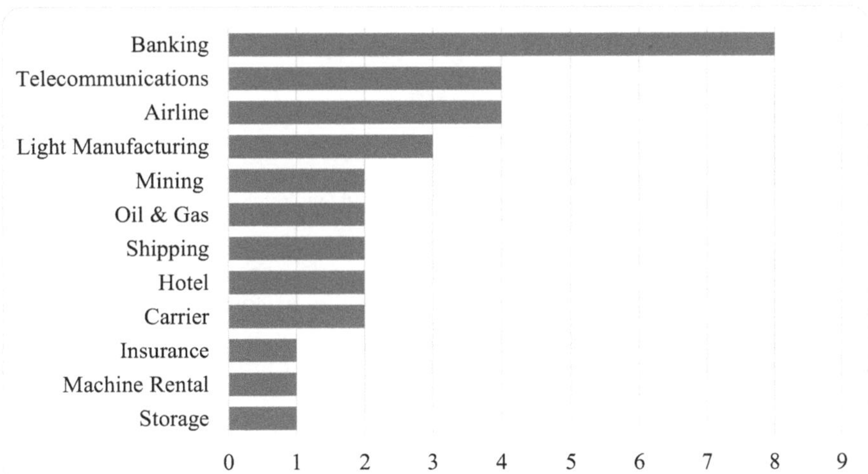

Figure 2.13 FDI distribution by sector 2007.

Source: Bank of Sierra Leone and UNCTAD (2010, p. 16)

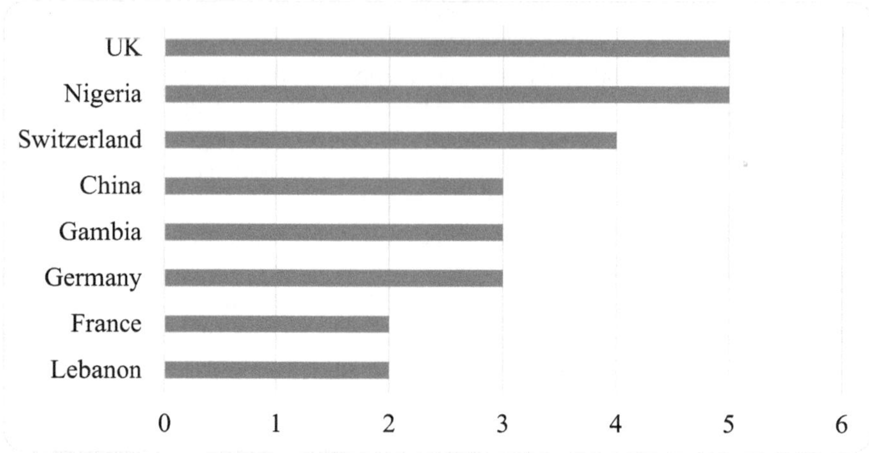

Figure 2.14 Top sources of inward FDI to Sierra Leone (2007).
Source: Bank of Sierra Leone and UNCTAD (2010, p. 20)

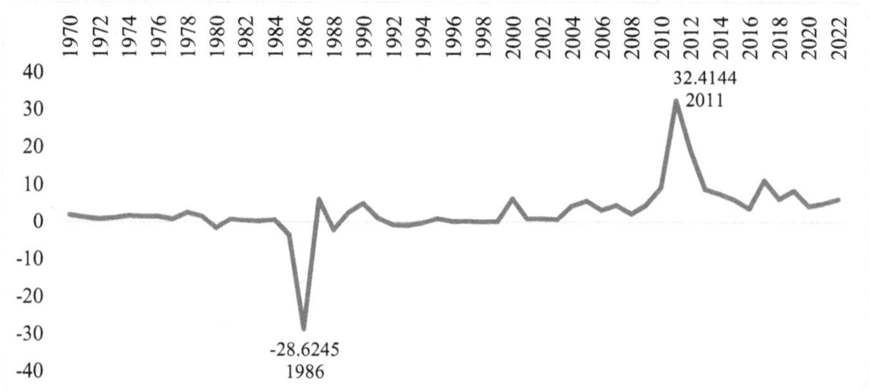

Figure 2.15 FDI inflows 1970–2021 (% GDP).
Data source: World Bank's WDI (2023) and Macrotrends, http://macrotrends.net

human capital). Of course, recall that the availability of human capital is just one of several pull factors that are required for FDI to flow into the country. Clearly, banking and telecommunications have been prominent inflows from some major sources (see Figure 2.14).

FDI is concentrated in Freetown, partly because of its relatively superior infrastructure, and in the three major mining areas – Kono and Kenema (in the west for diamonds) and Bonthe (in the south for rutile and bauxite). The remainder of the country has not attracted FDI because of the paucity and absence of economic attraction (review the push factor in the previous chapter); Nigerian investment has

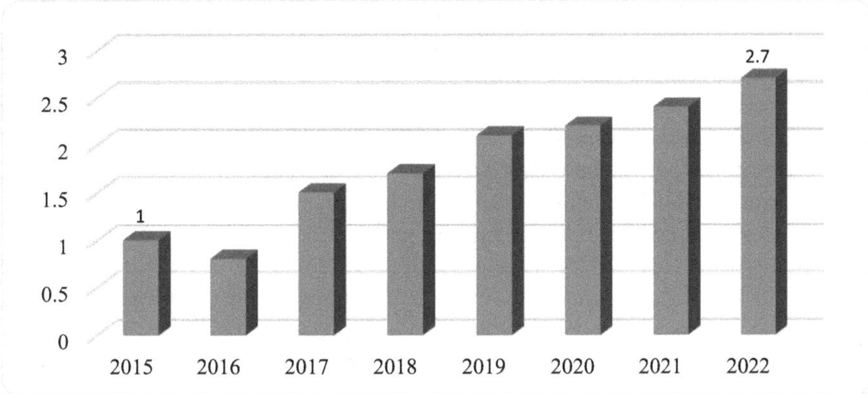

Figure 2.16 FDI inflows from the UK to Sierra Leone US $B.

Data source: Trade and Investments Factsheets (as reported by Sierra Leone): UK's Department for Business and Trade (2023 December, p. 11)

Note: In 2021, the stock of FDI from the UK in Sierra Leone was £66 million, 1.2% or £779.2 thousand lower than in 2020. In 2021, Sierra Leone accounted for less than 0.1% of the total UK outward FDI stock (p. 10).

heavy presence in the banking sector (UNCTAD, 2010, p. 20). The data show that FDI has contributed marginally to economic growth but for the spike in 2011 (see Figure 2.10). The post-2011 slump warrants some inquiry for policy readjustments or realignments if the 2011 flow was not merely a positive shock.

The UK continues to be a major source of FDI into Sierra Leone (see Figure 2.16). The US' FDI in Sierra Leone (stock) was $1 million in 2022, which remained unchanged from 2021.[15]

> *Foreign investors have equal access to the judicial system, which is slow and often subject to financial and political influence. However, Sierra Leonean courts may acknowledge foreign judgment from specific jurisdictions with reciprocal enforcement arrangements with Ghana, Nigeria, Guinea, and the Gambia. Generally, Sierra Leonean courts do not apply foreign law, but foreign judgment can be enforced when registered with the high court. However, the registration may be refused when enforcement is contrary to public policy.*
>
> (US DoS)

For obvious economic reasons, empirical support for FDI flows is rather persuasive. For example, FDI creates new jobs, boosts wages, increases the US exports, strengthens the US manufacturing and services, brings in new research, technology, and skills, and contributes to rising the US productivity in the US.[16] The contributions of FDI to economic growth have a storied presence in the literature (see

Lin, 2001). Data inadequacy makes it difficult to evaluate the impact of FDI on the social and economic development of Sierra Leone, but some foreign companies have made conspicuous impact on the socio-economic development of the country. Foreign telecommunication firms installed a mobile network infrastructure that has provided coverage for about 80 percent of the country. Mining has also contributed to the development of transport networks (UNCTAD, 2010, p. 21).

As expected, FDI has contributed to the employment of Sierra Leonean residents. It is estimated that alluvial mining, especially in the labor-intensive mining sector, has employed a substantial amount of people. The Titanium Resource Group reported that it employed over 2,000 employees, while Koidu Holdings reported the employment of approximately 600 people (UNCTAD, 2010, p. 21). It is noteworthy that there are always negative aspects of FDI flows in underdeveloped economies. Sierra Leone's environment can also be expected to come under pressure from activities that are less friendly to the environment or local politics.[17]

Governments routinely make cost–benefit analyses decisions when it comes to inviting FDI inflows. Hence, the Government of Sierra Leone (GoSL) takes a conciliatory position toward FDI that could foster the country's economic growth and development. The GoSL's Medium-Term National Development Plan (2019–2023) sets a growth agenda to support economic diversification and competitiveness toward promoting and developing a viable private sector to increase participation in global trade (US Department of State, US DoS).

> *The* Investment Promotion Act of 2004 *protects foreign entities from discriminatory treatment and permits foreign firms (investors) to compete with domestic firms. The Act creates incentives and customs exemptions, provides for investors to freely repatriate proceeds and remittances, and protects against expropriation without adequate compensation. The Act further provides for arbitration under the UNCITRAL rules in the event of a commercial dispute.*[18]
>
> (US DoS)

The Investment Promotion Act (IPA) of 2004 provides the basic legal framework for investment. Article 4 encourages any investor, domestic or foreign, to invest in any legitimate form of business. Though the GoSL hopes to invite investment in the areas of fishing, farming, and tourism, the poor or substandard quality of infrastructure and human capital continue to pose significant challenges and disincentives to foreign investment and commercial activity. Reforms to initiate investment in the country provide a counterbalancing consideration (see Table 2.1 and Figure 2.2). Significantly, foreign investments have legal limitations.

> *Foreign investors cannot invest in arms and ammunition, cement block manufacturing, granite and sandstone excavation, manufacturing of certain consumer durable goods, and military, police, and correctional officers' apparel and accouterments. Furthermore, there are limits to land ownership by foreign entities and individuals; the limitations vary depending on the location of the land being used and are discussed below in the "Real Property" section.*

Sierra Leone has few specific restrictions, controls, fees, or taxes on foreign ownership of companies that can outrightly own Sierra Leonean companies subject to certain registration formalities. However, investment in mining of less than $500,000 is an exception as this requires a 25 percent Sierra Leonean holding. Foreign technical and unskilled labor can be used but must seek approval from the Corporate Affairs Commission to transfer shares . . .

Small mining investments require a minority partnership with a Sierra Leonean company. The Sierra Leone National Carrier Ratification Agreement Act of 2012 *mandates the use of the Sierra Leone National Shipping Company for 40 percent of all goods imported or exported from Sierra Leone. The* Petroleum Act 2001 *restricts petroleum exploration and production licenses to companies registered or incorporated in Sierra Leone.*[19]

(US DoS)

Sierra Leone does not have antitrust laws that are comparable to that of the US or the European Union. I have extensively discussed the evolution and substantive provisions of the US antitrust law elsewhere (see Warburton, 2021, pp. 315–355). Such laws generally require competitive practices that optimize consumer welfare (see the introductory models and prior discussions of the competitive model in this chapter). Yet, foreign investments are not immune from legal expropriation (see also Warburton, 2021, pp. 439–459, and Collins, 2017). Analogously, preferential trade agreements may disadvantage some foreign investors who belong to countries that are not regionally integrated with Sierra Leone.[20]

The Constitution of Sierra Leone authorizes the GoSL to confiscate property only when necessary, in the interest of national defense, public safety, order, morality, town and country planning, or the public benefit or welfare. In such cases, the Constitution guarantees the prompt payment of adequate compensation, with a right of access to a court or other independent authority to consider legality, determine the amount of compensation, and ensure prompt payment (US DoS). This expropriatory position of the country is consistent with the provisions of international law. Naturally, disputes over points of fact and law are susceptible to judicial resolution. It was not until 1924 that the Permanent Court of International Justice (PCIJ) provided a legal definition of an international dispute.

A dispute is a disagreement on a point of law or fact, a conflict of legal views or of interest between two persons. Mavrommatis Palestine Concession Case.

(Jurisdiction) (1924) PCIJ, Ser. A, No. 2 at 11

Sierra Leone became a party to the International Convention on the Settlement of Investment Disputes (ICSID) in 1966 to arbitrate investment disputes and enforce ICSID awards. Also, Section 13 of the Arbitration Act 1960 . . . allows foreign arbitral awards to be registered in Sierra Leonean courts and

> *enforced in the same manner as a domestic judgment or court order. However, registration of foreign arbitral awards is not automatic but instead left to the presiding judge's discretion.*
>
> (US DoS)

Timely compensation and enforcement of arbitral awards are tricky propositions in countries with "sovereign rights." However, reluctance to abide by international investment laws elevates investment apprehension that discourages further investments in noncompliant countries. In fact, noncompliant countries expose themselves to economic retaliation or punitive measures by the aggrieved countries with deprived investors.

Notes

1 Marginal revenue is just the change in total revenue (TR) relative to a change in incremental quantity ($\Delta PQ/\Delta Q$).

2 For a comprehensive analysis of business organizations and operations, see the work of Parrino et al., pp. 1–6–1.20, and Mayo, pp. 272–290.

3 A minority interest is a stake in a company that is otherwise controlled by a parent or holding company that owns more than 50 percent of the voting shares. The concept is usually applicable to subsidiaries in which the minority has less than 50 percent of the voting shares.

4 The main cash crops grown in Sierra Leone are cocoa, coffee, and oil palm. Cocoa is responsible for the highest export earnings. Cash crops are produced for their commercial value rather than individual consumption. They tend to have competitive advantage when their comparative advantage in the international market is very high.

5 *Local buyers can help a nation's companies gain advantage if their needs anticipate or even shape those of other nations – if their needs provide ongoing "early-warning indicators" of global market trends. Sometimes anticipatory needs emerge because a nation's political values foreshadow needs that will grow elsewhere. Sweden's long-standing concern for people with disabilities has spawned an increasingly competitive industry focused on special needs. Denmark's environmentalism has led to success for companies in water-pollution-control equipment and windmills* (Porter, 1990, p. 82).

6 *The National Revenue Authority (NRA) was established by an Act of Parliament on 13th* September 2002 *and commenced operation in* January 2003. *This Act mandated the Authority to collect and account for both direct and indirect taxes in Sierra Leone and strengthen the enforcement of provisions in various tax laws (Customs Tariff Act,1978, (*Amended in 2011*), Income Tax Act,2000, Payroll Tax Act,1972, Foreign Travel Ticket Tax Act,1975, Entertainment Tax Act,197, Restaurant Food Tax Act,1989,* Sales Tax Act, 1995, *Hotel Accommodation Tax Act and External Telecommunications Act,1995 (now embedded into the* Goods and Services Tax Act 2009*),* Excise Act, 1982 *and a number of tax codes)* (NRA, 2011, p. 1).

7 The latter two treaties may not have been ratified at the time of this writing. Apart from tax benefits, the treaties protect investors against unlawful expropriation; see Warburton's Chapter 8 for the international law on expropriation.

8 In 1974, to objectionably suggest that the US was on the downward sloping segment of the Laffer curve, an American economist, Arthur Laffer, scribbled what influentially became known as the "Laffer Curve" on a piece of napkin in a Washington restaurant. The idea has formed the basis of tax cuts (Mankiw, p. 161). It is noteworthy that useful tax cuts must be properly targeted. Tax increases must be equitable and relevant to business cycles.

9 See Warburton (pp. 273–307) for a comprehensive discussion of tax evasion and avoidance in the US.

10 $\eta_S = \frac{dQs}{dP_W}$; elasticity of supply (e) = percentage change in supply relative to percentage change in world prices for continuous values. Higher supply elasticities in absolute terms have lower values because of the small change in quantity relative to price. It should be noted that excessive tariffs nearly always lead to trade wars and a reduction in aggregate welfare for the trading partners.

11 *In addressing corrupt practices, the country progressed 14 places up in the Transparency International Corruption ranking from 129/180 in 2018 to 115/180 in 2021. Similarly, the government passed the Millennium Challenge Corporation's indicator on the control of corruption four times in a row, from 71 percent in FY19 to 83 percent in FY22;* see US Department of State, *www.state.gov/reports/2022-investment-climate-statements/sierra-leone/. Corruption may also have implications for misinvoicing, selection of articles of trade, and enthusiastic imports of certain types of goods that contribute to loss of national revenue.*

12 *Out of a total of five (5) parastatals (Sierra Leone Commercial Bank, Rokel Commercial Bank, Sierra Leone Port Authority, National Insurance Company, and the Sierra Leone State Lottery) that usually pay dividend to Government, only the Rokel Commercial Bank paid dividend in 2008 and 2009. The remaining parastatals continued to either declare loss or ploughed back profits in their businesses* (NRA, 2009, p. 26).

13 *Overall, Sierra Leone's FDI inflows as a share of GDP, at 2.4 percent, were closely aligned with the averages of ECOWAS countries during the period 2001–2005. However, for the same period, FDI inflow per capita for Sierra Leone was considerably lower at $6.5 as compared to ECOWAS ($14.0), LDCs ($15.9), and developing economies ($47.2) . . . . These important differences are not surprising given the relatively short period of time between the end of the war in Sierra Leone and the resumption of economic activity under peace conditions* (UNCTAD, 2010, p. 15).

14 *De Beers was the primary foreign investor from the early 1930s through the mid-1980s, but even that investment was fairly limited due to the low-capital intensity of the type of mining being conducted. The significant decline in mid-1980s can be attributed to the exit of De Beers from Sierra Leone* (UNCTAD, 2010, p. 15). Sierra Leone utilizes two prominent methods of mining diamonds: (i) alluvial mining, which is less capital-intensive, and (ii) kimberlite mining, which is a capital-intensive form of mechanized mining of underground kimberlite pipes.

15 See countries and regions of the Office of the United States Trade Representative.

16 See US International Trade Administration https://legacy.trade.gov/investamerica/impacts.asp#:~:text=Foreign%20direct%20investment%20impacts%20the,4.6%25%20of%20private%20industry%20empl

17 A 121-acre resort project that was slated to use wetlands near Lumley Beach for tourism raised questions about the potential impact on the ecosystem and the environment (UNCTAD, 2010, p. 22). Extractive procedures do not necessarily protect the environment, and it is not unusual for foreign investors to have political favorites, which exposes their investments to legal and illegal expropriations.

18 The process of implementing the New York Convention in Sierra Leone was subjected to consideration of the lessons learned from other African countries that are already parties to the Convention.

19 *The Local Content Policy, adopted in 2012, promotes the utilization of locally produced goods and locally provided services and the employment of Sierra Leonean nationals. While failure to follow the policy previously resulted only in denying investment incentives, the* Sierra Leone Local Content Agency Act 2016 *requires compliance. More information is available below in the "Performance Requirements" section* (US DoS). *In addition to restrictions on services activities, other entry limitations apply to maritime and airport services. Foreign persons or firms are prohibited from holding licences*

for the activities of clearing or forwarding air or sea freight cargo operations (article 7 of the Cargo Clearing and Forwarding Act of 1974*). Private investors, foreign or domestic, cannot participate in other maritime port activities given that the Sierra Leone Ports Authority (SLPA) has exclusive responsibility for provision of port services cargo* (UNCTAD, 2010, p. 26).

20 *Sierra Leone offers more favourable treatment (full national treatment) to nationals from the Mano River Union19 and ECOWAS member countries (see the final list of the GATS article II most favoured nation exemptions in* WTO, 1995b*).20 For example, in the road transport sector (passengers and freight), only the vehicles registered in the Mano River Union and ECOWAS are allowed to provide services in Sierra Leone. ECOWAS provisions note that each member State accords non-discriminatory treatment to nationals and companies of other member States. If, however, for a specific activity, a member State is unable to reciprocate national treatment, other member States are not bound to accord non-discriminatory treatment* (UNCTAD, 2010, p. 25).

Further reading

Casey, K., Glennerster, R. & Suri, T. (2017). *The economic impacts of Ebola on firms in Sierra Leone* (Reference number: F-39204-SLE-1). International Growth Center.

Collins, D. (2017). *An introduction to international investment law*. Cambridge University Press.

Eickelpasch, A., Lejpras, A. & Stephan, A. (2010). *Locational and internal sources of firm competitive advantage: Applying Porter's diamond model at the firm level* (JIBS Working Papers No. 2010-6). Jönköping University. www.diva-portal.org/smash/get/diva2:552194/FULLTEXT01.pdf

Goolsbee, A., Levitt, S. & Syverson, C. (2020). Microeconomics (3rd ed.). Worth Publishers.

International Monetary Fund. (2021). Sierra Leone: *Technical assistance report – public investment management assessment* (IMF Country Report No. 21/90). IMF.

International Monetary Fund. (2023). *Global Debt Database*. IMF. https://www.imf.org/external/datamapper/datasets/GDD

Lin, E.-G. (2001). Determinants of, and the relationship between, *FDI and growth: A summary of the recent Literature* (IMF Working Paper, WP/01/175). IMF.

Mankiw, G.N. (2021). *Principles of macroeconomics* (9th ed.). Cengage.

Mayo, H.B. (2021). *Investments: An introduction* (13th ed.). Cengage.

National Revenue Authority. (2007). *Annual report January to December 2006*. Government of Sierra Leone.

National Revenue Authority. (2008). *Annual report January to December 2007*. Government of Sierra Leone.

National Revenue Authority. (2009). *Annual report January to December 2008*. Government of Sierra Leone.

National Revenue Authority. (2010). *Annual report January to December 2009*. Government of Sierra Leone.

National Revenue Authority. (2011). *Annual report*. Government of Sierra Leone.

Parrino, R., Bates, T.W., Gillan, S.L. & Kidwell, S.D. (2018). *Fundamentals of corporate finance* (4th ed.). Wiley.

Porter, M.E. (1990). The competitive advantage of nations. Harvard Business Review, 73–91.

Porter, M.E. (1998). *Competitive strategy* (pp. 17–23). Free Press.

Porter, M.E. (2000). Locations, clusters and company strategy. In G.L. Clark, M.P. Feldman & M.S. Gentler (eds) *The Oxford Handbook of Economic Geography* (pp. 253–274). Oxford University Press.

UNCTAD. (2010). *Investment policy review*. United Nations.

United States Department of State. (n.d.). 2023 Investment Climate Statements: Sierra Leone. www.state.gov/reports/2023-investment-climate-statements/sierra-leone/

Warburton, C.E.S. (2021). *Economic analysis and law: The economics of the courtroom*. Routledge.

World Bank. (2007). *Sierra Leone emergency power – meeting the challenge of turning on the lights*. World Bank.

World Bank. (2020). *Economy profile, Sierra Leone, doing business 2020: Comparing business regulation in 190 economies*. World Bank Group.

World Bank Group (2020). *Doing Business*. World Bank. https://archive.doingbusiness.org/en/data/exploretopics/starting-a-business

World Bank. (2023). *World development indicators*. World Bank.

World Bank. (2024). *World Development Indicators*. World Bank.

WTO. (1995b). *General Agreement on Trade in Services – Sierra Leone's Schedule of Specific Commitments*. WTO document GATS/EL/105. 30 August.

3 Economic growth, productivity, and sustainable development

3.1 Volatile economic growth

Per capita GDP growth reverted to the 2000 level of approximately zero growth after 20 years or more (Figure 3.6), and economic growth has been exceedingly volatile for the same period (see Figure 3.6). The capital stock (plants, equipments, and other long-term assets that are utilized for producing output) of the country grew sharply between 1991 and 1996 but never returned to the 1996 level by 2019 (Figure 3.1). Of course, there have been two episodes of substantial per capita economic growth (2002 and 2013), and two episodes of unusual economic growth (1998 and 2001). Information about human capital, inflation, and monetary policies in Chapter 1, and TFP in the preceding section are essential foundations before proceeding with this chapter. I provide a primer of economic growth theories and subsequently analyze episodes of volatile economic growth in Sierra Leone.

3.1 (a) A primer of growth theories: what are the drivers of economic growth?

For countries that want to grow, the drivers of economic growth are incontrovertible and very specific. The empirical evaluation of the drivers has empirically withstood the test of time. Growth models have influentially evolved since the 1940s and probably even earlier. All the theories have strongly suggested that countries must improve on national saving, human capital, and, much later, technology if they want to grow. By growth, I mean increases in national output as measured by nominal or real GDP.

Growth-oriented countries must invest in human capital, increase their level of national saving (more about this concept in Chapter 4), produce tradeable goods and services, increase total factor productivity (TFP), provide growth-oriented infrastructure, encourage long-term capital inflows, check unproductive population growth, conserve natural and environmental resources, reduce poverty, and guarantee the health care of their residents. The checklist is by no means exhaustive, but it is an adequate precondition for the complementarity of economic growth and sustainable development. The checklist implicitly indicates that it takes time and intentional public policies to attain economic growth and sustainable development. That is, economic growth and sustainable development are not chance occurrences.

DOI: 10.4324/9781003518464-4

Further, policymakers must spend some time trying to understand the determinants of saving, population growth, and technological change to provide better interventions in their macroeconomic systems for better economic growth and sustainable development.

One of the earliest and most influential growth models was provided by Roy Harrod and Evsey Domar in the 1940s. The Harrod–Domar model was notable for its emphasis on capital accumulation. The model specified a linear relationship between output (Y) and physical capital (K), which has a fixed coefficient, 1/v:

$$Y = \frac{1}{v}K \rightarrow Y = \frac{K}{v}, \qquad 3.1$$

where v is a fixed constant to be estimated. The capital stock, divided by the fixed constant, is indicative of the annual value of output. The constant, v, is a capital–output ratio, which could be derived from Equation 3.1. This ratio is fundamentally the productivity of capital or investment. A larger v implies that more capital is needed to produce output that could be produced with less capital stock. Sierra Leone has some very interesting historical episodes of capital stock acquisition and capital–output ratios (see Figures 3.1 and 3.2).

The monetary value of the capital stock of Sierra Leone increased sharply between 1988 and 1996 (Figure 3.1). This increase in capital stock was also reflected in the capital–output (K-O) ratio between 1988 and 1998. The ratio could also be used to make projections about the amount of capital that may be needed to

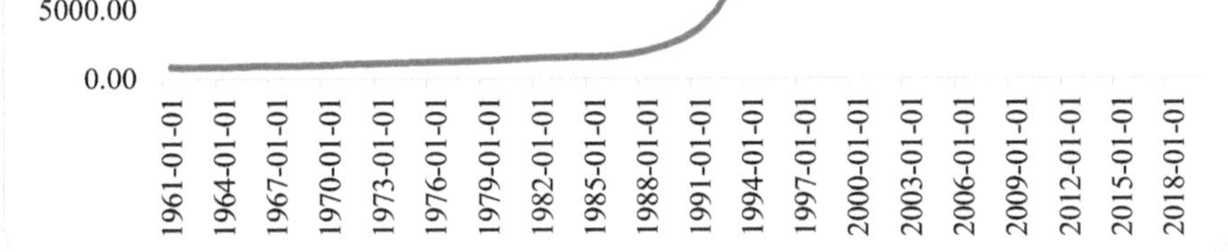

Figure 3.1 Capital stock for Sierra Leone, 1961–2019 (US$ million).

Data source: University of Groningen and University of California, Davis, Capital Stock at Constant National Prices for Sierra Leone, retrieved from FRED, Federal Reserve Bank of St. Louis; https://fred.stlouisfed.org/series/RKNANPSLA666NRUG, December 28, 2023

Note: Capital stock at Current Purchasing Power Parities for Sierra Leone, Millions of 2017 US Dollars, Annual, Not Seasonally Adjusted. The author considers capital stock to be plants, equipments, and other long-term assets that are used to produce output.

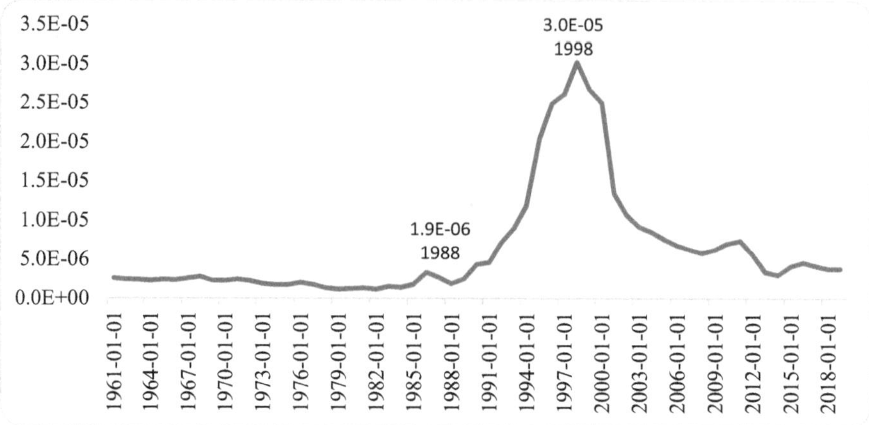

Figure 3.2 The annual capital–output (K-O) ratio for Sierra Leone (1961–2019).

Data sources: IMF/FRED and the World Bank's WDI (World Development Indicators)

Note: See Figure 3.1 for information about capital stock.

target a specific number of output growth. In effect, it could also be a multiplier (the product of targeted growth and the K-O ratio). It is noteworthy that the ratio does not have constant value over time (not even the incremental capital–output ratio) though it may be presumed to be constant for a given period.

The oversized increase in the K-O ratio, which is notable for a country that is not capital-intensive, is usually indicative of less-efficient methods of production (capital is not being utilized efficiently) (see Perkins et al. pp. 96–98). This may well have been a very inefficient phase in the production history of the country. Significantly, a civil war occurred in Sierra Leone from 1991 to 2002, reaffirming the destructive nature of political instability and civil wars when capital is diverted from productive uses to unproductive uses.

During the 11-year war, Sierra Leone redundantly utilized capital (denominated in US $) to produce US$1 worth of output on an annual basis. However, this ratio is a bit tricky because long-term capital depreciates over time, and it is utilized to produce output till the estimated terminal date of expiration. Essentially, the capital–output ratio defines the relationship between the value of capital that is invested in an economy and the value of output that is generated.

The incremental capital–output (ICOR) ratio determines the effect on output of an incremental increase or decrease in capital. As such, the ICOR measures the productivity of an additional value or unit of capital rather than the mere relationship between a country's total stock of capital and its output. I decompose the annual time series data into two periods, 1961 to 1989 and 1990–2019, to analyze the incremental capital–output ratio in logarithmic forms; the results of the inquiry are reported in Table 3.1.

Before 1989, a percentage increase in long-term capital stock contributed more than 1 percent (1.32) to an increase in output; between 1990 and 2019, a

Table 3.1 ICOR for Sierra Leone (1961–1989 and 1990–2019)

Dependent variable log output (t-stat in parenthesis)

	ICOR		*ICOR*
Log capital stock (1961–1989)	1.32 (7.32) **	Log capital stock (1990–2019):	0.6 (2.43) **
Observations	29	Observations	30
F-stat	53.55**	F-stat	5.89**

Data sources: IMF/FRED (capital stock, current PPP 2017 US$) and World Bank's WDI (output, current US$).

** Significant accommodation of less than 5% error. All data are estimated by Eviews12.

percentage increase in long-term capital stock contributed less than 1 percent to output. A caveat worth noting is that the latter period had noisy occurrences of wars and the Ebola epidemic. In the Harrod–Domar model, the capital–output ratio is presumed to be invariable (constant), which nullifies the concept of changes. Therefore, Harrod and Domar presumed that ICOR is equal to the K-O ratio.

The Harrod–Domar model could be rewritten to show the relationship between changes in capital stock and changes in output:

$$\Delta Y = \frac{\Delta K}{v}. \quad 3.2$$

Explicitly, the growth rate of output is just a function of investment:

$$g = \frac{\Delta Y}{Y} = \frac{\Delta K}{Yv} \rightarrow \frac{s}{v} - d, \quad 3.3$$

where $\Delta K = sY - dK$ (saving minus depreciation) (see Perkins et al., pp. 96–98). Solow and Swan improved on the Harrod–Domar growth model in the 1950s.

Solow (1956) proposed that economic growth should be studied by assuming a standard neoclassical production function with decreasing returns to capital. Taking the rates of saving and population growth as exogenous, he showed that these two variables determine the steady-state level of income per capita.

Because saving and population growth rates vary across countries, different countries reach different steady states. Solow's model gives simple testable predictions about how these variables influence the steady-state level of income. The higher the rate of saving, the richer the country. The higher the rate of population growth, the poorer the country.

Yet all is not right with the Solow model. Although the model correctly predicts the directions of the effects of saving and population growth, it does not correctly predict the magnitudes. In the data, the effects of saving and population growth on income are too large. To understand the relation between saving, population growth, and income, one must go beyond the textbook Solow model. We therefore augment the Solow model by including accumulation of human as well as physical capital (capital incubates human capital – a confounding problem).

The Solow model had a confounding problem. The exclusion of human capital from the textbook Solow model can potentially explain why the estimated influences of saving and population growth appear too large for two reasons. First, for any given rate of human capital accumulation, higher saving or lower population growth leads to a higher level of income and thus a higher level of human capital; hence, accumulation of physical capital and population growth have greater impacts on income when accumulation of human capital is considered. Second, human capital accumulation may be correlated with saving rates and population growth rates; this would imply that omitting human capital accumulation biases the estimated coefficients on saving and population growth.

To test the augmented Solow model, Mankiw et al. included a proxy for human capital accumulation as an additional explanatory variable in our cross-country regressions. We find that accumulation of human capital is in fact correlated with saving and population growth. Including human capital accumulation lowers the estimated effects of saving and population growth to roughly the values predicted by the augmented Solow model. Moreover, the augmented model accounts for about 80 percent of the cross-country variation in income. Given the inevitable imperfections in this sort of cross-country data, we consider the fit of this simple model to be remarkable. It appears that the augmented Solow model provides an almost complete explanation of why some countries are rich and other countries are poorer.

One can explain much of the cross-country variation in income while maintaining the assumption of decreasing returns. This conclusion does not imply, however, that the Solow model is a complete theory of growth: one would like also to understand the determinants of saving, population growth, and worldwide technological change, all of which the Solow model treats as exogenous.

The Solow–Swan model uses the Cobb–Douglas function with some regularity conditions.

$$Y(t) = K(t)^{\alpha}(A(t)L(t))^{1-\alpha} \quad 0 < \alpha < 1, \qquad 3.4$$

where Y is for output, K is for capital stock, L is for labor, and A is for the level of technology (say, in Sierra Leone). Labor and capital are assumed to grow at rates, n and g, respectively, that are not determined within the model (exogenously), so that:

$$L(t) = L(0)e^{nt}, \text{ and} \qquad 3.5$$

$$A(t) = A(0)e^{gt}. \qquad 3.6$$

The number of effective units of labor in Sierra Leone then grows at a rate of $n + g$.

The model assumes that rational and prudent social planners will invest a fraction of output, s.

When K is defined in terms of effective unit of labor (k), it could then be rewritten as

$$k = \frac{K}{AL}. \quad 3.7$$

Similarly, output (Y) could be rewritten in terms of effective unit of labor as

$$y = \frac{Y}{AL}. \quad 3.8$$

The evolution of the model to a steady state ($sy(t) = sk(t)^{\alpha}$) is governed by the rule that

$$\begin{aligned} \dot{k}(t) &= sy(t) - (n + g + \delta)k(t) \\ &= sk(t)^{\alpha} - (n + g + \delta)k(t), \end{aligned} \quad 3.9$$

where δ is for the rate at which capital depreciates. Equation 3.9 indicates that k converges to a steady-state value (k^*):

$$\begin{aligned} sk^{*\alpha} &= (n + g + \delta)k^* \\ k^* &= \left[\frac{s}{(n + g + \delta)}\right]^{\frac{1}{(1-\alpha)}}. \end{aligned} \quad 3.10$$

The central predictions of the Solow model concern the impact of saving and population growth on real income. Substituting (3.10) into the production function and taking logs, we find that steady-state income per capita is

$$\ln\frac{Y(t)}{L(t)} = \ln A(0) + gt + \frac{\alpha}{1-\alpha}\ln(s) - \frac{\alpha}{1-\alpha}\ln(n + g + \delta). \quad 3.11$$

Figure 3.3 shows that the Solow production function, ($f(k^*)$), has positive and diminishing marginal returns – output per worker rises at an increasing rate at the lower stages of production as an additional worker (input) is employed, but not continuously as more and more workers are employed (output diminishes). The 45-degree line shows the effects of depreciation and population growth, which increases linearly with capital per worker and output per worker. It is reasonable to concede that a fraction of the capital stock of a country will depreciate on an annual basis. However, the rate of depreciation is assumed to progress at an invariant (fixed) proportion of total capital stock. Since a given percentage of the stock of capital depreciates each year, depreciation per worker increases in proportion to the amount of capital per worker. Population growth is rather tricky for reasons to be discussed shortly. It is instantly revealed that a leftward rotation of the 45-degree line will decrease capital per worker and output per worker.

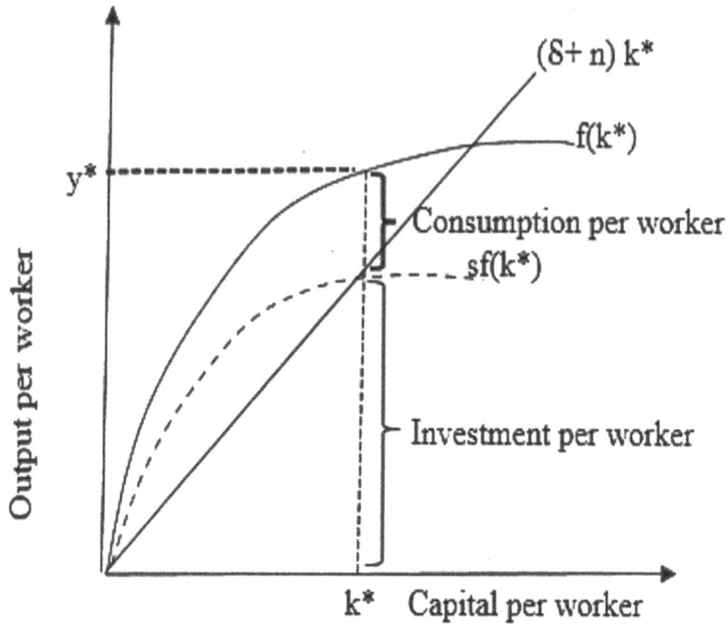

Figure 3.3 The Solow steady state.

At levels below the steady state, capital per worker (k*), investment per worker, sf(k*), is greater than depreciation per worker (δn(k*)). The net capital gain (additional capital less subtraction of capital (depreciation)) increases capital per worker. On the contrary, depreciation per worker exceeds investment per worker beyond *k**. Thus, in the relationship of investment per worker and capital per worker, social planners must expect to replenish their investment per work at different stages of economic growth. How could this replenishment take place?[1]

Solow and Swan propose capital accumulation and technological advance through the national saving channel. In the next chapter, I will discuss the effects of national saving and economic growth in East Asia. However, Trevor Swan (1956) noted that technological advances could also push countries out of the steady-state gridlock. Narrowly defined, technological changes are just applications of science to production that reduce the cost of production. In the previous section, I discussed the corollary total factor productivity (TFP) that could increase the output capacities of a country. A very liberal interpretation or definition of technology could encompass high-tech processes of computer banks, iPads, management techniques, and nutritional regimes (Mell and Worker, p. 211).

Nations that want to grow continuously must make improvements in technology to attain higher periodic steady-state levels of output per worker. Notice that by increasing the investment schedule, the investment function per worker shifts upward to increase both capital per worker and output per worker. Unfortunately,

Figure 3.4 Sierra Leone's nominal gross saving as a percentage of GDP (2000–2024).

Data source: International Monetary Fund, Nominal Gross National Saving for Sierra Leone, retrieved from FRED, Federal Reserve Bank of St. Louis; https://fred.stlouisfed.org/series/SLENGSGDPPT, December 28, 2023

Note: Nominal Gross National Saving for Sierra Leone, Percent of GDP, Annual, Not Seasonally Adjusted.

the saving record of the country has not been very robust (see Figure 3.4). Saving is highly contingent on the possession of human capital and job availability. Gross saving is a measure of saving that is available to support the nation's stock of fixed assets. It is the sum of personal saving, undistributed corporate profits with inventory valuation and capital consumption adjustments, net government saving, and consumption of fixed capital. It is also equal to gross national income less the sum of personal consumption expenditures, government consumption expenditures, and current taxes and transfer payments to the rest of the world.[2] Evidently, a productive rather than congestive population is good for saving, capital accumulation, and economic growth.

Economists do not have consensus on the effects of population growth on economic development. The issue of population growth is contingent on whether population growth merely increases production and consumption of consumer goods, or whether population growth enhances the productive capacities of a country by producing capital goods or newer capital. Consider Kremer's model depicting a positive correlation between population and economic growth when population growth generates the resources to produce new technologies within a country (an endogenization of population growth and technological progress):

$$\Delta A = qPA, \quad 3.12$$

where q is for the research productivity per person ($q > 0$), P is for population, and A is for the accumulated stock of knowledge and technology – a relationship between the growth of technology to the size of the population, augmented by technology.

$$\frac{\Delta A}{A} = g_A = qP. \quad 3.13$$

Equation 3.13 shows that technological change depends on a creative population even when the research productivity of people in a country remains constant.[3] That is, an intelligent population could be creative. Apart from the work of Mankiw et al. (1992), there is a very rich literature on the relationship between human capital and economic growth and development. For example, Guisan (2009) examined government effectiveness, education, economic development, and well-being in European countries, the United States, and Canada. She found that the most outstanding countries in the overall index – Norway, Denmark, Sweden, the United States, Austria, Ireland, Switzerland, Canada, Finland, Netherlands, and the United Kingdom – espouse a very good interaction of the variables, with some important positive effects of education on economic development and governance effectiveness.

The population of Sierra Leone has grown from 2.3 million in 1960 to 8.6 million in 2022 (about 3 percent in 62 years) – about 2 percent from 1960 to 1989, and 2.2 percent from 1989 to 2022 (see Table 3.2). A civil war broke out in the country in 1991, leading to tremendous loss of lives and a Malthusian decline in the population growth rate. The population growth rate poses a scary prospect for the continuous urbanization problem discussed in the introductory chapter of this book. Migration from disturbed neighboring countries puts an upward pressure on population growth. The problem for Sierra Leone is that most of the migrants – as discussed in the opening chapter of this book – do not have a sophisticated level of human capital.

Table 3.2 Population growth rates of Sierra Leone and the World (1961–2023)

Year	*World*	*Sierra Leone*	*Year*	*World*	*Sierra Leone*	*Year*	*World*	*SierraLeone*
1961	1.63	1.73	1982	1.84	2.1	2003	1.29	4.1
1962	1.9	1.79	1983	1.82	2.18	2004	1.28	3.41
1963	2.21	1.84	1984	1.79	2.24	2005	1.27	2.71
1964	2.24	1.89	1985	1.8	2.27	2006	1.27	2.22
1965	2.14	1.94	1986	1.82	2.49	2007	1.27	2.23
1966	2.08	1.95	1987	1.84	2.73	2008	1.27	2.55
1967	2.03	1.97	1988	1.81	2.74	2009	1.27	2.77
1968	2.05	1.98	1989	1.78	2.54	2010	1.27	2.83
1969	2.08	1.97	1990	1.77	4	2011	1.25	2.73
1970	2.06	1.97	1991	1.69	1.22	2012	1.25	2.66
1971	2.02	1.94	1992	1.6	−1.75	2013	1.24	2.6
1972	1.98	1.92	1993	1.54	−0.14	2014	1.22	2.52
1973	1.96	1.93	1994	1.49	0.45	2015	1.19	2.44
1974	1.92	1.92	1995	1.46	0.21	2016	1.17	2.45
1975	1.85	1.9	1996	1.43	0.54	2017	1.15	2.45
1976	1.8	1.86	1997	1.4	1.33	2018	1.1	2.39
1977	1.77	1.91	1998	1.37	1.02	2019	1.06	2.36
1978	1.75	1.99	1999	1.34	0.57	2020	0.98	2.33
1979	1.77	2	2000	1.34	2.43	2021	0.87	2.27
1980	1.8	2.04	2001	1.33	5.96	2022	0.83	2.2
1981	1.81	2.07	2002	1.31	5.83	2023	0.88	4.1

Data sources: From 1961 to the current year: elaboration of data by United Nations, Department of Economic and Social Affairs, Population Division. World Population Prospects: The 2022 Revision (Medium-fertility variant) (see also Worldometer) and FRED (see *Note* for Figure 3.5).

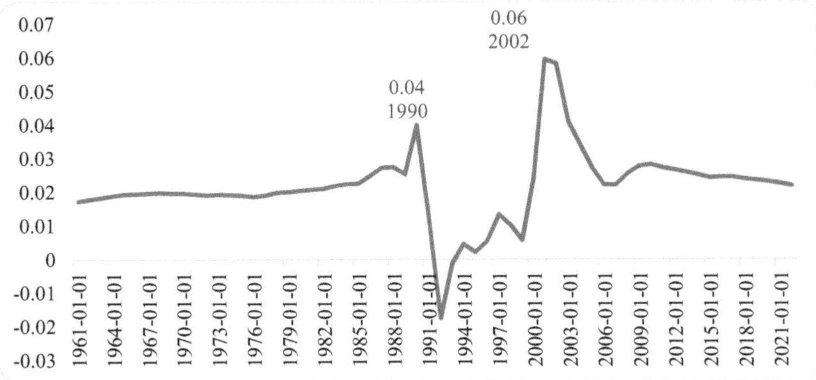

Figure 3.5 Sierra Leone's population growth (1961–2022).

Data source: World Bank, Population, Total for Sierra Leone [POPTOTSLA647NWDB], retrieved from FRED, Federal Reserve Bank of St. Louis; https://fred.stlouisfed.org/series/POPTOTSLA647N-WDB, December 29, 2023

Note: From the total population for Sierra Leone, Persons, Annual, Not Seasonally Adjusted. Total population is based on the de facto definition of population, which counts all residents regardless of legal status or citizenship – except for refugees not permanently settled in the country of asylum, who are generally considered part of the population of their country of origin. The values shown are midyear estimates. Author's computation of the annual growth rate.

Population growth creates a congestive problem rather than an increase in productive capacity (see Kremer's model). But for the civil war years and few instances apart, the population growth rate of Sierra Leone has exceeded the global benchmark rates since 1961 (see Table 3.2). The country stayed below the global average rate of population growth for the greater part of the 1960s and 1970s.

The Solow–Swan model assumes that factors are paid their marginal products, and the model predicts the signs and the magnitudes of the coefficients on saving and population growth. Mankiw et al. note that because capital's share in income is roughly one-third, the model implies an elasticity of income per capita with respect to the saving rate of approximately 0.5 and an elasticity with respect to $n + g + \delta$ of approximately -0.5. Figure 3.3 provides a depiction of the steady-state arguments and assumptions.

The natural question considered by Mankiw et al. is whether available data could support the Solow model's predictions concerning the determinants of standards of living. In other words, they became interested in investigating whether real income is higher in countries with higher saving rates are lower in countries with higher values of $n + g + \delta$. They propose a Solow-augmented model that takes the following form:

$$Y(t) = K(t)^{\alpha} H(t)^{\beta} (A(t)L(t))^{1-\alpha-\beta} \quad \alpha + \beta < 1, \tag{3.14}$$

The evolution of an economy is determined by

$$\dot{k}(t) = s_k y(t) - (n + g + \delta)k(t); \tag{3.15}$$

$$\dot{h}(t) = s_h y(t) - (n + g + \delta)h(t), \quad 3.16$$

where $h = \frac{H}{AL}$.

The augmented model predicts that an economy converges to steady states with the decomposition of capital stock:

$$k^* = \left[\frac{s_k^{1-\beta} s_h^{\beta}}{(n + g + \delta)}\right]^{\frac{1}{(1-\alpha-\beta)}}, \quad 3.17$$

$$h^* = \left[\frac{s_k^{\alpha} s_h^{1-\alpha}}{(n + g + \delta)}\right]^{\frac{1}{(1-\alpha-\beta)}}. \quad 3.18$$

From 2020 to 2024, there was no clearly defined trajectory of a positive per capita growth trend (see Figure 3.8). This problem mirrors the volatile economic growth rates of Sierra Leone between 1961 and 2022 (see Figure 3.6).

The volatilities or cycles of national output are not unusual occurrences. Advanced economies like the US and the UK also experience output volatility (see Figure 3.7). However, the average values of historical economic performance are also nested in output volatility; for example, the US and the UK economies grew at average annual rates of 3.62 and 2.85 percent, respectively, between 1961 and

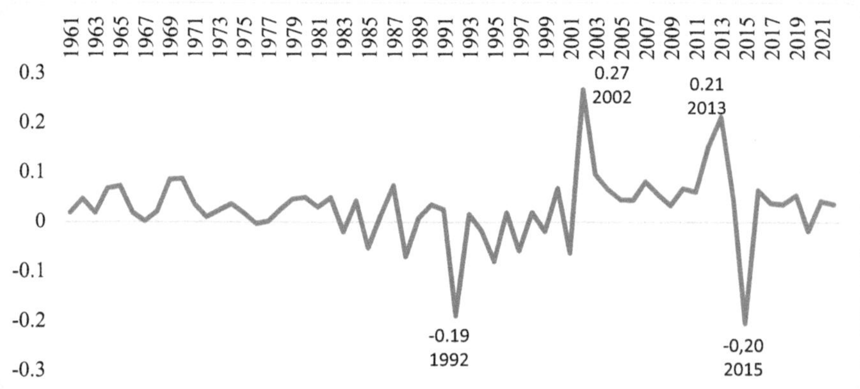

Figure 3.6 Sierra Leone's national output (GDP) growth rate (1961–2022).

Data source: World Bank's WDI (World Development Indicators, 2023)

Note: GDP (constant 2015 US$) at purchaser's prices is the sum of gross value added by all resident producers in the economy plus any product taxes and minus any subsidies not included in the value of the products. It is calculated without making deductions for depreciation of fabricated assets or for depletion and degradation of natural resources. Data are in constant 2015 prices, expressed in US dollars. Dollar figures for GDP are converted from domestic currencies using 2015 official exchange rates. For a few countries where the official exchange rate does not reflect the rate effectively applied to actual foreign exchange transactions, an alternative conversion factor is used (author's computation of annual growth rates).

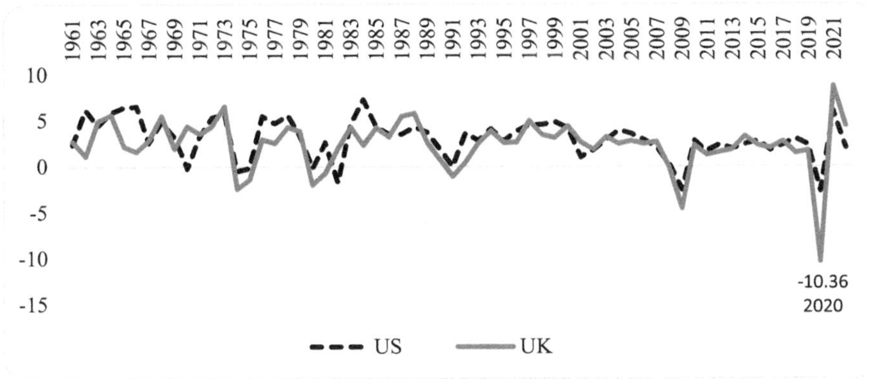

Figure 3.7 National output (GDP) growth rate for the US and the UK (1961–2022).

Data source: World Bank's (WDI) World Development Indicators

Note: Annual percentage growth rate of GDP at market prices based on constant local currency. Aggregates are based on constant 2015 prices, expressed in US dollars. GDP is the sum of gross value added by all resident producers in the economy plus any product taxes and minus any subsidies not included in the value of the products. It is calculated without making deductions for depreciation of fabricated assets or for depletion and degradation of natural resources.

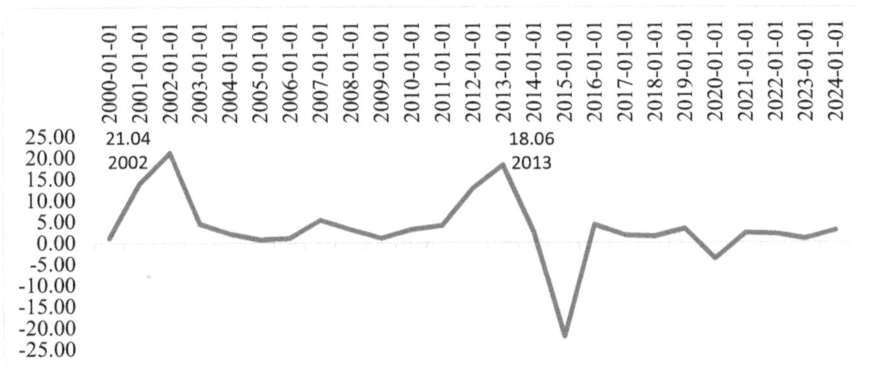

Figure 3.8 Sierra Leone's real GDP per capita growth (2000–2024).

Data source: International Monetary Fund, Real GDP Per Capita for Sierra Leone, retrieved from FRED, Federal Reserve Bank of St. Louis; https://fred.stlouisfed.org/series/SLENGDPRPCPCPPPT, December 28, 2023

Note: Real GDP Per Capita for Sierra Leone, Percent Change From Preceding Period, Annual, Not Seasonally Adjusted.

1989, and 2.4 and 1.9 percent, respectively, between1990 and 2022. Though the data suggest that TFP is relatively lower for both countries compared to Sierra Leone (see Figures 3.9 and 3.10), possibly because of differences in input costs and measurement variations. The average annual growth rates for Sierra Leone are about 2.5 percent and 3 percent for both periods. This finding is consistent with the

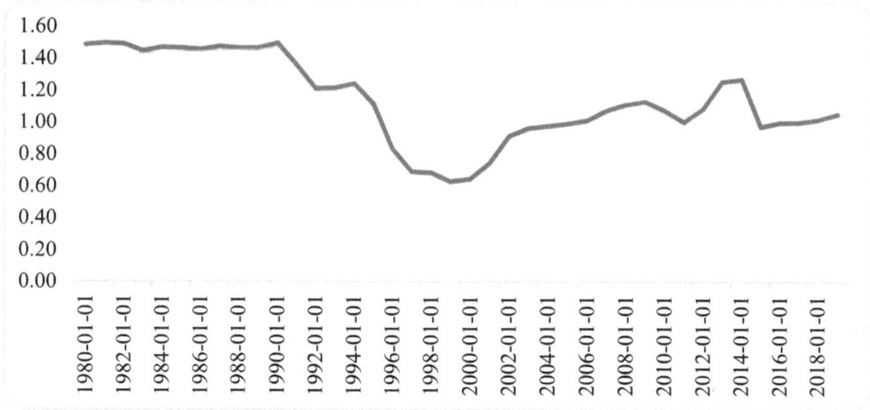

Figure 3.9 TFP in Sierra Leone (1980–2019).

Data source: Feenstra, R.C., Inklaar, R. & Timmer, M.P. (2015). The next generation of the Penn world table. *American Economic Review*, 105(10), 3150–3182, www.ggdc.net/pwt and FRED (Federal Reserve Bank of St Louis)

Note: Total Factor Productivity at Constant National Prices for Sierra Leone, Index 2017=1, Annual, Not Seasonally Adjusted.

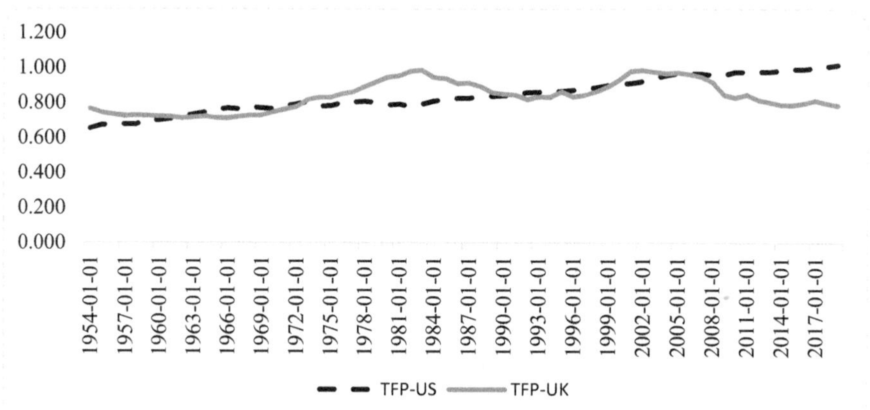

Figure 3.10 TFP for the US and the UK (1954–2019).

Data source: University of Groningen and University of California, Davis, Total Factor Productivity at Constant National Prices for the US and the UK, retrieved from FRED, Federal Reserve Bank of St. Louis; https://fred.stlouisfed.org/series/RTFPNAUSA632NRUG, December 29, 2023, and https://fred.stlouisfed.org/series/CTFPPPGBA669NRUG, December 30, 2023

empirical analysis of the relationship between TFP and economic growth, but it is also notable that Sierra Leone had two unusual spikes in output growth in 2002 and 2013 (see Figure 3.6), and two unusual troughs in 1992 and 2015. The UK had an unusual trough in 2020. Growth data nearly always raises issues about distributional problems.

Economic growth *per se* does not provide sufficient answers to socio-economic issues of political instability, excessive rural–urban migration, higher levels of poverty, increases in trade imbalances (excessive imports more than exports), and high sovereign debts. These developmental and economic issues require stringent scrutiny and analyses of leakages and maldistribution of economic resources that are beyond the scope of this book. In Chapter 5, I will extend the deliberate choices to include external shocks and threats to economic growth and sustainable development. The next section examines the concepts of productivity and the implications of multifactor productivity for growth and development in Sierra Leone.

3.2 Multifactor/total factor productivity (TFP)

Productivity (least cost production of output for a given period) is integral to economic growth and sustainable development. In fact, it drives the competitiveness of businesses and a nation. However, its measurement is not unimodal, and researchers may formulate different specifications of productivity to obtain targeted objectives. Researchers may target production efficiencies in terms of input costs, or they might use the contributions of input to output to evaluate the efficiencies of production. The latter procedure is particularly tricky because of the omission variable bias and mischaracterization of errors as estimation of TFP. I addressed this issue in 2020 and will revisit it in this chapter.

Productivity is more commonly defined as a ratio between the output volume and the volume of inputs. Pointedly, it measures the efficiency with which production inputs, such as labor, capital, and energy consumption, are being utilized in an economy to produce a given level of output. As such, productivity significantly contributes to economic growth by decreasing the cost of production and increasing the competitiveness of firms and countries. Unsurprisingly, it provides essential econometric information for international comparisons of macroeconomic performances. Productivity growth is also an important criterion for modeling and determining the productive capacity or utilization of economies, which in turn allows policymakers to evaluate business cycles and forecast economic growth (Krugman, 1994).

The most basic measure of productivity is TFP, otherwise known as "multifactor productivity,"

$$TFP = \frac{Output}{\sum Inputs}, \qquad 3.19$$

where the sum of inputs is usually denominated in costs; such costs may include labor, capital, materials, and rental costs (at the micro level). It is probably evident that the measurement of TFP in Equation 3.19 poses some dynamic problems – the standardization of inputs to be considered, variations in levels of inflation, and disparities in currency values without a numeraire that is adjusted for inflation.

Before Solow's 1957 specification of multifactor productivity Equation 3.20, a more prominent and explicit measure of TFP was the Solow residual, the use of an omitted variable bias in regression models. Of course, the Solow–Swan model endogenized the contribution of technology to output growth, which has not resolved the issue of specification bias and misclassification of the error expression. The typical Solow model that endogenizes multifactor productivity takes a form (Equation 3.18) that has been reproduced by Jones (2002, pp. 45–46):

$$Y = BK^{\alpha}L^{1-\alpha}, \qquad 3.20$$

where Y is for output, B is a Hicks-neutral productivity expression, L is for labor, and the exponents are for the marginal contributions of capital and labor to output as has been extensively discussed in the previous section. Taking the logs of Equation 3.20 and differentiating the function show that the change in output is a function of capital accumulation, the change in labor, and the growth of multifactor productivity:

$$\frac{\dot{Y}}{Y} = \alpha\frac{\dot{K}}{K} + (1-\alpha)\frac{\dot{L}}{L} + \frac{\dot{B}}{B}. \qquad 3.21$$

Equation 3.21 can be rewritten to obtain the growth rate per worker (per capita GDP growth); see Figure 3.8.

$$\frac{y}{y} = \alpha\frac{\dot{k}}{k} + \frac{\dot{B}}{B}. \qquad 3.22$$

The decomposition of Equation 3.20 shows that output per worker is a function of physical capital per worker and the contribution from multifactor productivity growth.

Real GDP per capita growth in Sierra Leone has hovered around zero with two notable and unusual spikes (exceptions) in the series (2002 and 2013) – after the end of the civil war and before the Ebola pandemic (see Figure 3.8). Equation 3.4 has limited usage that is centered around the productivity of labor and multifactor productivity in a regression specification. Alternative forms of estimation have relied on the Solow residual. In 2020, I examined the residual of a growth specification in terms of public investment in human capital to make the growth residual intentionally useful.

A major problem with Equation 3.20 is that the omitted variable bias remains unresolved with a loss of generality – only the confounding capital, labor, and TFP are endogenized. That is, the specification provides limited utility to measure the general effects of productivity beyond the effects of capital accumulation and TFP on output per worker (labor). That is, per capita output is merely induced by capital accumulation and multifactor productivity. Interest in productivity could be very extensive. As such, the effects of other significant and less significant variables remain elusive. Yet the error expression could be defined and utilized with meaningful effect. Consider the presentation of Perkins et al. (p. 69), which I have empirically estimated elsewhere for some comparative results that are revealing (Warburton, 2020):

$$g_y - a = (rK * gK) + (wL * gL), \quad 3.23$$

where

gy = GDP growth rate,
gK = growth rate of capital stock,
gL= growth rate of the labor force,
wL= the share of labor in national income,
rK = the share of capital in national income, and
a = omitted variable bias [residual, error, or TFP].

GDP per capita is gross domestic product divided by midyear population. This variable controls for disparities in national wealth and facilitates comparative analysis. GDP is defined as

> the sum of gross value added by all resident producers in the economy plus any product taxes and minus any subsidies not included in the value of the products. It is calculated without making deductions for depreciation of fabricated assets or for depletion and degradation of natural resources.

The data are in constant 2010 US dollars, and they have been provided by the World Bank (WDI). The notation for the growth of GDP per capita is *gy*.

A general problem with econometric specifications of growth and productivity is that land is persistently considered to be neutral in the production process. The productivity of land is nearly always excluded from econometric measurements because of an assumption of the fixity of land. Equation 3.23 is flexible enough to accommodate considerations of omitted variables. The stock of capital and land improvement by capital (K) is instrumental in computing the contribution of human capital to economic growth or output (K/Y= rK). Land could be reclaimed, and its quality could be improved by physical and human capital for robust economic growth. Traditional models have generally disregarded the value of land, which also includes marine resources and atmospheric conditions (in economics), and its interactive capacity with human capital. Variable interactions pose multicollinearity problems (measurement errors) in regression models. In 2020, I examined economic variables to reflect the indispensable interaction of the factors of production. The growth of the capital stock is captured by gK.

Gross fixed capital formation,

> *formerly gross domestic fixed investment, is used to show the interaction of human capital, physical capital and land improvement." Therefore, the variable includes "land improvements (fences, ditches, drains, and so on); plant, machinery, and equipment purchases; and the construction of roads,*

> *railways, and the like, including schools, offices, hospitals, private residential dwellings, and commercial and industrial buildings. According to the 1993 System of National Accounts (SNA), net acquisitions of valuables are also considered capital formation.*

The data are in current US dollars and made available by the World Bank and the OECD (see the World Bank's World Development Indicators (WDI) for 2019).

The labor force (stock) comprises people in the age category of 15 and older who supply labor to produce goods and services during a specified period.

> *It includes people who are currently employed and people who are unemployed but seeking work as well as first-time jobseekers. Not everyone who works is included, however. Unpaid workers, family workers, and students are often omitted, and some countries do not count members of the armed forces. Labor force size tends to vary during the year as seasonal workers enter and leave.*
>
> (World Bank, 2019)

Using the unemployment rate (the percent of total labor force, national estimate) of the sampled countries, the labor force was readjusted to compute the effective labor force (L_E) since everyone in the labor force cannot be productive or gainfully employed. Therefore, the effective labor force defines the contribution of labor to output ($L_E/Y= wL$). The World Bank defined unemployment as "the share of the labor force that is without work but available for and seeking employment." However, definitions of labor force and unemployment differed from country to country (WDI, 2019). Consequently, the general theoretical specification of the growth residual can be specified in terms of Equation 3.23.

Equation 3.23 makes the TFP measurement puzzle, which is simply the part of measured growth that cannot be explained by data on the traditional factors of production (Perkins et al., p. 69), less refractory and contingent on the quality of information (data) to be estimated. The error expression suddenly becomes useful when it is evaluated in terms of specific investments or decision variables to obtain economic growth (it is not as worthless as it might seem), for example, residuals could be evaluated against investments in human capital (public investment in education) across various countries.

Lower error-investment ratios mean that investments, say public investment in human capital, have greater effect on economic growth than the unexplained variables. That is, the errors are finally estimated as a percentage of public investment in human capital. Public investment in education (I_G) or general government expenditure on education (current, capital, and transfers) as a percentage of GDP could be very informative. It includes expenditure funded by transfers from international sources to government. "General government" usually referred to local, regional, and central governments (WDI, 2019).

Between 1967 and 2006, the interactive effects of human capital have been well documented for several countries in America, Europe, Eurasia, Africa, and Asia-Pacific. Empirical studies show interactions between: (i) education and the production function; (ii) education and investment per inhabitant; (iii) education, fertility, and economic development; (iv) education and social capital; (v) human capital, industry, and foreign trade; and (vi) human capital and regional development (Guisan & Neira, 2008). The data were classified into nine periods of annual growth (1969–78, 1979–88, 1989–98, 1999–2008, 2009–17) to derive the contributions of investment in human capital to economic growth. Main findings of the study are reported in Table 3.3.

Table 3.3 Residual–investment ratios (1990–2017)

United States	*1990–98*	*1999–2008*	*2009–17*
Residual (TFP)	0.02	0.02	0.01
RES/Investment	–	0.39	0.26
Canada			
Residual (TFP)	–	0.02	0.02
RES/Investment	–	0.46	0.32
Denmark			
Residual (TFP)	–	0.01	0.001
RES/Investment	–	0.18	0.0006
Finland			
Residual (TFP)	0.02	0.03	0.001
RES/Investment	0.34	0.53	0.02
France			
Residual (TFP)	0.02	0.02	0.01
RES/Investment	0.36	0.29	0.14
Germany			
Residual (TFP)	0.02	0.01	0.01
RES/Investment	0.11	0.12	0.11
United Kingdom			
Residual (TFP)	0.02	0.02	0.01
RES/Investment	0.41	0.5	0.21
Australia			
Residual (TFP)	0.03	0.03	0.02
RES/Investment	0.53	0.6	0.47
Ghana			
Residual (TFP)	–	0.04	0.07
RES/Investment	–	0.73	1.09
Sierra Leone			
Residual (TFP)	–	0.01	0.04
RES/Investment	–	0.24	1.42
South Africa			
Residual (TFP)	0.01	0.03	0.02
RES/Investment	0.15	0.54	0.3
Brazil			
Residual (TFP)	0.02	0.03	0.01
RES/Investment	0.33	0.69	0.22
Mexico			
Residual (TFP)	0.02	0.02	0.02
RES/Investment	0.83	0.36	0.39

Source: Warburton (2020, p. 15).

Note: See the Appendix to the source for further expositions.

For a variety of reasons, the prototypical growth residuals of the Solow model could be utilized with some precaution: (i) the model was not used as an estimated regression model that absorbs the regularity conditions of the ordinary least squares (OLS) models, (ii) the residuals can be associated with factors that are unrelated to investment in human capital or TFP, and (iii) the percentage of error that is unrelated to investment in human capital is generally unknown. Notwithstanding, the productivity of investment in human capital could be estimated in terms of endogenous and exogenous variables of a growth specification.

Of the 13 sampled countries, a small sample of arduous work to be regionally representative of the world, Denmark and Sierra Leone had the lowest and highest residual-to-investment ratios, respectively. In the case of Denmark, investment in human capital could account for all the residual in one form or another between 2009 and 2017. In the case of Sierra Leone and Ghana, investment in human capital could not account for any portion of the growth residual.[4] Finland's investment in human capital accounted for 98 percent of the growth residual in the same period. The UK's investment in human capital accounted for about 79 percent of the growth residual. The study provides interesting opportunities for further inquiry. However, the finding is consistent with the concept of the rise and fall of human capital in the introductory chapter of this book. Accordingly, the finding is not entirely surprising.

The relatively poorer countries have loud noises that could not be directly associated with investment in human capital or TFP. Some African countries are saddled with sovereign debt and repayment regimes that constrain the ability of their policymakers to engage in robust social spending or investment in educational (human capital) programs. Public debt stifles capital formation, and higher levels of poverty impede capital accumulation via the saving channel. The sovereign debt problem will be discussed in Chapter 5.

The next section examines the long-run prospects of the most productive sectors of the Sierra Leonean economy and the probable time frame for their rejuvenation (before reaching steady-state conditions). The Markov chain could best be utilized as a forecasting algorithm for proactive public policies.

3.3 Markov chain process and long-run equilibria of productive sectors in Sierra Leone

In this section, I use the Markov chain process to forecast the performance of the most productive sectors of the economy (based on the assumption that future conditions are contingent on current/state conditions). Notably, Markov chain uses transition matrices to make projections. The Markov forecasting algorithm suggests that the services sector in Sierra Leone has great long-run potential, reaching a steady state in about two decades. The product of the probability transition and state matrices has been utilized to generate conformable state vectors.

The Markov chain is a very useful paradigm for forecasting economic outcomes, based on contemporary situation and probabilistic transition matrices. Consider the following succinct definition of the Markov process. The Markov process could be defined as a discrete time process with finite or countable state space $\mathscr{H}$, and having a sequence of $X_0, X_1, \ldots$ of $\mathscr{H}$-valued random variables, such that for all states $i, j, k_0, k_1, \ldots$ and all times $n = 1, 2, \ldots,$

$$P(X_{n+1} = j, X_n = i, X_{n-1} = k_{n-1}, \ldots) = p(i, j), \tag{3.24}$$

where $p(i, j)$ depends only on the states i, j, and not on the time n or the previous states $K_{n-1}, n-2 \ldots$. The numbers $p(i, j)$ are characterized as the transition probabilities of the chain.[5]

In this section, the Markov process has been adopted to evaluate the long-run performance of the most productive sectors in the Sierra Leonean economy because supportive measures are required for continuous productivity and long-term economic growth and sustainable development. Equation 3.25 presents a column of stochastic probability matrix (the columns add up to 1), which is based on percentages of output and the sum of values that are associated with the use of labor, CO_2 emissions, and land in relation to the output of the most productive sectors of the Sierra Leonean economy – agricultural, industrial, and service sectors.[6] Average Co_2 emissions – excluding residential buildings and commercial and public services – hovered around 12 percent in the lower income Sub-Saharan countries for about 14 years (2000–2014). This information has been adopted to proxy for the data on Co_2 emissions in Sierra Leone.[7] Agricultural land, excluding forest area (% of land area), is generally reported to be about 44 percent of national income for the low-income Sub-Saharan countries (WDI).

The state vector, which has been defined by the most productive sectors of the Sierra Leonean economy, constitutes agriculture (Agric.) (% of 2021 GDP, $b), industry (Ind.) (including construction), value added (% of 2021 GDP, $b), and services, value added (% of 2021 GDP, $b); where GDP is estimated at constant 2015 US dollars. Equation 3.25 gives the probability transition matrix and state vectors required to project the long-run performance of the productive sectors (in Table 3.4) for policy analysis:

$$\begin{array}{ccc} Em & C0_2 & Land \end{array} \quad VGDP$$
$$\begin{bmatrix} 0.43 & 0.56 & 0.44 \\ 0.12 & 0.13 & 0.28 \\ 0.46 & 0.33 & 0.28 \end{bmatrix} * \begin{bmatrix} 3.12 \\ 1.43 \\ 2.5 \end{bmatrix} \begin{array}{l} Agric. \\ Ind. \\ Servs. \end{array} \tag{3.25}$$

It is noteworthy that the model is sensitive to some regularity conditions or theoretical assumptions that are unavoidable: (i) that subsequent production is sensitive to the use of critical environmental resources and public commitments to environmental conservation, (ii) that available commercial special land is fixed and susceptible to deterioration, and (iii) that supervening occurrences do not disturb the transitions to the steady state.

The contribution of the service sector to national income, which has been trending downward (as a percentage of GDP) since 2014 (see Figures 3.11 and 3.12), has

Table 3.4 Markov's steady state for productive sectors of Sierra Leone (US$ b)

	2022	*2032*	*2043*	*2044*
Agriculture	3.22	3.47	3.8	3.8
Industry	1.25	1.37	1.5	1.5
Services	2.59	2.81	3.1	3.1

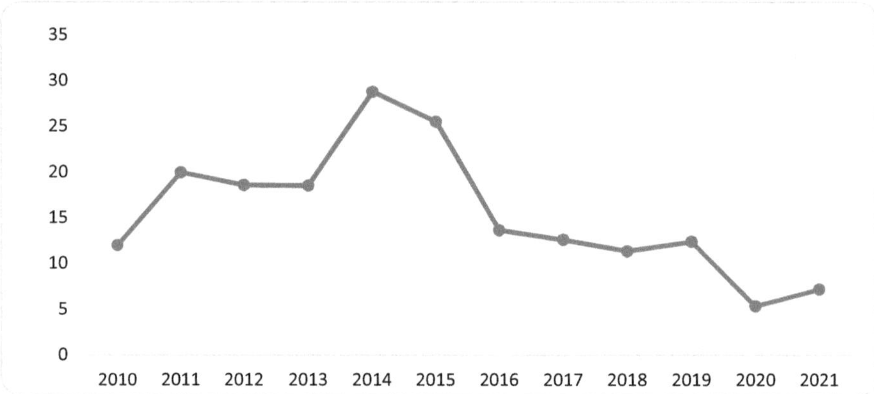

Figure 3.11 Sierra Leone's trade in services (% of GDP).

Data source: World Development Indicators (WDI) 2023

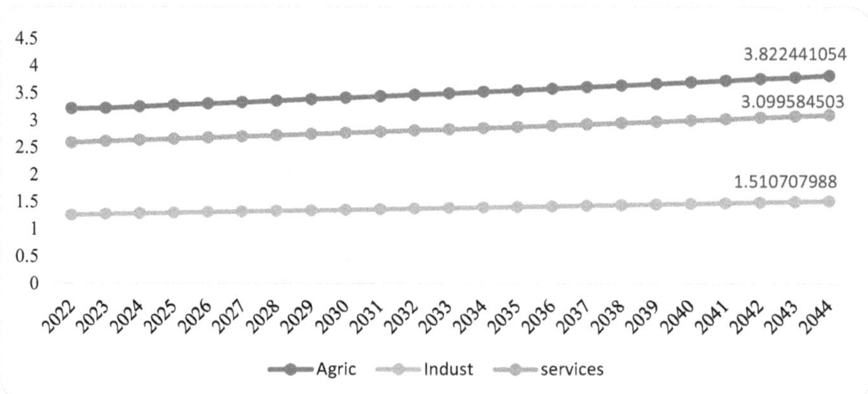

Figure 3.12 Markov's long-run steady state (US$ billion).

Data source: World Bank's *WDI* (2023)

attractive long-run potential. Accordingly, the need to develop human capital and service-oriented infrastructure is rather compelling. Unsurprisingly, the sector provides lucrative opportunities for long-term domestic and foreign direct investment.

Naturally, the steady-state conditions require proactive policy interventions for revitalization (review the steady-state theories of economic growth in this chapter). Pointedly, productive resources are depleted over time. Interventions are naturally contingent on productivity, domestic and foreign saving, technological innovation, human capital, sound macroeconomic policies, and sensitivities to intergenerational equity (preservation of environmental resources) – it should be helpful to review the Solow–Swan growth model in the previous section, and the Porter model in the previous chapter.

3.4 Energy, technology, and sustainable development

Human activities and inefficient uses of energy and environmental resources have engendered undesirable threats to human existence and sustainable development – the use of environmental resources that does not compromise the ability of subsequent generations to harness environmental resources for growth and sustainable development.

Productivity refers to cost-reducing measures to produce output. Accordingly, it is unclear why poorer or low-income countries would continue to embrace costly energy consumption that increases liabilities, reduce standards of living, and compromise the prospects of sustainable development.

Since the mid-1800s, scientists have known that carbon dioxide (CO_2) is one of the main greenhouse gases of importance to Earth's energy balance. Direct measurements of CO2 in the atmosphere and in air trapped in ice show that atmospheric CO_2 increased by more than 40 percent from 1800 to 2019 (Royal Society). CO_2 has both natural and human sources, but CO_2 levels are increasing primarily because of the combustion of fossil fuels, cement production, and deforestation, which reduces the CO_2 taken up by trees and increases the CO_2 released by decomposition of the detritus (waste/debris) and other land use changes. Scientists have argued that increases in CO_2 are the single largest contributor to global warming. Methane (CH_4) has both human and natural sources, and methane levels have risen significantly since pre-industrial times due to human activities such as raising livestock, growing paddy rice, filling landfills, and using natural gas, which is mostly CH_4, some of which may be released when it is extracted, transported, and used. Nitrous oxide (N_2O) concentrations have risen primarily because of agricultural activities such as the use of nitrogen-based fertilizers and land use changes.

Halocarbons, including chlorofluorocarbons (CFCs), are chemicals used as refrigerants and fire retardants. In addition to being potent greenhouse gases, CFCs also damage the ozone layer. The production of most CFCs has now been banned, and their impact on the environment is starting to decline. However, many CFC replacements are also potent greenhouse gases and their concentrations, and the concentrations of other halocarbons continue to increase (Royal Society).

Naturally, the sources of greenhouse gases (GHGs) are diverse, but they have become highly contingent on inescapable economic activities in richer and poorer (or impoverished) countries like Sierra Leone. Yet the exacerbation of the levels of GHGs is highly contingent on population growth, per capita income, and energy consumption. The functional relationship between emission and its drivers is influentially known as the Kaya Identity:

$$M = P\left(\frac{Y}{P}\right)*\left(\frac{E}{Y}\right)*\left(\frac{M}{E}\right) \to M, \qquad 3.26$$

where M is for emissions, P is for population, Y is for gross domestic product, and E is for primary energy consumption. The identity, which is rather analogous to Dupont's financial identity, is more instructive when it is respecified in proportional growth rates over time:

$$\frac{\partial \ln M}{\partial t} = \frac{\partial \ln P}{\partial t} + \frac{\partial \ln^{Y}/_{P}}{\partial t} + \frac{\partial \ln^{E}/_{Y}}{\partial t} + \frac{\partial \ln^{M}/_{E}}{\partial t}. \qquad 3.27$$

Consider the growth rate for of a random variable, X:

$$\frac{\partial \ln X}{\partial t} = \frac{1}{X}\frac{\partial X}{\partial t} = \frac{\dot{X}}{X}. \qquad 3.28$$

The growth rate of emission is contingent on the cumulative growth rates of population, per capita income, energy intensity, and carbon intensity (see Tol, p. 18). The threatening effects of population growth on human existence are not entirely new. The eighteenth-century Reverend gentleman and British economist, Thomas Malthus, reported the alarming prospects of the dissonance between arithmetic food production and geometric population growth in his *Essay on the Principle of Population* (1798). The theory of doom postulated that natural disasters and wars should realistically be welcomed adversities to bring population growth in conformity with food production (positive check). Though scientific progress dampened the unsettling specter of the Malthusian prognosis, the COVID-19 pandemic gave it a new lease of life, albeit momentarily (Warburton, 2021). Apparently, population growth continues to threaten human existence because of the increasing consumption of critical environmental resources – even in the poorer countries of Africa – which coexists with newer and sophisticated technologies of human ingenuity.

Since 2010, energy intensity in Sierra Leone is marginally lower than that of its Sub-Saharan cohorts (see Figure 3.13) but higher than the energy intensities of the US, Britain, and France. Intensities in the more developed countries are reported to be 4.21, 2.23, and 3.23, respectively, in 2021, indicating that the poorer countries have tremendous potential to produce one unit of output with minimal energy (megajoule, MJ). Poorer countries could converge with the relatively wealthier countries if the poorer countries choose to use energy more efficiently. A transition

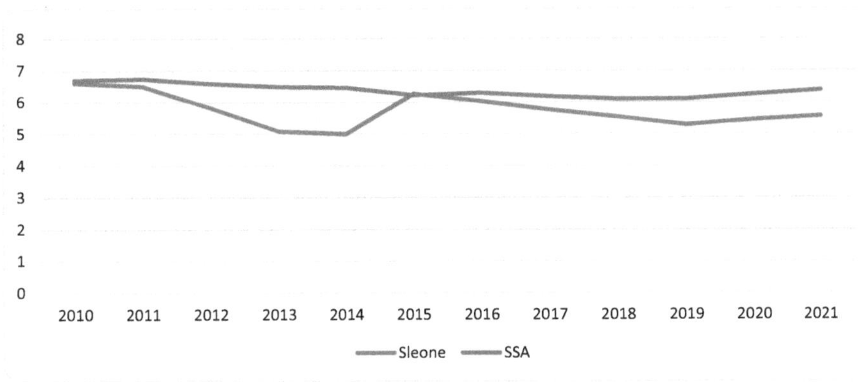

Figure 3.13 Energy intensity use in Sierra Leone and Sub-Saharan Africa (excluding high-income countries).

Data source: World Bank's *WDI* (2023), megajoule (MJ, unit of energy)

Note: Energy intensity level of primary energy is the ratio between energy supply and gross domestic product measured at purchasing power parity [2017]. Energy intensity is an indication of how much energy is used to produce one unit of economic output. Lower ratio indicates that less energy is used to produce one unit of output.

In 2020, to keep income classification thresholds fixed in real terms, the thresholds were moved up in line with the inflation measure. The thresholds (to be compared with GNI per capita in current USD, Atlas method) in 2020 were as follows: Low income <1,036; lower-middle income, 1,037–4,045; Upper-middle income, 4,046–12,535; and high income, >12,535.

to the strategic use of energy could also collaterally reduce undesirable levels of GHG emissions.

Empirical evidence is increasingly supporting the theory that the growth rate of GHG emissions has undesirable consequences for human existence on earth. Some of the effects of GHGs have been reported in Table 3.5, including direct impact on human health, agricultural productivity, the ecosystems, and weather patterns. Various forecasts have projected a reduction in grain yields of up to 50 percent in Africa and extinction of valuable plant and animal species (Perkins et al., p. 758).

The continuing recognition of climate change as a serious threat to the world's environment is becoming increasingly intense, and the issue is being proactively addressed through the United Nations Framework Convention on Climate Change (UNFCCC). Governments throughout the world responded to the concerns about climate change at the 1992 UN Conference on Environment and Development by adopting the Framework Convention on Climate Change (UNFCCC). Membership of UNFCCC has increased to about 198 members, including Sierra Leone, in 2023.

Total GHG emissions in kt of CO_2 equivalent are composed of CO_2 totals excluding short-cycle biomass burning (such as agricultural waste burning and savanna burning) but including other biomass burning (such as forest fires, post-burn decay, peat fires, and decay of drained peatlands), all anthropogenic CH_4

Table 3.5 Damages associated with greenhouse gas emissions

Impact area	*Damages included in the study*
Health impacts	Expansion of the area amenable to parasitic and vector-borne diseases
Agricultural impacts	Changes in area suitable for certain crops and technical changes, e.g., irrigation
Water supply impacts	Changes in water resources
Sea-level rise	Losses of land and wetlands; costs of protection; migration effects
Impacts on ecosystems	Valuations based on estimates of species loss
Hazards of extreme weather events	Changes in frequency and severity of cold spells, heat Waves, drought, floods, storms, and tropical cyclones

Source: Eyre et al. (1998)

Figure 3.14 GHG emission in Sierra Leone and Sub-Saharan Africa (excluding high-income countries, % change).

Data source: World Bank's *WDI* (2023)

sources, N_2O sources, and F-gases (HFCs, PFCs, and SF6) (2009–2021, % change) (World Development Indicators, 2023).

The percentage changes in GHG emission in Sierra Leone and Sub-Saharan Africa (SSA, excluding high-income countries) are oscillatory and occasionally uncorrelated (Figure 3.14). However, the band of vacillation became narrower after 2012. There have been increases in atmospheric concentrations of anthropogenic greenhouse gases (GHGs), consisting of CO_2, methane (CH_4), nitrous oxide (N_2O), as well as halogenated compounds – such as chlorofluorocarbons (CFCs), hydrofluorocarbons (HFCs), and perfluorocarbons (PFCs) – over the past century.

> *Greenhouse gases such as carbon dioxide (CO_2) absorb heat (infrared radiation) emitted from Earth's surface. Increases in the atmospheric*

concentrations of these gases cause Earth to warm by trapping more of this heat. Human activities – especially the burning of fossil fuels since the start of the Industrial Revolution – have increased atmospheric CO_2 concentrations by more than 40%, with over half the increase occurring since 1970. Since 1900, *the global average surface temperature has increased by about 1 °C (1.8 °F). This has been accompanied by warming of the ocean, a rise in sea level, a strong decline in Arctic Sea ice, widespread increases in the frequency and intensity of heatwaves, and many other associated climate effects. Much of this warming has occurred in the last five decades.*

(Royal Society)

The causes for the levels of GHGs are rather variegated but mainly associated with transportation, manufacturing, and the inefficient use of energy (e.g., see Tol's pie chart of distribution, p. 16).[8] Energy efficiency could be an imprecise or nebulous concept, but it could be operationally standardized for comparative analysis. Frazier (2023) provides a standardized workable unit of measurement, dollars per MMBtu (1 million British thermal unit). The central concept could be reasonably discerned as net usage, which defines useful output minus leakages as a fraction of total energy input:

$$Efficiency = \frac{Useful\ Energy\ Output}{Total\ Energy\ Input} = \frac{Total\ Energy\ Input - Waste\ Energy}{Total\ Energy\ Input}. \quad 3.29$$

Invariably, cost of equipments, installation costs, and the relative costs of energy sources are indispensable to informed energy decisions. Hence, policymakers will be well advised to engage in thoughtful cost–benefit analysis that incorporates intergenerational benefits over an extended period to realize returns on energy investments. Table 3.6 provides a basic framework of relative costs for energy preferences. Of course, energy preferences are not without external costs.

Table 3.6 Cost of energy (2022, megawatt hour, MWh)

Source of Energy	*Cost*
1. Solar, standalone	\$32.78 per MWh
2. Geothermal	\$36.40 per MWh
3. Wind, onshore	\$36.93 per MWh
4. Combined cycle	\$37.11 per MWh
5. Solar, hybrid	\$47.67 per MWh
6. Hydroelectric	\$55.26 per MWh
7. Coal	\$72.78 per MWh
8. Biomass	\$89.21 per MWh
9. Battery storage	\$119.84 per MWh
10. Wind, offshore	\$120.52 per MWh

Source: Robertson, J., solar insights.

Solar energy is by far the cheapest of energy options, in terms of not only its natural sources and cost of panel installation but also its positive externalities or environmental protections. According to the US Energy Information Administration, the share of renewables in global energy generation reached nearly 28 percent in 2020 and is projected to approach 49 percent by 2050 (Robertson). Yet the cost of renewable energy has been progressively declining, making it more accessible and more feasible as a long-term alternative to fossil fuels. Closely aligned with solar energy is wind, both of which are abundant natural resources in Sierra Leone and preconditions for higher productivity levels, international competitiveness, and sustainable development.

Ironically, most underdeveloped countries, including Sierra Leone, have not harnessed and optimized the lower costs of energy and the accompanying positive externalities. Pointedly, lower cost energy increases productivity through the cost-reducing channel (see Equation 3.19), which enhances sustainability through the sparing use of environmental resources and reduction of GHG emissions.

Less-efficient energy choices have historically dominated the menu of energy options in Sierra Leone and poorer or impoverished countries of Africa. Energy consumption in Sierra Leone is dominated by biomass, which accounts for over 80 percent of energy in use at the time of this writing. The largest source of biomass energy is wood fuel, which is followed by charcoal,[9] while the use of agricultural crop residues and bagasse in the sugar industry remains limited. In addition, there is considerable potential (without impacting food production) to produce biofuels from energy crops such as maize and cassava, and processing of charcoal into biochar.

About 96.8 percent of the population in Sierra Leone uses firewood or charcoal for cooking. Other sources, including gas, kerosene, or electricity, account for the remaining 3.2 percent. Household use of firewood and charcoal are 64.7 percent and 32.1 percent, respectively, with variations in the use by districts (Energypedia, and SSL, 2015), see Box 3.1 for the use of firewood and charcoal as sources of energy.

Box 3.1 Energy usage in Sierra Leone

In the Northern, Eastern, and Southern regions, an average of 83.7 percent of the population cooks with firewood and an average of 14.5 percent uses charcoal. In the Western Region, where the capital Freetown is situated, 83.3 percent of the households use charcoal as the main source of energy for cooking, 8.9 percent use wood, and 7.8 percent other sources. By way of conclusion, the main energy source for cooking in rural areas is firewood, the main energy source for cooking in urban areas, especially in Freetown, is charcoal . . . .

The rate of consumption of fuel wood far exceeds the replenishing rate to such an extent that desert encroachment, soil erosion, and loss of soil fertility are now serious problems in the country. The nation's 2.726 million hectares of forest and woodland reserves could be depleted within the next 136 years, if not properly managed. These would result in negative impacts on the environment, such as soil erosion, desertification, loss of biodiversity, microclimatic change, and flooding. Most of these impacts are already evident in different ecological zones in the country, amounting to huge economic losses.

Wood fuel is the dominant and cheapest fuel available in the Sierra Leonean market; the production, transportation, and sale of wood fuels are all undertaken by the private sector. There is no official government pricing regulatory body responsible for setting the prices of wood fuels in Sierra Leone.

Sources: Energypedia (2020, June) and SSL (2015, 2017)

Imported petroleum products are the next largest source of power (approximately 13 percent). Imported petroleum products consist of refined products like gasoline or petrol, diesel, marine fuel oil, and kerosene, due to the absence of a domestic refinery. These imports, in lieu of domestic supply of clean energy, perversely expand trade imbalances, deplete the reserves of the country, cause inflationary pressures, and destroy the competitiveness of the local currency. Sierra Leone currently imports all its petroleum products. Petroleum product importation volume per annum increased by more than 100 percent between 2000 and 2011. Petroleum product consumption averaged 184,290 toe per annum (Energypedia). The country needs to invest in technology for clean and efficient energy usage.

I have stated elsewhere that structural changes in the global economy were demanding investments in the service and technology sectors (Warburton, 2018). Yet the service and technology sectors require competent and efficient human capital, reliable infrastructure, and political stability. Consumption of environmental resources (critical capital) need not follow a degrading paradigm to attain economic growth and development. Strategic consumption of environmental resources could simultaneously improve intergenerational equity and economic growth, meaning that the agonizing trade-off between the use of environmental resources and economic growth is not an inevitable occurrence of development.

Accordingly, I reiterated an unavoidable question in 2018: Can long-term investments increase consumption and conservation at the same time? The trade-off between consumption of environmental resources and economic growth could be avoided if saving and consumption could be proportionally increased over time. Skillful investment – driven by policy choices – could lead to increased income and proportional consumption of critical environmental resources when the economic and natural spheres are interdependent. Van den Berg's depiction of the interdependence of the economic and natural spheres has been provided in Figures 3.15 and 3.16 for ease of reference.

Consider Figures 3.15 and 3.16, depicting income per capita ($y, f(k)$), conservation costs $C(s)$, the services that nature could offer (s), the production function in the natural sphere ($F(S)$), available capital per worker (k), depreciation of capital

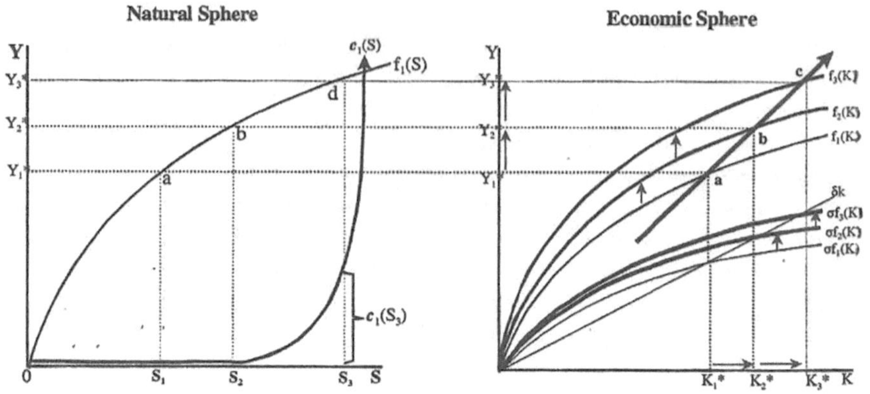

Figures 3.15 The natural and economic spheres.

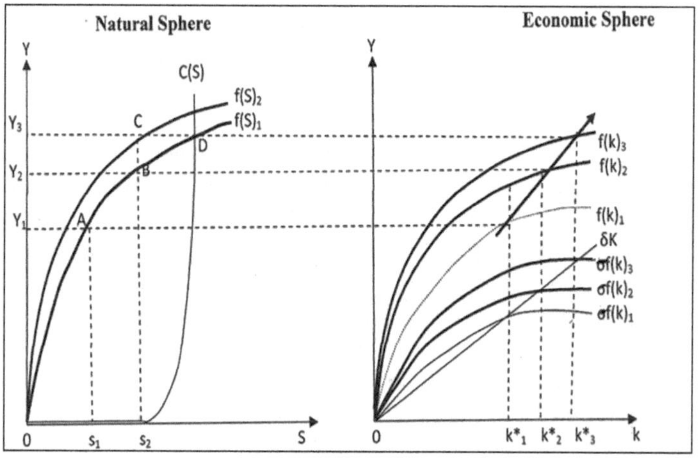

Figure 3.16 Natural and economic spheres with technological innovation.

Source: Van den Berg, Hendrik, *Economic Growth and Development* (2017, pp. 280 and 283)

(δk), and investment ($\sigma f(k)$), based on the Solow model discussed earlier in the chapter. At lower levels of production, the use of nature's services is not intensive, and the marginal conservation cost is zero. As a result, the conservation cost curve is flat (see 0-s_1-s_2 in Figure 3.15). At higher levels of output, corresponding to intensive use of nature's resources (s), conservation cost increases with physical capital per worker (k) and the conservation cost begins to rise. Therefore, increases in output beyond k^*_2 will require an increase in conservation cost (see also Warburton, 2018). The positive correlation between output and consumption of nature's services can be modified by targeted investment in green technology and the reduction of poverty in a low-income country like Sierra Leone, where poorer people depend heavily on accessible environmental resources for fuel/energy and food.

The growth and saving-augmenting effects of investment are depicted in Figure 3.15. Progress in the economic sphere, which increases capital per worker, can alter the production function of the natural sphere to such an extent that long-term investment and technology in the natural sphere generates efficiencies in the natural sphere. Instead of increasing output and the cost of conservation in tandem from B to D (see the Natural Sphere of Figure 3.16), output can be increased from B to C, thereby stabilizing the use of nature's resources.

Evidently, Sierra Leone is endowed with critical (natural) resources, which provides lucrative opportunities for long-term foreign direct investments (FDIs), energy independence, and sustainable growth and development. The latent capacities to provide self-sufficient energy supply would also require improvement on the level of human capital that is required to absorb and maintain long-term technological investments in energy production.

3.5 Sustainable development and the latent capacities of Sierra Leone

Sierra Leone has a lot of underutilized energy capacities; capacities that could increase productivity by reducing energy cost and guaranteeing environmental sustainability. Though Sierra Leone is endowed with sources of energy in various forms, including the less-efficient biomass from agricultural wastes, its wind, hydro, and solar power are underutilized. Energy consumption, as noted earlier, is largely dominated by biomass from fuel wood, which accounts for around 80 percent of the energy consumption. Imported petroleum products, the next largest source of energy, are mainly for power generation, which accounts for 13 percent of energy consumption. Several rivers with numerous waterfalls and the abundance of sunlight for solar energy create considerable capabilities for sourcing energy for a country with a spatial dimension of 71,620 sq km.

It is sensible for the country to focus on the cheapest sources of renewable energy (see Table 3.6) to maintain reasonable trade imbalances, competitiveness in the global economy, conservation of foreign reserves, a viable currency, and price stability. Renewable energy is source of energy from natural phenomena such as sunlight, wind, tides, plant growth, and geothermal heat. As such, renewable energy is derived from natural processes that are constantly replenished. The potential use of solar energy in Sierra Leone is virtually limitless.

3.5 (a) Solar potential

Approximately 1460 kWh/m of solar radiation can be expected annually in Sierra Leone.[10] The country signed the Energy Africa Policy Compact with the UK as a pioneer at a time when there was no solar power capacity installed in Sierra Leone (IREA, 2017, p. 50); but according to Sierra Leone Investment and Export Promotion Agency (SLIEPA), some big and smaller solar projects were eventually implemented around the country.[11]

The country has very competitive solar irradiation in the subregion, where solar irradiance is defined as the power per unit area received from the sun in the form of electromagnetic radiation in the wavelength range of the measuring instrument.

Solar irradiance is measured in watts per square meter (W/m^2) in SI units, established by the General Conference on Weights and Measures. The Joint Research Centre (JRS) of the European Commission estimates the solar potential of Sierra Leone to be as high as 2200 kWh/m (Energypedia, 2020). Figure 3.17 also reveals the irradiation competitiveness of the country in the subregion. Figure 3.18 shows that over 80 percent of the country's land area could get about 14–16 annual generation per unit of installed PV capacity (MWh/kWp) and about 10 percent could get 12–14. The country is in an enviable position to benefit from solar energy. Figure 3.19 shows that solar energy was severely underutilized in 2022.

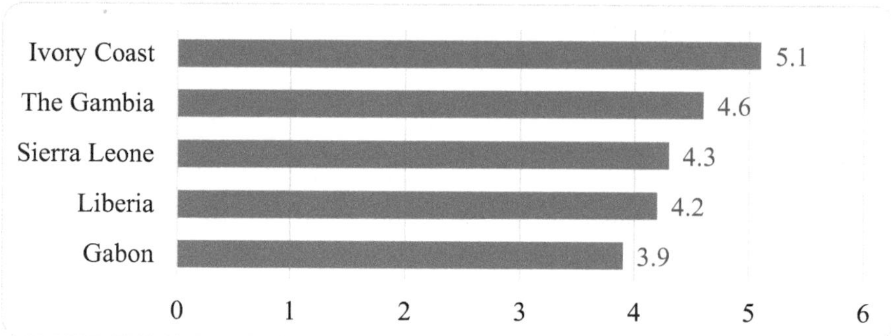

Figure 3.17 Solar irradiation (kilowatts per square meter, 2021).

Sources: Global Solar Atlas, 2021 and SLIEPA (Sierra Leone Investment and Export Promotion Agency)

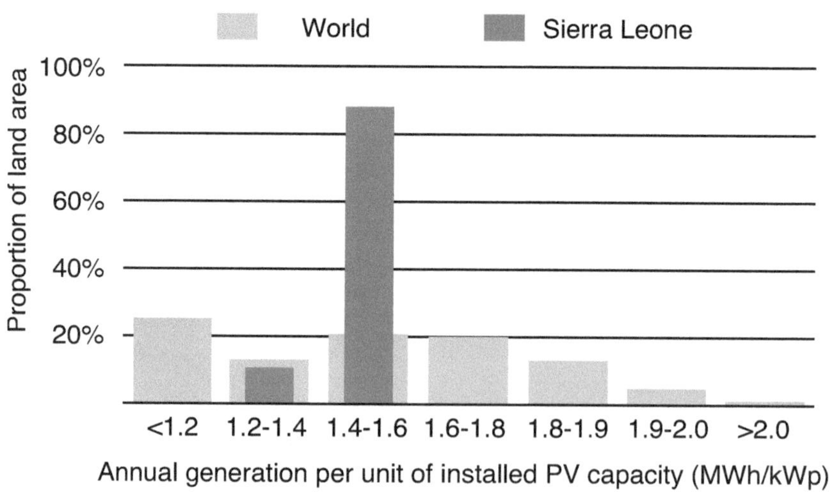

Figure 3.18 Distribution of solar potential.

Source: International Renewable Energy Association (IREA)

Note: Solar resource potential has been divided into seven classes, each representing a range of annual PV output per unit of capacity (kWh/kWp/yr). The bar chart shows the proportion of a country's land area in each of these classes and the global distribution of land area across the classes (for comparison).

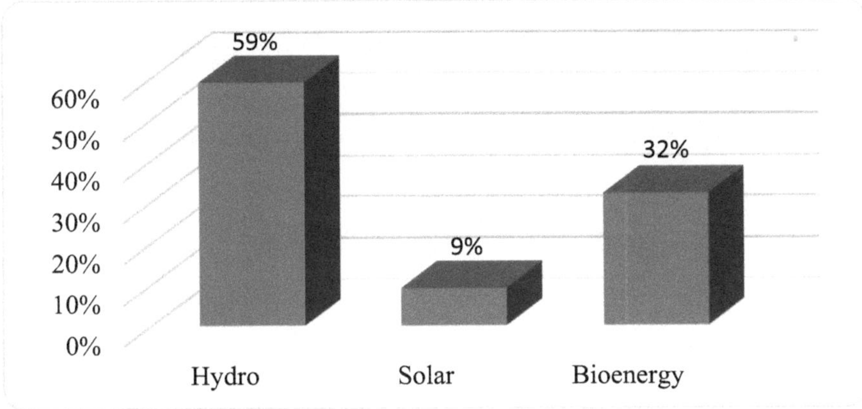

Figure 3.19 Renewable capacity in 2022.

Data source: IRENA

Note: Geothermal and wind are insignificant.

3.5 (b) Wind energy

Wind farms are possible at certain locations including along the **coastline, offshore,** and at some **mountainous locations** in the country. Prospective evaluations indicate that wind farms are possible at certain locations including along the coastline, offshore, and at some mountainous locations in the country.

With the availability of low wind speed turbines in global markets, there is a strong potential for the use of wind as a reliable source of energy in the areas of the country for which wind energy is most propitious, especially the northern rural areas of the country. There is a known wind energy system of 5kw in Sierra Leone, located in the Bonthe District, along the south coastline area. Sierra Leone's best wind velocities indicate a country-wide average of between 3 m/s and 5 m/s, increasing to approximately 8 m/s in some mountainous areas (Energypedia). There is some indication that wind speeds of 12 m/s are possible in parts of the country, implying that wind energy could be a viable option in selected locations. Wind farms are, for instance, possible at certain locations such as along the coastline, at sea near the coastline, and at some locations in the country. Figure 3.20 also shows that the country has a latent capacity for using wind energy. Notwithstanding the underutilized capacities of clean and cost-efficient sources of energy, there are inherent problems that challenge the movement to energy diversification. Some of these problems could be found in Box 3.2. Governments of the country have made treaties and enacted laws, but the practical and substantial economic effects of the treaties and laws are yet to be realized. A cross section of the laws has been provided in Box 3.3.

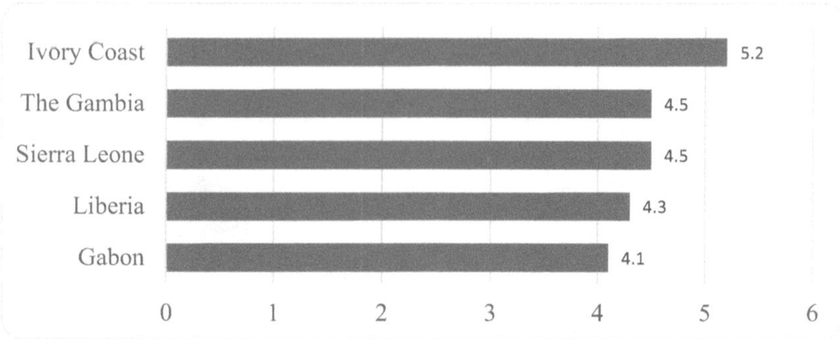

Figure 3.20 Average wind speed in Sierra Leone (meters per second, 2021).

Sources: Global Wind Atlas, 2021 (data shown is an average of speeds recorded onshore and up to 200 km offshore) and SLIEPA

Box 3.2 Key problems of the energy sector

Financing/Investment: *Especially lack of private investments, lack of economic incentives, support and implementation for PAYGO availability necessary, microfinance should be available for solar businesses, no fully functioning mobile money platform exists.*

Enabling Legal Framework: *Need for clear regulations of private-sector participation in electricity generation, need for mini-grid licensing and concessions, need for standardized Power Purchase Agreements (PPAs), need for less bureaucratic process of receiving tax/duty waivers for private companies importing certified solar products, no Rural Electrification Agency exists.*

Infrastructure and Services: *Transmission and distribution infrastructure need to be improved, most parts of the country have no access to any grid, many distribution lines were destroyed during the civil war, old equipment is in place and needs to be replaced, poor energy efficiency, the existing network is very old, and there are immense power losses in the generation, transmission, and distribution (40% transmission losses), generation capacity does not cover the demand, especially in the industry many companies are forced to rely on diesel generators, service standards of EDSA are poor, use of inefficient cook stoves/3-stone-fires and kerosene lights/battery torches,*

Lack of accurate data: *Lack of data collection in the energy sector, absence of detailed research.*

Lack of awareness: *Missing awareness on quality standards for solar, especially PicoPV products, missing awareness on Improved Cook Stoves, missing awareness on environmental benefits (climate change, health, etc.) of solar and improved cook stoves, recycling program for old batteries necessary.*

Source: Energypedia.

Box 3.3 Sustainability and regulation

The Sustainable Energy for All (SE4ALL) Action Agenda for Sierra Leone. *The Action Agenda was part of a 2014 agreement of ECOWAS member states that agreed on the development of National Renewable Energy Action Plans (NREAPs) and SE4ALL Agendas. In its agendas, Sierra Leone outlined goals, such as the electrification of all district-headquarter towns, increased installed power capacity, 1.229MW in 2030, increased access to Renewable off-grid solutions, but also objectives such as increased access to improved cooking technologies or improved charcoal production. The goals are outlined for 2020 and 2030, respectively.*

The Energy Africa Policy Compact. In February 2016, *Sierra Leone was the first African country to sign the Energy Africa Policy Compact with the Government of the UK. As a result, the Government of Sierra Leone launched the Energy Revolution, a government-led initiative to promote the solar home system market with activities in the areas of Demand Creation, Technical Assistance for Businesses, Policy Reform, and Access to Finance. The initiative is committing to reach 250,000 households with modern solar solutions by 2018 and achieve "Power for All" by 2025. A DFID-financed Power for All Campaign was launched and an "Energy Task Force Meeting" was established.*

The Finance Act, 2017 (Energypedia, 2020). . . *Finance Act guaranteeing Duty Waivers for imported solar products that fulfill IEC Standards. In practice, it is difficult for private companies to impose the measures, due to unclear administrative processes and long delays.*

The . . . Renewable Energy Policy of Sierra Leone and the Energy Efficiency Policy of Sierra Leone, *ratified by the* Parliament in 2016 *and launched in 2018, outlining the status of Renewable Energy in the country and objectives and measurements in the sector.*

Source: Energypedia (2020).

Notes

1 See also Mankiw (2013, pp. 205–231), Gylfason (1999, pp. 129–145), and Jones (2002, pp. 20–91) for a comprehensive discussion of exogenous and endogenous growth models.

2 See the Bureau of Economic Analysis, *www.bea.gov/help/glossary/gross-saving#:~:text=A%20measure%20of%20the%20saving,and%20consumption%20of%20fixed%20capital*.

3 See van den Berg (pp. 412–414) for an extension of Kremer's (1993) model, including the Malthusian theory that population grows whenever per capita income is above subsistence per capita income (the congestive theorem); see also Warburton (2021).

4 Agriculture accounts for about 20 percent of GDP and employs more than half of the workforce, mainly small landholders, in Ghana. Education is highly privatized in Sierra Leone; see the rise and fall of human capital in the introductory chapter of this book,

5 For further clarifications and expositions, see *https://galton.uchicago.edu/~lalley/Courses/312/MarkovChains.pdf.*
6 Employment in agriculture (% of total employment) (modeled ILO estimate), employment in industry (% of total employment) (modeled ILO estimate), and employment in services (% of total employment) (modeled ILO estimate).
7 Higher levels of methane, a relatively dangerous gas, are associated with agriculture. However, it is noteworthy that agricultural methane emission (% of total emissions) in 2008 was about 57 percent for Sierra Leone (WDI). Co_2 data have been extrapolated from the sub-region of comparable countries to satisfy the probabilistic requirements of the model. The author has considered CO_2 emissions from other sectors, excluding residential buildings and commercial and public services (% of total fuel combustion) for residual emission. CO_2 emission from manufacturing industries and construction (% of total fuel combustion) for the sub-region in 2014 is utilized as a proxy for industrial CO_2 emission.
8 Sierra Leone puts almost all its refuse in landfill sites [landfill emit methane gas]. The energy content of the total domestic and industrial refuse disposed of in 2012 amounted to 594,000 tons per annum. Options for energy production from municipal waste should be examined including biogas projects as well as methane gas from landfills (Energypedia, https://energypedia.info/wiki/Sierra_Leone_Energy_Situation#:~:text=Sierra%20Leone%20puts%20almost%20all,as%20methane%20gas%20from%20landfills).
9 See Statistics Sierra Leone (2015) Population and Housing Census. (SSL, 2015) and Energypedia.
10 See SLIEPA, *www.sliepa.gov.sl/industries/energy/diverse-sectoral-opportunities.*
11 These include installation and operation of three solar mini grids in Segbwema, Panguma, and Gbinti, installation of SHS for approximately 100 charging centers, 20 energy hubs for Agricultural Business Centers, 20 clinics, 12 schools, and 12 financial service associations. Equipment and training for three Energy Laboratories in cooperation with Polytechnics. Sales of Pico PV products through local retailers. Other projects include Promoting Renewable Energy Services for Social Development (PRESSD) (2014–2018), Rural Renewable Energy Project (2017–2020), Installation of Solar Street Lights, and some smaller projects.

References

Energypedia. (2020, June). Sierra Leone Energy Situation. https://energypedia.info/wiki/Sierra_Leone_Energy_Situation

Extension Service, BAE-1408. https://extension.okstate.edu/fact-sheets/true-cost-of-energy-comparisons-apples-to-apples.html

Eyre, N., Downing, T., Hoekstra, R., Rennings, K. & Tol, R.S.J. (1998). *ExternE: Externalities of energy: Global warming: Warming damages*. The European Commission.

Feenstra, R.C., Inklaar, R. & Timmer, M.P. (2015). The next generation of the Penn World Table. *American Economic Review,* 105(10), 3150–3182. www.ggdc.net/pwt

Frazier, R.S. (2023, March). *True cost of energy comparisons apples to apples*. Oklahoma Cooperative.

Guisan, M.C. (2009). Government effectiveness, education, economic development, and well-being: Analysis of European countries in comparison with the United States and Canada, 2000–2007. Applied Econometrics and International Development, 9(1), 39–55.

Guisan, M.C. & Neira, I. (2008). Direct and indirect effects of human capital on world development, 1960–2004. Applied Econometrics and International Development, 6(1), 17–34.

Gylfason, T. (1999). *Principles of economic growth*. Oxford University Press.

International Renewable Energy Association (IREA). (2017). *Renewable energy statistics 2017*. IREA.

Jones, C.I. (2002). *Introduction to economic growth* (2nd ed.). Norton.

Kremer, M. (1993). Population growth and technology change: One million BC to 1990. *Quarterly Journal of Economics*, 108, 681–716.

Krugman, P. (1994). Defining and measuring productivity. The Age of Diminishing Expectations, 1.

Mankiw, G.N. (2013). *Macroeconomics* (8th ed.). Worth.

Mankiw, G.N., Romer, D. & Weil, D.N. (1992, May). A contribution to the empirics of economic growth. *The Quarterly Journal of Economics*, 107(2), 407–437.

Mell, A. & Walker, O. (2014). *The rough guide to economics: From first principles to the financial crisis*. Rough Guides.

Perkins, D.H., Radlet, S., Lindauer, D.L. & Block, S.A. (2013). *Economics of development* (7th ed.). Norton.

Robertson, J. (2022). Types of energy ranked by cost per megawatt hour. *Solar Energy Insights*. https://solarpower.guide/solar-energy-insights/energy-ranked-by-cost

Solow, R.M. (1956). A contribution to the theory of economic growth. *Quarterly Journal of Economics*, LXX, 65–94.

Solow, R.M. (1957). Technical change and the aggregate production function. *Review of Economics and Statistics*, 39, 312–320.

Statistics Sierra Leone. (2015/17). *Sierra Leone 2015 population and housing census*. Sierra Leone.

Swan, T.W. (1956). Economic growth and capital accumulation. *Economic Record*, 32(63), 334–361.

The Royal Society. (2020). *Climate change: Evidence and causes,* update 2020. National Academy of Sciences. https://royalsociety.org/topics-policy/projects/climate-change-evidence-causes/

Tol, R.S.J. (2019). *Climate economics: Economic analysis of climate,* climate change, and climate policy (2nd ed.). Edward Elgar.

Van den Berg, H. (2017). *Economic growth and development* (3rd ed.). World Scientific.

Warburton, C.E.S. (2018). Positive time preference and environmental degradation: The effects of world population growth and economic activity on intergenerational equity, 1970–2015. Applied Econometrics and International Development, Euro-American Association of Economic Development, 18(2), 5–24.

Warburton, C.E.S. (2020). The acquisition of human capital and economic growth: An international survey. *Applied Econometrics and International Development,* 20(2), 5–24.

Warburton, C.E.S. (2021). Positive check: The Malthusian theorem and the Covid-19 pandemic. *Journal of Smart Economic Growth,* 6(3), 1–7.

World Bank. (2019). *World development indicators*. World Bank.

World Bank. (2023). *World development indicators*. World Bank.

4 International trade and economic growth

4.1 Theories of international trade

Theories of international trade generally provide explanations for international transactions and the way countries could improve their collective welfare through international trade. Trade theories often raise controversies because of conflicting national interests, which could sufficiently challenge competing interests. Of course, these conflicts are not new. Since ancient times polities and countries have been in search of financial assets, raw materials that they do not have, and markets to sell finished products. These desires have led to coercion, expansionary wars of conquest (colonialism), and diplomatic overtures when coercion and wars became costly and impracticable. In the final analysis, serious nations are interested in improving the aggregate welfare of their citizens through a variety of mechanisms, including international trade. How?

Sometimes the best intentions of political leaders are not adequately captured by the choices that they make to maximize aggregate welfare. To maximize the welfare of their citizens, political leaders could make innocent mistakes when dealing with the rest of the world, or they could be outrightly callous about the welfare of citizens. Intellectual and contemporary trade theories started with the former – an innocent mistake to maximize aggregate welfare that has been widely characterized as "mercantilism." Conceivably, the mercantilist thought still has residual appeal within the protectionist mode of international trade.

Mercantilist thoughts were loosely conceptualized until Adam Smith gave it theoretical dimensions in terms of its fallacies in resolving balance of payments problems and achieving and national prosperity.

> *Mercantilism is nothing but a tissue of protectionist fallacies foisted upon a venal Parliament by our merchants and manufacturers, grounded upon the popular notion that wealth consists in money. Like an individual, a country must spend less than its income if its wealth is to increase.*
>
> (Blaug, p. 11)

In effect, mercantilism has been associated with the acquisition of money (bullion) by spending less and acquiring more money for nations to become richer and

DOI: 10.4324/9781003518464-5

wealthier. A fundamental problem is that trade will be contractionary if all nations think as such. Nations become poorer when they cannot sell their own goods and they will eventually not have money to continue to import goods from other nations that are not reciprocating. Accordingly, the beggar-thy-neighbor concept of international trade is unsustainable.

However, not all mercantilists measured national wealth in terms of the stock of bullion. It was apparent to some mercantilists that economic activity could be constrained, leading to an upward pressure on prices when money is withdrawn from circulation and hoarded; for example, Thomas Mun (1571–1641), John Locke (1632–1704), and Charles Davenant (1656–1714) highlighted the complexity of measuring national wealth. Adam Smith recalled the definition of wealth by mercantilists such as Thomas Mun and John Locke: *wealth of a country consists of not only gold and silver but also its lands, houses, and consumable goods of all different kinds* (Blaug, p. 11).

The inflationary effects of excess money supply were captured via the transaction velocity of money that was later popularized by David Hume (1711–1776).

$$\begin{aligned} TP &= MV, \\ \log T + \log P &= \log M + \log V, \end{aligned} \tag{4.1}$$

where T is for the transaction volume of goods per unit of time, P is for the general price level, M is for money in circulation, and V is for the velocity of money per unit of time – the number of times a unit of money could be used to purchase final goods [and services]. The logarithmic transformation shows that there is a direct link between the money in circulation and the general price level if the volume of transactions and velocity of circulation are constant.[1] The retroactive effects of rising prices on international competitiveness and the trade balance were granted undue attention. This connection was later made by David Hume (Kurz, p. 13).

The nationalist sentiment of mercantilism was accepted in England, France, and Germany from the sixteenth to eighteenth centuries; for example, Thomas Mun (1571–1641) pointed out that: [England's wealth is increased] *wherein wee . . . sell more to strangers yearly than wee consume of theirs in value* (*England's Treasure by Forraign Trade*, c.1630) (Kurz, p. 12). Though the mercantilist theorem had a common denominator of protection, regulation, and monopolization of trade, the economic conditions in the mercantilist countries were not homogeneous. In France, luxury goods such as silks, linens, tapestries, furniture, and wine were heavily regulated because of their value. Under the leadership of Jean Baptiste Colbert (1619–1683), the minister of finance for more than 20 years during the reign of Louis XIV, national guilds were set up to regulate major industries in France (Fusfeld, p. 16). The popularity mercantilist theory of international trade started to wane more prominently by the middle of the eighteenth century.

Small businesses were crushed by monopoly power and farmers hated taxes that were intended to boost the income and wealth of nations. British policy of taxation without representation did not work out too well in America. Similarly, corrupt government in France faced opposition over taxes on peasants and independent farmers, while the nobility was largely exempted from onus taxes. The Physiocrats started to toll the death knell of mercantilism as a dominant trade theory of the eighteenth century.

The Physiocrats (French anti-mercantilists) were repulsed by the burden of taxation on peasants and the devastating effects of taxes on what they conceived as the most productive elements of the economy of France, Agriculture provided both the livelihood and money to finance the French feudal economy. Quesnay structured the French economy into three component parts: (i) the productive agrarian sector of farmers who produced food and pay rents to the consumer class of landlords, (ii) the consumer class of landlords who collected rents (income) and taxes from the farmers (peasants), and (iii) the sterile class of artisans (manufactures) that generated no taxes or surplus (profits) to finance the French economy.

Now and then, the thought that the manufacturing class was sterile is rather counterintuitive. However, it was premised on the notion that competition ensures that the prices of manufactures are no more than the raw material and labor costs required to produce them. Presumably, there was no allowance for profits in the prices of manufactures. In general, Quesnay's work suggests that the wages that manufacturers received were very close to the modern concept of a "normal profit" (Eltis, 176). Hence, the Physiocrats proposed that artisans produced no surplus over costs, while agriculture can produce a surplus if it is sufficiently capitalized (Eltis, pp. 176–178). The surplus that the farmers produced went to the landed aristocracy, the Church, and the King. A schematic representation of the transfers of economic activities could be found in Appendix A. Half of the income of the productive and sterile components were consumed but the artisans had nothing to contribute to national revenue.[2] However, the doubling of advances in agriculture produced a surplus from which taxes could be paid (the middle column of Appendix A).

Quesnay assumed here that landlords, farmers, and artisans each spend half the money they receive on the outputs of the "productive" sector, that is, on the products provided by "agriculture, grasslands, pastures, forests, mines, fishing, etc.," and the remaining half on the products of the "sterile" sector, that is, on "manufactured commodities, house-room, clothing, interest on money, servants, commercial costs, foreign produce, etc." (Eltis, 181). The productive sector was generating revenue for the sterile sector. Money that was reinjected into the system by the landlords for equal redistribution came from the rents of the farmers.

Physiocracy was not a theory of international trade. It barely exposed the flaws of the mercantilist theory of trade in significant ways, which enabled Adam Smith to develop the international trade theory of absolute advantage in 1776. The central issue was, how could nations become wealthy? In his *Wealth of Nations* (1776), Smith postulated the theory of absolute advantage that is based on factor abundance.

The theory of absolute advantage simply states that, rather than hoarding bullion and constraining international trade, nations could become richer if they freely trade with one another by specializing in the production of goods for which they have absolute advantages. Pointedly, though the gains of international trade are asymmetric, trade is welfare-enhancing and not a zero-sum game as the mercantilists had postulated. Various variables account for differences in supply-side factors, including geographic conditions, natural resources, factor availability, production cost, and technology. Therefore, abundant and cheap inputs should be the basis for international trade. Smith writes:

> *The natural advantages which one country has over another in producing particular commodities are sometimes so great that it is acknowledged by all the world to be in vain to struggle with them . . . . As long as the one country has those advantages, and the other wants them, it will always be more advantageous for the latter rather to buy of the former than to make. It is an acquired advantage only, which one artificer has over his neighbor, who exercises another trade; and yet they both find it more advantageous to buy of one another than to make what does not belong to their particular trades.* (Smith, 1776 [1994], p. 487)
>
> *If a foreign country can supply us with a commodity cheaper than we ourselves can make it, better buy it of them with some part of the produce of our own industry employed in a way in which we have some advantage. The general industry of the country, being always in proportion to the capital which employs it, will not thereby be diminished, no more than that of the above-mentioned artificers; but only left to find out the way in which it can be employed with the greatest advantage.*
>
> (Smith, 1776 [1994], p. 486)

The natural complements of endowment and skill are specialization and freer trade. Specialization increases productivity and competitiveness. This was borne out by production in England's pin factory.

> *[O]ne man draws out the wire, another straights it, a third cuts it a fourth points it, a fifth grinds it at the top for receiving the head; to make the head requires two or three distinct operations . . . but if they had all wrought separately and independently, and without any of them have been educated to this particular business, they certainly could not each of them have made twenty, perhaps not one pin a day.*
>
> (Smith, 1776 [1994], p. 4)

Thus, nations are more likely to discover easier and readier methods of production as they intensify or increase their levels of specialization to trade freely with other nations. But the benefits of trade can be stymied by protections and taxes if trade is not managed properly to prevent antagonisms.

> *But if foreigners, either by prohibitions or high duties, are hindered from coming to sell, they cannot always afford to come to buy; because coming without a cargo, they must lose the freight from their own country to Great Britain. By diminishing the number of sellers, therefore, we necessarily diminish that of buyers, and are thus likely not only to buy foreign goods*

> *dearer, but to sell our own cheaper, than if there was a more perfect freedom of trade. As defence, however, is of much more importance than opulence, the act of navigation is, perhaps, the wisest of all the commercial regulations of England.*
>
> (Smith, 1776 [1994], p. 494)

In effect, absolute freedom is incompatible with international trade.

In the final analysis, the benefits from trade among nations need not be symmetric.

> *First, though it were certain that in the case of a free trade between France and England, for example, the balance would be in favour of France, it would by no means follow that such a trade would be disadvantageous to England, or that the general balance of its whole trade would thereby be turned more against it. If the wines of France are better and cheaper than those of Portugal, or its linens than those of Germany, it would be more advantageous for Great Britain to purchase both the wine and the foreign linen which it had occasion for of France than of Portugal and Germany. Though the value of the annual importations from France would thereby be greatly augmented, the value of the whole annual importations would be diminished, in proportion as the French goods of the same quality were cheaper than those of the other two countries. This would be the case, even upon the supposition that the whole French goods imported were to be consumed in Great Britain.*
>
> (Smith, 1776 [1994], p. 505)

An extension of the theory of absolute advantage has been provided in Figure 4.6.

Though Smith's theorem of absolute advantage was an elegant improvement on the mercantilist theory of trade, it was an insufficient theory of international trade. Factor abundance, skill, or technology did not quite explain the basis for international trade when a country is more efficient in the production of many goods. The theory that supplanted absolute advantage became known as comparative advantage, which is based on relative costs or the opportunity costs of production. There are various shades of the theory of comparative advantage that are beyond the scope of this chapter.

The theory of comparative advantage by David Ricardo (1772–1823) provided an alternative and improved theory of international trade in terms of resource allocation and comparative cost (*Principles of Political Economy and Taxation*, 1817). Unlike Smith, he argued that even if a nation is comparatively less efficient in the production of multiple goods, there is still a basis for mutually beneficial trade if the nation specializes in the production of the good for which its comparative disadvantage is less (Warburton, 2021, p. 376).

The illustration in Figure 4.1 shows that China has an advantage in the production of both manufactures and farm products. Both nations, China and Sierra Leone, can produce and consume at autarkic levels (A) on the demand diagonal (DD) line. However, the autarkic levels are suboptimal because both nations can

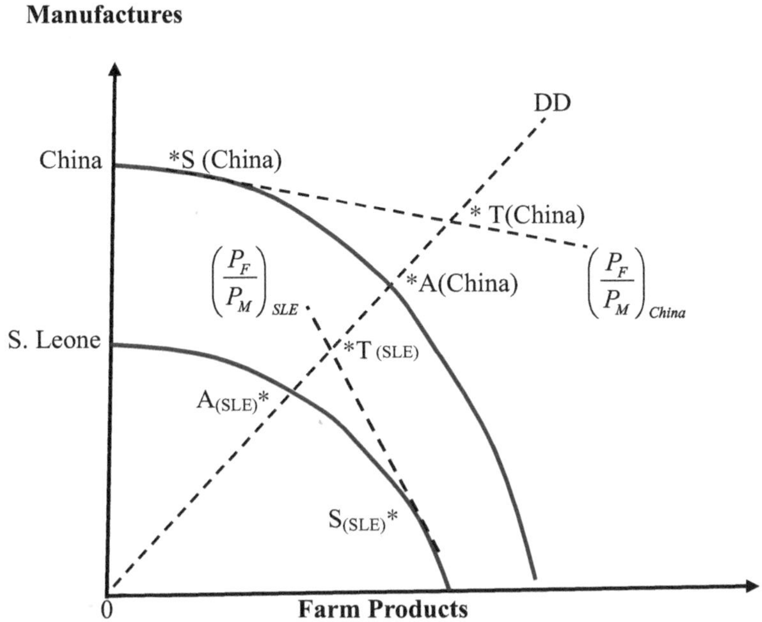

Figure 4.1 Comparative costs of manufactures and farm products in China and Sierra Leone.

consume at superior levels (T) beyond their respective autarkic positions (A) after specializing (S) in the production in the goods for which they have comparative advantage. Notice that in this case China has an advantage in the production of both categories of goods, but that China has a comparative advantage in the production of manufactures.

$$\left(\frac{P_F}{P_M}\right)_{China} > \left(\frac{P_F}{P_M}\right)_{SLE} \rightarrow \left(\frac{P_M}{P_F}\right)_{SLE} < \left(\frac{P_M}{P_F}\right)_{China}$$

The relative price lines that are the opportunity (relative) costs are given by relative prices, where the opportunity cost of producing manufactures is the cost of producing farm product relative to manufactures (P_F/P_M). Since the cost of producing farm product in lieu of manufactures is greater in China, China is better off producing manufactures. The opposite must be true for Sierra Leone. Evidently, the illustration shows that by specialization and consumption both countries are better off than not trading at all though the gains are asymmetric. The welfare effect must be noteworthy even with trade that is based on comparative advantage (see also Warburton, 2021, pp. 369–379).

Since trade is mutually beneficial, all nations engage in international trade, except when they are ostracized by the international community because of bad behavior that disturbs international peace and security. Even so, they engage in a

Table 4.1 Foreign trade indicators (percentage of GDP in parenthesis)*

Foreign Trade Indicators	*2017*	*2018*	*2019*	*2020*
Imports of Goods (US$m)	1,301	1,354	1,576	1,257
Exports of Goods (US$m)	567	554	619	368
Imports of Services (US$m)	420	370	404	N/A
(% GDP)	–48	–39	–38	–36
Exports of Services (US$m)	145	92	64	NA
(% GDP)	–26	–17	–18	–15
Foreign Trade (% GDP)	–74	–57	–56	–52

Sources: World Trade Organization (WTO) and the World Bank

* Trade in services for 2020 is somewhat counterintuitive

limited amount of trade with nonconforming nations. We have now fitted Sierra Leone into one of the theories of international trade.

Even with competitive disadvantages in Sierra Leone, there is still a basis for Sierra Leone to trade with the rest of the world and grow. Table 4.1 provides a snapshot of Sierra Leone's trade with the rest of the world from 2017 to 2020.

Imports as a percentage of GDP were higher compared to exports. This means that the country is buying more than it is selling to other countries which adversely affects the trade balance for a small open economy. The rest of this chapter will examine all the major issues of international trade and their implications for economic growth and sustainable development in Sierra Leone. I first examine the evolution of international trade treaties.

4.2 The evolution of contemporary international trade treaties

Trade agreements predate World War I; for example, the British and the French struck the Cobden–Chevalier Treaty of 1860, which prefaced a series of other European trade treaties. Bilateral trade agreements and accompanying most favored nation (MFN) clauses led to reduction in tariffs (taxes on traded goods). However, European free trade started to decline between 1879 and 1914. During the Great European Depression between 1873 and 1896 prices of internationally traded goods progressively plummeted (WTO, 2007, p. 9), and countries with large agrarian sectors in continental Europe started to increase tariffs.

As production shifted to wartime needs during WWI, extensive government controls replaced private commercial transactions during the interregnum (1918–39). High tariff levels, quantitative restrictions, and foreign exchange controls contracted the volume of international trade within the framework of beggar-thy-neighbor policies. The international framework for cooperation, embodied in the League of Nations (1920), proved inadequate to foster political and economic cooperation. Much more consequential efforts to foster multilateral trade arrangements emerged after World War II within the frameworks of the International Trade

Organization (ITO), General Agreement on Tariffs and Trade (GATT), and the World Trade Organization (WTO).

After America and Britain made a proposal to the United Nations to form a multilateral trade organization, the Economic and Social Council of the United Nations called a conference to establish the International Trade Organization (ITO). The ITO Charter was drafted by a preparatory committee (1946–48) and signed in Havana Cuba in March 1948. However, huge opposition to the Charter in the US Congress and elsewhere in the US prevented President Truman from presenting the Charter to the Congress for Congressional approval in 1950. However, the thought of a multilateral trade agreement was enduring.

The GATT emerged as an offshoot of the ITO negotiations though it was intended to be a temporary multilateral trade agreement pending the ratification of the ITO Charter. In 1948, the United States and 22 other countries established the General Agreement on Tariffs and Trade (GATT) to formulate and enforce rules that govern international trade. The treaty was signed by 23 countries on October 30, 1947, and entered into force on January 1, 1948. The GATT emerged as a strong multilateral organization till the 1990s, and it was responsible for multiple rounds of international negotiations for trade liberalization (see Table 4.2). GATT was enhanced during the Uruguay Round (1986–1993) to deal with trade disputes, trade in services, and intellectual property rights,[3] and it subsequently morphed into the World Trade Organization with specific principles: (i) promotion of trade liberalization (freer trade), (ii) nondiscriminatory trade practices, and (iii) fairness (equity) in international trade.

Table 4.2 GATT-WTO multilateral trade talks

Round	*Trade Objectives*
Kennedy Round (1964–67)	Tariff reduction
Tokyo Round (1973–79)	Tariff reduction, including most favored nations (MFNs) tariffs, and nontariff barriers (NTBs)
Uruguay Round (1986–93)	Tariffs and investment, Dispute Settlement Understanding (DSU) and Mechanism (DSM), the WTO Charter, General Agreement on Trade in Services (GATS), Trade-Related Intellectual Property Rights (TRIPS)
Doha Round (2001–2015)	Market access in agriculture and manufactured goods, TRIPS, environmental conservation technological transfer

Note: The Kennedy Round cut tariffs on manufactured goods by an average of 35 percent to an ad valorem value of 10.3 percent. The average tariff on manufactured goods of the nine major industrial countries was cut from 7 percent to 4.7 percent during the Tokyo Round of negotiations (Carbaugh, p. 188). NTBs included customs valuation, import licensing procedures, government procurement policies, subsidies and countervailing measures, technical barriers to trade, and antidumping agreement (WTO, pp. 187–188). The Doha Round was partially successful till the US called for its termination in 2015.

Box 4.1 GATT-WTO multilateral treaty

By 1994, *GATT had expanded to include 128 member countries, and most tariffs rarely exceeded 10 percent, especially among developed nations. Trade liberalization under GATT is widely referred to as multilateral liberalization primarily because of the many countries participating in that agreement. A crucial element of GATT is the concept of most favored nation (MFN) status.*

Under GATT, all members agree to grant one another MFN status, meaning that any favorable trade terms extended to the imports from any GATT member country must be extended to imports from all GATT member countries. GATT has been an important factor behind the substantial increase in global trade and has contributed to global economic growth since its inception. In 1994, *the Uruguay Round of GATT negotiations established the World Trade Organization (WTO) to serve as a permanent forum for negotiating further trade liberalization and to monitor members' compliance. Because GATT reduced tariffs and eliminated quotas, multilateral trade negotiations under the WTO expanded to include rule-based reforms.*

Those reforms address legal issues such as investment protections, market access for trade in services, intellectual property rights, and labor and environmental standards. The WTO instituted those reforms to further facilitate trade and investment among its members by creating standardized rules for businesses operating in one another's countries. For example, in 1995, the WTO established minimum protections for intellectual property rights for member countries through the Agreement on Trade-Related Aspects of Intellectual Property Rights (commonly known as TRIPS). In addition, WTO negotiations in 1995 addressed liberalization of trade in services through the Global Agreement on Trade in Services. Perhaps most significantly, the Uruguay Round established a dispute settlement mechanism that enables aggrieved countries to place punitive tariffs on the imports of countries judged to have violated the WTO's rules.

In the late 1990s, multilateral trade negotiations under the WTO began to stall. The Doha Round of negotiations began in 2001 but still has not concluded, even after several attempts to reach agreement. Global trade talks have proven particularly difficult in this round of negotiations because rule-based reforms tend to be more complicated and contentious than simply eliminating tariffs on industrial goods. For example, the WTO's negotiations to increase intellectual property protections have failed in part because less-developed countries are reluctant or unable to offer additional protections.

Source: Congressional Budget Office.

4.3 Trade treaties of Sierra Leone

Sierra Leone is a small open economy in which trade accounts for around 58 percent of the country's GDP (World Bank, 2021). Sierra Leone is a member of the Mano River Union (MRU), consisting of Guinea, Sierra Leone, Liberia, and Côte d'Ivoire. Sierra Leone is also a member of the Economic Community of West African States (ECOWAS), which includes 15 countries: Benin, Burkina Faso, Cape Verde, Côte d'Ivoire, The Gambia, Ghana, Guinea Bissau, Guinea, Liberia, Mali, Niger, Nigeria, Senegal, Sierra Leone, and Togo.

Trade treaties generally have three targeted provisions: (i) promotion of trade and investment by lowering import tariffs, removing nontariff barriers (NTBs) and improving market access for service providers and investors; (ii) setting commercial rules and standards; and (iii) establishing legal rules and mechanisms through which disputes can be resolved; for example, in addition to regional arrangements. Sierra Leone has bilateral investment treaties with Germany (in force since 1966), the United Kingdom in 1981 (revised in 2001), and China, signed in 2001 (yet to enter into force at the time of this writing). These treaties are theoretically intended to protect investors against unlawful expropriation and provide guarantees of fair and equitable treatment. Investment disputes could be contentious and unresolved in a timely manner.[4] It is in the best interest of developing countries to resolve these disputes in a timely manner to encourage long-term investments.

The trade agreements of Sierra Leone transcend the subregion of Africa to include the US and countries in Europe, Asia, calling into question the widespread applicability of the gravity theorem – the theory that national income and geographic proximity play a major role in the direction and volume of trade. Thus, Sierra Leone has preferential trade agreements (PTAs) with the European Union, the United States, and a multilateral pact with the African Continental Free Trade Agreement (a trade agreement among 55 African Union member states to create a common market and a currency union).

However, PTAs do not necessarily and completely explain the patterns of international trade of Sierra Leone. This anomaly may reflect the trade-diverting effects of unionization, dynamism of international trade, and the incapacities of regional members as well as the preferences of public officials and domestic consumers. Table 4.3 provides a list of the major trading partners of Sierra Leone in 2018 (the readily available data in 2023).

PTAs are generally useful not only because they help to foster liberalized international trade but also because they help to develop and strengthen international trade law by harmonizing the rules of trade among their members and reaffirming multilateral trade laws in various areas, including the removal of tariffs (liberalization), environmental preservation, protections of intellectual property, protections of foreign investors, subsidies and dumping, and trade dispute resolutions. PTAs eliminate tariffs such as the per unit taxes on goods illustrated in Figure 4.8. The benefits and drawbacks of such tariffs will be subsequently discussed in this chapter. However, the effects of PTAs on trade balances are generally imprecise, partly because of the sizes of the economies in the PTAs. Notwithstanding, some positive

Table 4.3 Major trading partners of Sierra Leone (2018)

Importers of Sierra Leonean Exports	*2018* (*% of Exports*)	*Importers of Sierra Leonean Imports*	*2018* (*% of Imports*)
China	18.3	China	20.1
South Korea	14	United Arab Emirates	8.4
Netherlands	13.5	Belgium	7.5
Somalia	10.8	India	7.2
Ghana	8	United States	5.4
Romania	7.8	Turkey	5.2
Germany	5.3	South Africa	4.6
Guinea	4.5	Pakistan	3.7
Senegal	3	United Kingdom	3.3
Ivory Coast	1.9	Guinea	3

Source: Comtrade and United Nations Statistics

external effects could be achieved via increases in productivity, increased output, improvements in consumer welfare (as more goods become available at cheaper prices), and increases in the employment of domestic residents. It should also be noted that PTAs have the potential to displace workers because of competitive imports and cause structural unemployment, which imposes new challenges for policymakers. This issue will also be addressed later in this chapter.

The top destinations for goods exports are China (18.3% of total exports), Korea (14%), the Netherlands (13.5%), Somalia (10.8%), Ghana (8%), Romania (7.8%), and Germany (5.3%). The main partners for imports of goods are China (20.1% of total imports), the United Arab Emirates (8.4%), Belgium (7.5%), India (7.2%), the United States (5.4%), and Turkey (5.2%).

Sierra Leone joined the General Agreement of Tariff and Trade (GATT) in 1961 and the World Trade Organization (WTO) in 1995. Sierra Leone is committed to the multilateral trading system and has not notified the WTO of any inconsistent measures with the WTO's Trade-Related Investment Measures (TRIMs) obligations. It acceded to the Kyoto Protocol in 2006 and the International Convention on the Simplification and Harmonization of Customs Procedures, otherwise referred to as the Revised Kyoto Convention in 2015. It became a contracting party to the International Convention on the Harmonized Commodity Description and Coding System (HS Convention) in 2015. It replaced its pre-shipment inspection with a destination inspection in 2009 and notified the WTO of the Agreement on Trade Facilitation in May 2017. The Customs Act of 2011 upheld the WTO Customs Valuation Agreement, which prohibits the use of arbitrary or fictitious values (US Department of State, DoS).

After several years of mixed successes in various WTO trade talks, trade negotiations stalled during the Doha Round of negotiations. The most significant impasse between developed nations led by the European Union (EU), the United States (US), Canada, and Japan and the major developing countries led and represented mainly by India, Brazil, China, and South Africa revolved around the maintenance of agricultural subsidies in the EU and the US. The Tokyo Round dealt with NTBS like subsidies and other forms of trade barriers that are not characterized as tariffs.

The bulk of trade negotiations shifted from the multilateral format to bilateral, regional, and plurilateral formats (between two and among few after the demise of the Doha Round of trade negotiations) – the second best compared to multilateral arrangements.[5] PTAs were not creations of the 1990s. Between 1948 and 1990, there were about 70 PTAs. By 2010, there were about 300 PTAs in force (Trebilcock et al., p. 86). A fundamental problem with PTAs is their trade-diverting effects – the ironic unionization with high-cost producers rather than low-cost producers. The theory was first pioneered by Viner (1953) in the context of customs union – consisting of countries with common tariff policies – of the 1950s. Yet the initial focus was on the production effect rather than the production and consumption effects (Salvatore, p. 340). The theory was subsequently expanded by Meade (1955) to include the consumption effect. Consider Figure 4.2.

Sierra Leone could get a bundle of petroleum products from Libya at a price, P_L, from Nigeria at a price, P_N, and the rest of the world at various prices. It is instantly revealing that the cheaper source of the products will be Libya (P_L). Suppose Sierra Leone imposes a nondiscriminatory tax on the two countries, amounting to P_{L+T} and subsequently forms a union with Nigeria (as in the Economic Community of West African States (ECOWAS)); Sierra Leone will now be paying a higher price than the prevailing import price from Libya. Because Sierra Leone is paying a higher price for the products from Nigeria, the union will be a trade-diverting union, on the contrary, trade-creating.

Imports from Libya amounted to $(q_5\text{-}q_0)$ *Le/P_L. The union with Nigeria reduced imports to $(q_4\text{-}q_1)$ *Le/P_N. Consumers in Sierra Leone will reduce consumption

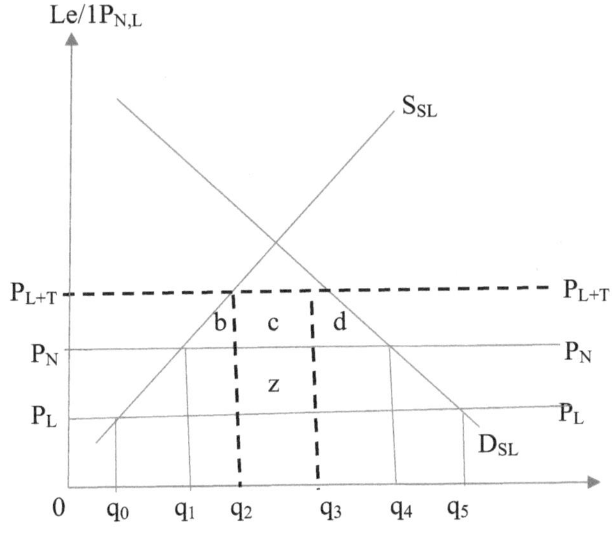

Figure 4.2 Prospects of diverting trade.

from q_5 to q_4 and pay the higher price of Le/P_N. The union would have been trade-creating if the price in Nigeria had been cheaper. Domestic producers (if any in Sierra Leone) lose area *b*, consumers gain area *b*, the trade diversion effect is area *c*, and the revenue effect is area *e* (taxes on the products from Libya). Trade-diverting effect is areas *e*. The welfare gain in Sierra Leone would be areas *b* and *d,* but the government would lose area *c* after the removal of the tax. The cost of importing is z, which is the trade-diverting effect of the union. The net diverting effect is area $z - (b+d)$.

Tables 4.4 and 4.5 report the country's major articles of trade. It is reasonable to presume that the country's comparative advantage has not changed since the data were released, where the comparative advantage is more meaningful for appraising the export capacities of the country relative to its preferences for imports. It is immediately apparent that cereals, which include rice, are taking the lion's share of the reserves of the country. It is worth recalling that the country used to export rice and invest in the education of farmers (review the salient sections of the introductory chapter of this book). The trade statistics suggest that the country must be more strategic in its choices of investment, production, and diversification of its export articles, especially articles of trade reflecting the current trends and needs of the domestic market and global economy (review the diamond model of Chapter 2 for a nation's competitive advantage and innovation). The transaction of international trade beyond geographic proximity raises new issues for regional trade organizations. Why are the major trading partners of the country in distant areas of the world? (see Table 4.3). What could be done to make international trade more

Table 4.4 Top goods exported by Sierra Leone in 2018

Rank	*HS*	*Commodity*	*$USD million*	*% of total goods exported*
1	3	Fish and crustaceans	42	20.50
2	26	Ores, slag, and ash	32	15.70
3	18	Cocoa and cocoa preparations	22	10.90
4	44	Wood and articles of wood; wood charcoal	20	9.90
5	87	Vehicles other than railway or tramway stock	20	9.80
6	84	Machinery and mechanical appliances	13	6.10
7	15	Animal or vegetable fats and oils	12	5.60
8	36	Explosives, pyrotechnic products; matches	6	2.70
9	20	Preparations of veg. fruit or nuts	5	2.50
10	25	Salt, sulfur, earths, and stone	5	2.40
		All goods exported	**205**	**100**

Data source: Trade and Investments Factsheets (as reported by Sierra Leone): UK's Department for Business and Trade (2023 December, p. 13).

Note: Minerals are not included as commodities. Top goods traded with the world by Sierra Leone, in current prices (UNComtrade).

Table 4.5 Top goods imported from the world by Sierra Leone in 2018

Rank	*HS*	*Commodity*	*$USD million*	*% of total goods exported*
1	10	Cereals	153	15.50
2	84	Machinery and mechanical appliances	112	11.30
3	87	Vehicles other than railway and tramway stock	93	9.40
4	85	Electrical machinery and equipment	63	6.40
5	39	Plastics and articles thereof	56	5.70
6	73	Articles of iron or steel	48	4.90
7	25	Salt, sulfur, earths, and stone	46	4.60
8	72	Iron and steel	35	3.50
9	30	Pharmaceutical products	24	2.40
10	11	Products of the milling industry	24	2.40
		All goods exported	**987**	**100**

Data source: Trade and Investments Factsheets (as reported by Sierra Leone): UK's Department for Business and Trade (2023 December, p. 13).

regionally integrated and less costly? How can a country reduce its dependence on others? The key is investment in human capital and innovation.

The foregoing discussion and newer patterns of international trade raise issues about the gravity theory of international trade, which emphasizes geographic proximity to markets, per capita income, and population inter alia. However, the theorem seems to be compatible with a North–North and a North–South trading pattern rather than a South–South trading pattern; more precisely, trade is more robust among advanced economies than among poorer or underdeveloped economies.

4.4 The gravity theorem of international trade

The gravity theorem of international trade postulates that bilateral trade between two countries is proportional to the product of the national income of two countries and in inverse relationship of the distance between the two countries (Frankel, 50), meaning that geographic proximity enhances bilateral trade. The regression specification of bilateral trade has been made flexible to include other regressors like population and the dimensions of land.[6] Equation 4.2 presents a functional representation of the gravity theorem:

$$\log T_{ij} = \eta_1 \log(GNP_i GNP_j) + \eta_2 \log[(GNPpc_i)(GNPpc_j)] - \eta_3 \log(Dis_{ij}), \quad 4.2$$

$$\eta_1, \eta_2 > 0,\ \eta_3 < 0,$$

where T_{ij} is for trade between two countries (*i* and *j*), GNP is for gross national income, GNP_{PC} is for gross national income per capita, *Dis* is for distance, and *ηs* are the elasticity coefficients for the variables. The signs of the coefficients are illustrative of the sensitivities of trade (exports and imports) to incremental percentage changes in the regressors. Significantly, distance is presumed to be inversely related to trade.

The gravity theorem gained widespread theoretical appeal in the 1960s with considerable number of successes and skepticism through the 1990s. Modern trade arrangements and the desires of relatively poorer countries have posed renewed challenges for the once-vaunted gravity theorem. Countries no longer rely on the common denominators of per capita income, population, and their geographic locations to forge trade alliances; for example, Sierra Leone can now trade extensively with China and the US rather than Liberia or Guinea. This is not to say that the theory is extinct and without merit. It does seem to have some explanatory sway over explanations for bilateral trade with countries in the North–North nexus; for example, the US could engage in robust trade with Canada and Mexico though the US' income per capita is exceedingly larger than that of Mexico (contrary to the income and per capita components of the gravity theorem). As such, the theory could have limited applications and relevance to international trade theory but not general applications.

Trade patterns of Sierra Leone do not strongly support the gravity theorem. Merchandise export to high-income countries relative to low-income countries have been traditionally higher in the trade pattern of the country. But for 2020, Figures 4.3 and 4.4 show that merchandise exports from Sierra Leone to low- and middle-income countries of Sub-Saharan Africa have been comparatively lower when compared to merchandise exports from Sierra Leone to high-income countries. Table 4.3 highlights the territorial amorphousness of the directions of trade flows.

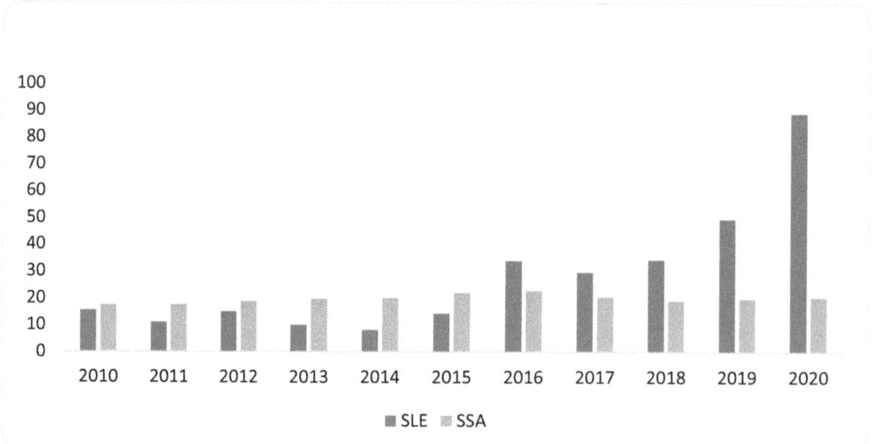

Figure 4.3 Merchandise exports to low- and middle-income economies in Sub-Saharan Africa (% of total merchandise exports).

Data source: World Bank's WDI (2023)

Except for 2020, merchandise exports from Sierra Leone to low- and middle-income Sub-Saharan African (SSA) countries were generally low, ranging from about 20 percent of total merchandise exports to about 40 percent (Figure 4.3). By contrast, merchandise exports from Sierra Leone to high-income countries were as high as 80 percent in 2015 and comparatively lower for very few years (2013, 2014, and 2020). For about five out of ten years, Sierra Leone's export of merchandise to high-income countries exceeded that of the SSA region (Figure 4.3).

Similarly, merchandise imports from distant high-income countries range from 30 to 50 percent of total merchandise imports (see Figure 4.5).

Figure 4.4 Merchandise exports to high-income economies (% of total merchandise exports).

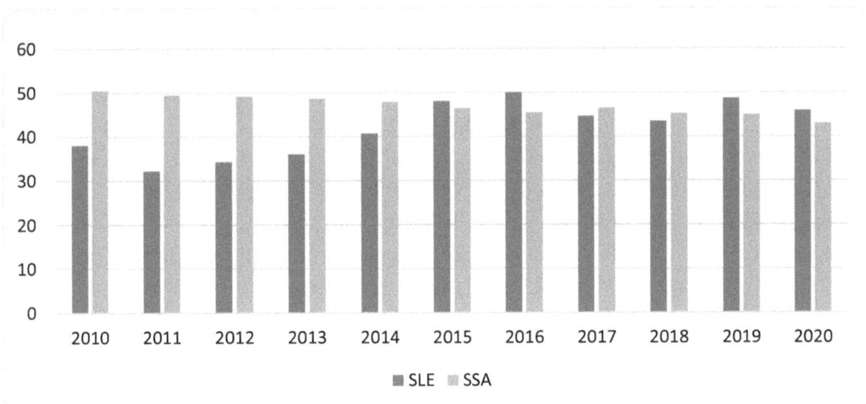

Figure 4.5 Merchandise imports from high-income economies (% of total merchandise imports).

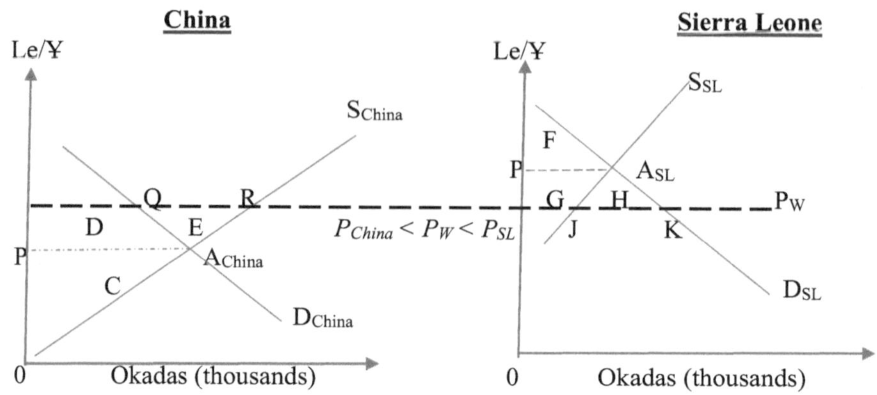

Figure 4.6 Comparative statics and trade between China and Sierra Leone.

Therefore, one could reasonably argue that contemporary international trade is highly contingent on relative advantages.

Figure 4.6 illustrates some fundamental properties of hypothetical international trade in Okadas. It shows that trade is heavily dependent on supply-side factors. In this illustrative example, distant China has abundant resources in the production of Okadas, and therefore its autarkic price (without international trade), *P*, is lower than that of Sierra Leone, PA_{SL}, meaning that Sierra Leone is less efficient in the production of Okadas; Sierra Leone does not have as much human capital and resources to produce Okada like China. Therefore, China must specialize in the production of Okadas and sell Okadas to Sierra Leone at the world price, P_W. It is instantly revealing that the world price, P_W, is less than the price, $P(A_{SL})$, at which Sierra Leoneans would have purchased Okadas without international trade. This type of trade is not without public policy implications.

By increasing production of Okadas in China, the producers of Okadas in China will become happier. They will now sell Okadas at a higher price and gain producer surplus, amounting to areas of *CDE*. The consumers of Okadas in China will be unhappy because they will now have to buy Okadas at a higher price. Consumers of Okadas in China will want the Chinese governments to liberalize the import of Okadas from countries where Okadas are relatively cheaper.

The consumers of Okadas in Sierra Leone will be happy because they can now purchase Okadas for transportation at a cheaper price, P_W, relative to the higher autarkic price, PA_{SL}, in Sierra Leone. Unhappy and relatively inefficient producers of Okadas in Sierra Leone will want the Sierra Leonean government to protect them from the importation of Okadas by imposing a tariff on Okadas. Sierra Leonean consumers will gain a surplus, amounting to areas *FGH*. The Sierra Leonean and Chinese governments will then be caught in a quandary, partly because the advocates of tariffs seldom consider the prescriptions of international trade law and the retaliatory consequences (or exposures) of undesirable tariffs. These issues will be dealt with in the next section.

4.5 International trade regulation

Aforesaid, trade restrictions could fall under two broad categories, tariffs (taxes), and everything else that could not be a tax, but which restricts the free flow of trade (nontariff barriers, NTBs). NTBs may have some underlying issues of unfairness, which could be discriminatory or prohibitive. NTBs consist of unfair subsidies, voluntary export restraints, government procurement policies, licensing requirements, dumping products (selling products in foreign countries below their fair market values), product quality, and sanitary and phytosanitary prohibitions. Many NTBs cannot be found in Sierra Leone, which makes Sierra Leone relatively open to trade than some other countries. This is partly because of the types of goods that are being imported into Sierra Leone. While the US does not impose taxes on exports, most developing countries impose import and export taxes to collect revenue.

Sierra Leone imposes import duties though restrictions on plants (phytosanitary restrictions) are not very prominent. Generally, a phytosanitary certificate is required for the international movement of any plant material or product that is listed under the WTO agreement. However, animals are subject to livestock inspection. It should be recalled that taxes do not generally apply to members of a PTA; recall the trade-creating and diverting effects. Accordingly, as a member of the ECOWAS community, Sierra Leone grants duty-free preference to products originating from ECOWAS members, where they are wholly produced, sufficiently transformed, or with 35 percent value added.

Sierra Leone's Customs and Excise Tariff is based on the Common External Tariff of the Economic Community of West African States (ECOWAS), which uses the Harmonized Commodity Description and Coding System (HS) to classify goods.[7]

> *It is a five-band regional tariff categorized as follows: zero percent for basic social goods; 5 percent for basic goods, raw goods, and capital goods; 10 percent for inputs and semi-finished goods; 20 percent for finished goods; and 35 percent for specific goods for economic development. For most imports, taxes are assessed based on the Cost, Insurance, and Freight (CIF) value while others are specific, mostly based on the weight, volume, and quantity. Excise duty is also levied on imports depending on the nature of the goods. Excises are either ad valorem or specific and are levied on juice, energy drinks, tobacco, alcoholic beverages, luxury cars, and petroleum products, among others.*
>
> (US ITA, 2021)

Imported products must be properly labeled. The Ministry of Trade and Industry requires that products be labeled in English to identify the name, weight, manufacture dates, expiration dates, ingredients, and product origin. Identification of marks and product origins is useful for customs verification and clearance of goods.

Some products may enter the country temporarily, that is, for goods that are imported for a specified period without payment of duty. Such goods may be

Table 4.6 Sierra Leone's Trade Regulation (2021)

Regulation	*Target/Objective*
Customs and excise tariff	Protecting the economy, residents, jobs, environment, etc. plus targeted taxes
Import tariff	Taxes on imports (with some exemptions)
Import licenses	Classifications of imports and documentation
Labeling and marking requirements	Intellectual property protections
Temporary entry	Goods without the assessment of customs duty for re-export and potential destruction
Prohibitions and restrictions	To protect human and animal lives, safeguard national security, as well as protect artistic, cultural, and intellectual property
Standards for trade [product quality]	Ascertainment of weights and measures, calibration of industrial and laboratory equipments, and validation and authorization of the metric system of measurement in Sierra Leone

Source: US International Trade Administration.

re-exported or destroyed after their assigned period of duration within the country by the customs authority, usually 3 months from the date of importation. Failure to re-export or destroy the goods as per the customs regulation will result in liquidated damages (US ITA).[8] A summary of trade regulations could be found in Table 4.6.

Certain goods are prohibited or granted restricted importation; for example, food products, drugs, pharmaceuticals, environmentally hazardous products, seeds, weapons, explosives, and antiques.[9] Additionally, there are licensing requirements for the provision of certain professional services such as banking, medical, engineering, legal, accounting, auditing, and architectural.

The effects of regulatory trade are bifurcated and not always harmful. It is very common to regard international trade regulations as trade restrictions. It is noteworthy that restrictions generally have negative connotations in the context of trade liberalization or freer international trade. Every nation has some form of restriction on the international flow of goods, services, and financial assets for good reasons. This does not mean that ostensible and surreptitious economic and political reasons could not be disingenuously couched as good reasons. This is precisely because every nation has historically managed international trade to conform with its national interest and aspirations. Accordingly, nations are left with the arduous task of evaluating the fairness of international trade and the intensity of restrictions on the flow of goods and services across international boundaries.

The percentage of imports into Sierra Leone coincides with higher tariff lines (see Figure 4.7). The World Bank defines the share of tariff lines with international peaks as *the share of lines in the tariff schedule with tariff rates that exceed 15 percent. It provides an indication of how selectively tariffs are applied* (World Bank, 2023). By implication, Figure 4.7 suggests that tariffs tend to be more selectively applied in Sierra Leone than in the subregion. Tariff rates of more than 15 percent on goods that are traded in an import-oriented country will put upward pressure

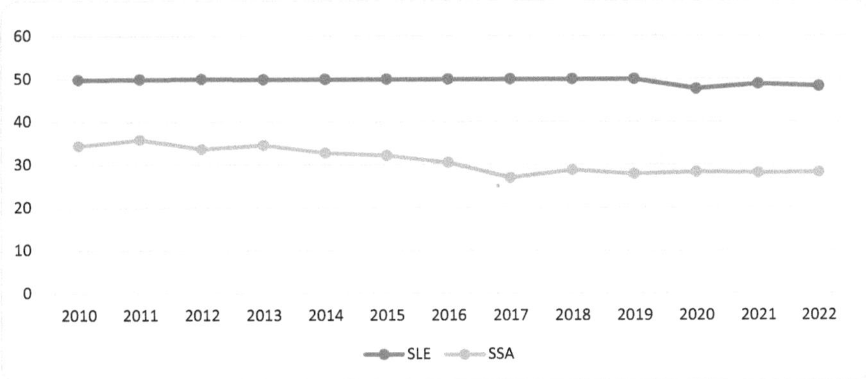

Figure 4.7 Share of tariff lines in Sierra Leone.

Data source: (World Bank, 2023). * Missing values = 2-yr rolling average, SLE = 2013–2019 and 2021–2022.

SSA (excluding high-income countries) = 2018–2022

on some consumer prices. Increases in domestic production (when appropriate or advantageous) and some amount of import substitution could stabilize prices at lower levels.

Contrary to the theories of animosities against international trade, international trade is a mutually beneficial exchange. Obviously, the benefits are not symmetric, which makes the asymmetry of benefits a policy challenge. Asymmetry requires sound redistributive public policies and readjustments to structural changes and unemployment.

As a small open economy, Sierra Leone has relatively fewer regulations compared to some other countries of the world.[10]

Realistically, it is reasonably practical to talk about "managed trade" in the contemporary world. No nation would permit all types of goods or volume of trade to destabilize its economy.

However, unnecessary, or poorly targeted tariffs are virtually always bad for consumers and national welfare (recall the discussions of taxes in Chapter 2). Higher taxes diminish the value of the disposable income of consumers, concomitantly reduce the standard of living of poorer consumers, and discourage investment or commerce. Ironically, it is very common for unsuspecting consumers to impulsively advocate for higher tariffs. Of course, what if the trading parties, say China and Sierra Leone, are members of bilateral, preferential, and multilateral trade arrangements? Alternatively, what if the Sierra Leonean government with a small open economy decides to impose a tariff? Consider the effects of the tariff on a small open economy in Figure 4.8.

Aforesaid, without international trade with China, consumers in Sierra Leone paid P for Okadas (assuming some Okadas could be produced in Sierra Leone).

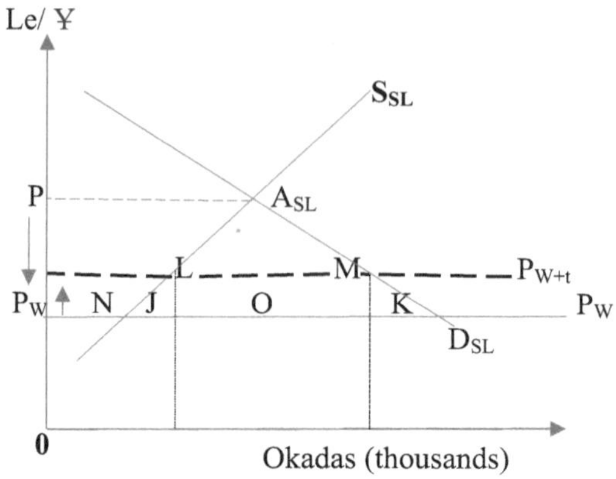

Figure 4.8 Tariff in a small open economy like Sierra Leone.

The consumers in Sierra Leone paid P_W for Okadas after the government of Sierra Leone liberalized trade with China. Sierra Leone imported *JK* (P_W) Okadas from China at the world price of P_W, and China exported *QR* (P_W) (the trade need not be balanced in a global economy). Assuming that the government of Sierra Leone accommodates the relatively inefficient producers of Okadas, the government will impose an import tariff of *t* on Okadas, thereby raising the per unit price of Okadas from P_W to P_{W+t}. The tariff reduces imports from *JK* (P_W) to *LM* (P_{W+t}).

The foregoing discussions suggest that there are at least four effects of the tariff: (i) a transfer of surplus from consumers to producers (the trapezoid *N*) because of the higher price that consumers have to pay for inefficient production, (ii) a production effect (defined by the triangle with a hypotenuse of JL), which is also a protection of inefficiency, (iii) a revenue effect, the revenue (taxes) that the Sierra Leonean government will collect, amounting to the rectangle *O* ($P_{W+t} - P_W$), assuming there is no leakage (corrupt or otherwise), and (iv) a consumption effect represented by the triangle with a hypotenuse *MK* (consumers reduce consumption or purchases of Okadas because of the inflated price of Okadas) (see also the work of Reinert, pp. 27–35). It may well be that the infant producers of Okadas in Sierra Leone (if any at all) need some time to be competitive in the global economy. Yet, the protection cannot be perpetual. Perpetual protection of the producers of Okadas in Sierra Leone means perpetual inefficiency; that is, protective tariffs are only beneficial when producers of domestic goods can be productive and innovative in the global economy. Historical support for time constraints exists.

It took the US a while to become competitive in the production of automobile and steel after a period of government protection from external competition. Unsurprisingly, some economists have argued that there is a positive correlation between higher levels of development and higher volumes of freer international trade. Unlike industrialized or high-income countries, governments of relatively poorer agrarian economies depend heavily on taxes for a large share of their budget (Frankel, p. 58).

What are the policy implications of undesirable trade tariffs? Governments must be willing to compensate losers and productively invest tariff revenues. Additionally, governments must proactively make plans to combat structural unemployment whenever they prefer trade liberalization or managed trade, as they must.

It is noteworthy that the impositions of tariffs and beggar-thy-neighbor policies could quickly degenerate into trade wars. The historical evidence of this fact is abundant and incontrovertible. Resolution of international trade disputes in structured or ad hoc environments (arbitral tribunals) is usually preferable and widely supported when paradoxical retaliations are legitimately authorized. Consider the US' Smoot-Hawley Act of 1930 (see Table 4.7) and the comparatively recent US–China trade wars of 2018.

As a result of the Smoot-Hawley Act, the US exports fell from $7 billion in 1929 to $2.5 billion in 1932. Farm exports fell to a third of their 1929 level by 1933. Global trade plummeted by 65 percent, which made it difficult for American manufacturers to remain in business (Amadeo). The tariff is believed to have worsened the Great Depression. The Chinese Ministry of government imposed a 25 percent charge on $16 billion worth of US goods, including vehicles such as large passenger cars and motorcycles in response to the US tariffs in 2018.

> *Trade wars are usually bad for the countries involved. After the US and China launched tit-for-tat tariffs on imports from each other in 2018, prices rose for American consumers, jobs were lost and corporate profits fell. Economic growth in both countries slowed.*
>
> (Totty, 2023)

which does not mean that other sectors of a macroeconomy should be neglected. Of course, nations could be less worried about trade wars when they are inured to import-oriented trade strategies with less retaliatory exposures to their targets. The insular assurances could be reinforced by domestic employment strategies.

Table 4.7 Smoot-Hawley retaliations*

Country	*Retaliation*
Spain	Wais tariff in response to the US tariffs on cork, oranges, and grapes
Switzerland	Boycotted the US exports in protest of tariffs on watches and shoes
Canada	Increased tariffs threefold in reaction to the US tariff on logs and food, inter alia
Italy	Retaliated against the US tariffs on olive oil and hats
Mexico	Reduced the US imports by 53.8% (1929–1932)
Cuba	Reduced the US imports by 45.9 % (1929–1932)
Australia and	Reduced the US imports by 67.1% (1929–1932)

Source: Carbaugh, *International economics*, p. 183, and Mitchener et al., p. 30.

*Average tariffs on the US tariffs on protected imports were raised to about 53%. Twenty-five trading partners of the US retaliated.

Nations always have non-outsourceable or secured job opportunities in their energy and service sectors. Further, nations that are productive and competitive will always create trade disruptions in international markets. Entrepreneurs – sometimes with the help of governments – spend lots of time and money to create, for a given period, new products that are unavoidably acceptable for consumption (innovation) in global markets. Notably, innovation is susceptible to a Schumpeterian "creative destruction." Ever so often, new items are displaced in international markets because of newer and better products. It is incumbent on the policymakers of poorer or impoverished countries to deal with issues of equity and realignment of productive domestic resources (review Porter's Diamond theorem in Chapter 2) whenever they are confronted by inevitable displacements in the global economy.

4.6 International trade and local currency valuation

Sierra Leone has a relatively liberal trade orientation compared to the comparable cohort of Sub-Saharan countries in the subregion of Africa (excluding high-income countries), but imports of goods and services as a percentage of GDP have been considerably higher (see Figure 4.9) suggesting that this also signals the inadequacy of domestic production for domestic and international consumption, which adversely affects the long-term competitiveness of the country and the value of its local currency (see Figure 4.9).

Deliberate policy intervention to lower the value of currencies is known as "devaluation" (loss of value). Devaluation or revaluation (appreciation of value) maybe used to correct fundamental disequilibria (persistent and destabilizing imbalances) in the balance of payments of nations (usually approved by the International Monetary Fund, IMF).[11] Market-based (market demand and supply) transactions

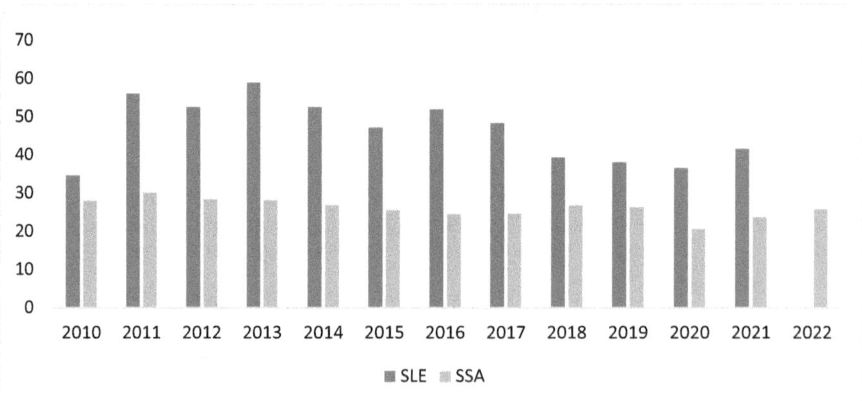

Figure 4.9 Sub-Saharan Africa and Sierra Leone's Imports of goods and services (%GDP).
Data source: (World Bank, 2023) * SSA excludes high-income countries

could cause a deterioration in the value of a currency (depreciation), when a currency's exchange rate is above its market clearing equilibrium price as a result of low demand for a currency, or excessive consumption of foreign goods (imports) inter alia (see Table 4.8 for factors that could affect the value of a local currency). Note that trade policies affect exports, imports, and the value of currencies. Figure 4.10 shows the depreciation and devaluation of the leone from 1980 to 2022.

Consider an illustrative and hypothetical example of a significant decrease in net exports in Figure 4.11. In 2022, Sierra Leoneans paid Le 2717.65 for 1¥, which is less than Le19,750.0 for a US dollar – a cross-exchange rate of about ¥7.27/$1. Suppose the consumers of Sierra Leone had decided to buy more goods and services from China without Chinese reciprocation; the demand curve would have shifted from D ¥ to D ¥ $_2$, generating a new equilibrium at E_2. The Chinese would have had to increase the supply of yuan to get back to the original exchange rate at

Table 4.8 Determinants of the value of local currencies

Determinant	*Effect (market-based)*
Excessive imports	Depreciation
Relative price inflation	Depreciation
Long-term capital inflows	Appreciation
Interest rate hikes for convertible currencies and capital inflows	Appreciation
Relative productivity increases	Appreciation
Purchases and sales of currencies by the monetary authorities	Appreciation (purchases) Depreciation (sales)

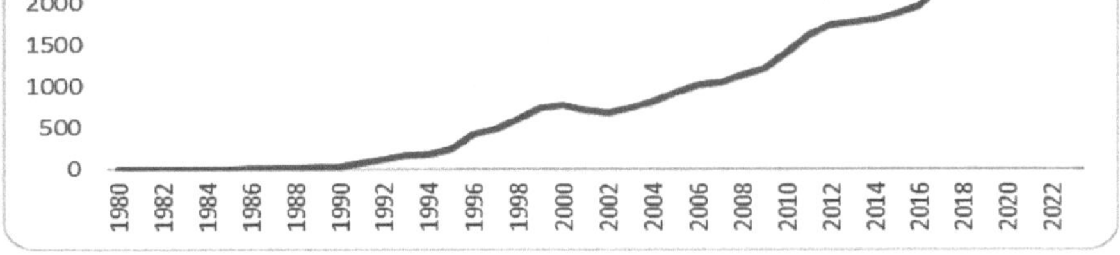

Figure 4.10 The depreciation and devaluation of the leone (leone/$,1980–2022).*

Data source: International Monetary Fund (IMF).

* International dollar: An international dollar would buy in the cited country a comparable amount of goods and services a US dollar would buy in the United States. This term is often used in conjunction with Purchasing Power Parity (PPP) data (World Bank).

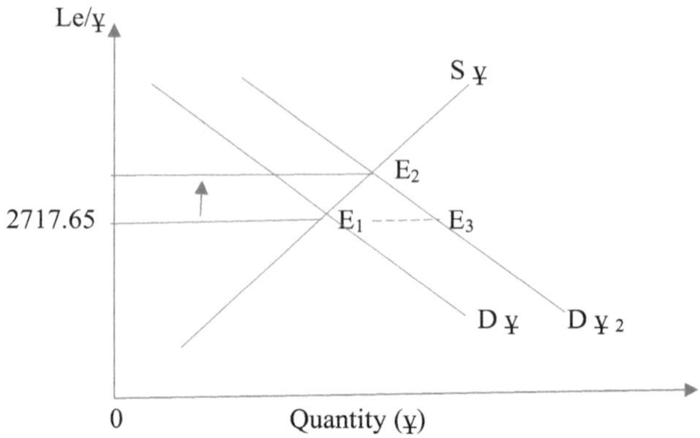

Figure 4.11 A decrease in net exports: An increase in imports relative to exports.

Le 2,717.65 and E_3, without which the monetary authorities of Sierra Leone would have had to use foreign reserves to defend the exchange rate, assuming that the exchange rate was fixed (pegged).

Notably, some African countries are without autonomous central banks – that is, political leaders determine the monetary policies of the central banks rather than professional bankers, and it is not unusual for the leaders to use the central banks as their depository institutions. Nevertheless, most countries now operate under a variety of flexible exchange rate regimes rather than the fixed regime, which makes it very easy for some countries to have precipitous depreciations like that of Figure 4.10 to accommodate large trade imbalances.

The movement from E_1 to E_2 shows a depreciation of the leone (an overvaluation) without Chinese reciprocation because consumers in Sierra Leone were using more leones to get goods and services that are denominated in Chinese yuan. Sierra Leone needs to produce goods and services that are attractive to the Chinese for the Chinese to reciprocate. However, reciprocation is not automatic in international trade, though persistent trade imbalances must be addressed (not left unchecked) for a currency to have greater international appeal in international markets (gain substantial convertibility). A major problem is that public international transactions and payments can quickly become elusive and opaque in various parts of Africa, for example, revenue from the "star of Sierra Leone," a diamond of unusually large physical size and concomitant value at the time, vanished into thin air in the 1970s.[12]

4.7 International trade shocks

International trade is prone to shocks or perturbations/disturbances, and policymakers are never going to have control over all aspects of international trade. Pandemics, foreign trade regulations, unanticipated domestic and international foreign wars, collective sanctions on rogue actors, sudden changes in demand and supply of exports, changes in international prices for the goods and services of small open economies, and exchange rate movements are just some of the occurrences that could disturb the ability of nations to engage in stable and fruitful international trade. Some countries have experienced very robust trade. One of the most significant influences on the Australian economy over the past decade has been the booming terms of trade which has risen by almost 80 percent. The terms of trade are currently around their highest level in the 140-year history of the series (Jääskelä & Smith, 2011).

The consequences of rising terms of trade will ultimately depend on the characteristics of the underlying shock, as well as the policy response. In a related work, Kilian (2009) and Peersman and Van Robays (2009) demonstrate the responses of monetary policy to shocks. In the US and euro area economies responses to oil price shocks also depend on the nature of the shock. Of course, shocks could have positive and negative effects. Jääskelä and Smith (2011) find that a positive world demand shock is associated with a pick-up in global economic activity and an increase in export and import prices. A positive commodity-market-specific shock increases export prices without a corresponding pick-up in global economic activity.

Schmitt-Grohé and Uribe (2018) argue that the conventional wisdom suggesting that terms-of-trade shocks represent a major source of business cycles in emerging and poor countries may not necessarily be supported by structural vector autoregression (SVAR) models. Significantly, model choices and available data tend to influence frequentist findings. In this section, I evaluate the probabilistic shock results of a VAR by using the Bayesian estimation, previously utilized in Chapter 2 of this book for a different purpose under different assumptions. This methodology eliminates a frequentist dilemma by focusing on probabilistic outcomes.

Essentially, Sierra Leone had long spells of insignificant macroeconomic activity for the lost generation – those who were born between 1961 and 1983. The inertial (lost) decades of macroeconomic stasis in Sierra Leone have provided a very shaky foundation for long-term economic growth and development. Today, the contemporary structural changes in the global economy are highly consequential, and the opportunities for very profitable international trade are very challenging for nations without adequate human capital and technological exposures. The newer global conditions and demands are no longer what they used to be in the 1960s or 1980s, and contemporary underdeveloped economies must quickly readjust to the changes that are occurring around them to be competitive and prosperous.

With superior human capital and infrastructure for economic growth and sustainable development, many nations are now relatively developed with a very strong competitive posture in the global economy. Evidently, opportunities for late starters have diminished. Nations that invested in economic growth and development during the formative years of their autonomy have moved away from the periphery. White-elephant projects – unprofitable projects with prohibitively high maintenance cost – should no longer exhaust the scarce economic resources of underdeveloped economies facing the specter of external shocks. Only profitable and socially rewarding public and private investments should be undertaken to withstand the effects of adverse international shocks. In fact, it is equally important to identify those variables that are badly exposed and highly vulnerable to international shocks, including national income, its constituent components (aggregate consumption, investment, and net exports), and the local currency of an underdeveloped economy. Invariably, it is a truism that conscionable social planners will consider the effects of external shocks on the most vulnerable segments of their population – the elderly and the poor.

At a very fundamental level, a country must be able to have adequate foreign reserves to dampen the effects of economic and financial shocks that emanate from abroad, invest in agriculture, feed itself, and avoid reliance on external sources for livelihood. It could then staunch the bleeding of foreign reserves and reasonably create the prospects of linkages to industrialization or light manufacturing for sustainable economic growth (national income), gainful employment (optimal use of domestic resources), and increased productivity or competitiveness in the global economy. It might just be too unsettling for some needy Sierra Leoneans to recall that Sierra Leone, once a net exporter of rice, now imports a colossal amount of rice, in addition to wheat and corn, at exorbitant cost for loss of foreign reserves. The import of cereals, amounting to US$160.8 million (up by 22.13% since 2021), has significantly helped to increase the negative trade imbalance of the country with deep international trade deficits under the cereals category.[13]

Historical experiments of export-led growth (ELG) and imports to enhance or augment domestic industrialization (Import-Substituting Industrialization, ISI), which will be discussed subsequently, are paradigms for takeoff. Consequently, the prospects of sound macroeconomic policy choices are highly contingent on valuable historical experiences, which are abundantly clearer today.

Lubik and Teo (2005) and Schmitt-Grohé and Uribe (2018) have examined the effects of interest rate shocks and terms of trade on economies. Lubik and Teo find that interest rate shock is more important. Using data information from 38 countries, Schmitt-Grohé et al. find that terms-of-trade shocks explain less than 10 percent of movements in aggregate activity. Interest rate is a natural transmission mechanism for aggregate economic performance.

A small open economy like Sierra Leone is not immune from the vagaries of trade shocks that require policy responses. To examine the macroeconomic exposures of the Sierra Leonean economy to trade shocks, I first examine the interaction of the native and significant trade variables – exports of goods and services as a percentage of GDP, imports of goods and services as a percentage of GDP, the implicit price deflator (an aggregate measure of inflation rather than consumer inflation), and the value of the local currency from 1987 to 2021. Aforesaid, most studies tend to focus on frequentist parameter estimates with time inconsistencies. I take a probabilistic Bayesian approach to analyzing the interaction of the variables for long-lasting policy implications. The Bayesian methodology uses the Monte Carlo Markov Chain (MCMC) process to compensate for data inadequacies. The results are reported in Table 4.8.

A range of values (credible interval) within which a parameter is likely to fall is of greater appeal to this work for a variety of reasons, including data limitations or accuracy of information and elusive parameter estimation of values. Therefore, the Bayesian probability estimation has some attractive properties for long-term policy decisions without reliance on shifting and questionable parameter estimations. Recall that the typical Bayesian posterior distribution and the probable value of a parameter, previously discussed in Chapter 2 of this book takes the form:

$$P(\theta \mid \xi) = \frac{P(\xi \mid \theta) * P(\theta)}{P(\xi)}; \qquad 4.3$$

Equation 4.3 defines the probability of observing a parameter (θ, theta) within a range of distributed values, given the probability of having the desired data (ξ, chi). The left-hand side defines the posterior Bayesian distribution that is sought (the probable range of the parameter of interest, given the desired data that have been generated from simulations of the available data). Ever so often there are data issues with less developed economies more so than relatively advanced economies. Therefore, the Bayesian method, unlike the frequentist approach of parameter estimates, is useful to capture the probabilities of parameter uncertainties. Elaborate data are not needed to capture probabilistic parameter estimates (see Chapter 2).

The right-hand side of Equation 4.3 is given by the probability of the prior parameter, P(θ), independently occurring, multiplied by the sampling density for the data (the likelihood), divided by the probability of observing the desired data p(ξ), generally considered to be the evidence. The probability of observing the desired data or evidence incorporates a prior distribution, the likelihood of the evidence given the expected parameter, and the posterior distribution, belief of hypothesis after seeing the evidence (updated information) (Equation 4.4):

$$P(\xi) = \frac{P(\xi \mid \theta) * P(\theta)}{P(\theta \mid \xi)}; \qquad 4.3$$

The Bayesian generative model (a model from which data could be derived/simulated) becomes robust for empirical analysis. Bayesian approach utilizes a distribution that fits the data rather than a model that fits the data and does not quantify parameter uncertainty.

Probability distributions are utilized to update beliefs about parameter uncertainty: (i) probability distribution of the data generating process (normal distribution, Bernoulli, etc.), and (ii) distribution of current beliefs about the parameters (regression coefficients) using probability distributions (e.g., t-distribution for small samples). The two conditions define the generative model. Data need not be random and simulations from Markov chain or Monte Carlo are used to extract information from the posterior (predictive) distribution to determine the probable future distributions, based on the data generating process of probability distributions (steps 1 and 2).

The main objective is to find the mean, standard deviation, and probability of success in predicting the value of a parameter, essentially trying to find the posterior distribution for model parameters. In an endogenous simultaneous Bayesian model (BVAR), the distribution of all variables is sought. The most likely value of interest is usually the means of the distribution, though median values may be considered as well. The variances and standard deviations provide information about the possible ranges of parameter locations in the posterior distribution. Table 4.9 reports covariances associated with GDP growth in Sierra Leone after controlling for exports and imports of goods and services as a percentage of GDP, the general price level (in terms of the implicit deflator), and the value of the leone relative to the international dollar price from 1989 to 2021.

Controlling exports and imports of goods and services as a percentage of GDP, aggregate inflation, and exchange rate (the value of the local currency), the probable value of GDP growth, given the data, is very small. It is highly probable that the value of the exchange rate could push GDP growth into negative territory after adjusting for the effects of exports and imports of goods and services and the general price level. The variance decomposition results are reported in Table 4.10.

Table 4.9 Bayesian analysis of covariance (standard errors in parenthesis)

	XGDP	*MGDP*	*DEFL*	*XR*
GDPg(–1)	0.01	–0.02	0.004	–0.001
	(0.05)	–(0.07)	–(0.07)	–(0.01)
Adjusted sample 1989–2021				
(33 observations)				
Prior type: Litterman/Minnesota				
Hyperparameters: Mu 1.1, L1: 0.1, L2:0.99, L3:1, L4: inf				
Sampling draw of 10,000 and burn-in rate of 10%				

Note: *GDPg* = GDP growth, *MGDP* = Import of goods and services as a percentage of GDP, *XGDP* = Export of goods and services as a percentage of GDP; *XR* = Implied PPP conversion rate of the leone (national currency per international dollar), and *DEFL* = inflation in terms of the GDP deflator. *The GDP implicit deflator is calculated as the ratio of GDP in current local currency to GDP in constant local currency* (WDI). All values have been estimated by Eviews 12. Hyperparameters are the primitive prior parameters defined in terms of mu, alpha (L1, the strength of prior belief (tightness parameter), L2, a measure of association or variance (overall parameter), and L3 (decay parameter, >1 fast decay, <1 slow decay)). The choices ensure that the hyperparameters will converge to optimal values. Tightness converges to 0.99. The pseudo-statistics are unreported here.

Table 4.10 Variance decompositions (2026 forecasts)

	GDPg	*XGDP*	*MGDP*	*DEFL*	*XR*
GDPg	–	2%	2%	0.11%	0.05%
XGDP	7%	–	10%	0.03%	0.01$
MGDP	5%	0.45%	–	0	0.04%
DEFL	13%	8%	0.15%	–	2%
XR	4%	0.77%	0.32%	24%	–

Note: Response variables are vertically listed. *GDPg* = GDP growth, *MGDP* = Import of goods and services as a percentage of GDP, *XGDP* = Export of goods and services as a percentage of GDP; *XR* = Implied PPP conversion rate of the leone (national currency per international dollar), and *DEFL* = inflation in terms of the GDP deflator (estimation by EViews 12).

The probability estimates are without imprecise or shifting parameter estimates (parameter uncertainties akin to frequentist evaluations of fixed but unknown estimates) since the parameters are random variables in a distribution of values. Though imports and exports of goods and services show wide variations, the range of probable values for the local currency shows virtually no such variation in the credible interval of 80 percent after scientific updates of available information (posterior distribution). Confidence interval (CI) creates a range of values that could be used to estimate the population parameter. Significantly, the probabilities show that serious policy measures are required for robust international trade and economic growth.

A projection of five years from the terminal date of the data illustrates that exports and imports of goods and services will account for about 4 percent of the variation in GDP growth of the country. Imports of goods and services as a percentage of GDP and GDP growth will account for about 17 percent of the variation in the exports of goods and services as a percentage of GDP. Of the variables considered, the most important determinant of the variation in imports of goods and services will be GDP growth, which accounts for 5 percent of the variation in imports of goods and services as a percentage of GDP. Exports of goods and services as a percentage of GDP, which is rather tepid, and GDP growth, which is also anemic, will substantially account for the variation in aggregate price inflation (about 21%). Aggregate inflation (defined in terms of the implicit price deflator) will account for about 24 percent of the variation in the value of the local currency (see Table 4.8 for the determinants of the values of local currencies).

Invariably, policymakers do not have control over all aspects of international trade, but they could proactively anticipate shocks and take proactive measures to deal with international trade shocks. Impulse response functions highlight some eventualities and the probable duration of diverse shocks. I subsequently examine trade disturbances of some trade variables and their potential effects on GDP growth. The response of the general price level to an export shock is also evaluated. The impulse response function is generally suitable for such an inquiry.

The impulse response function is derived from an orthogonal moving average VAR that gives meaning to the error expressions as innovations or shocks to targeted variables in a system of equations. A typical VAR can be written in moving average form by backward substitution as

$$y_t = \mu + \sum_{i=0}^{\infty} \phi_i u_{t-i}, \qquad 4.4$$

where y_t is a vector of variables – GDP growth, export of goods and services as a percentage of GDP, import of goods and services as a percentage of GDP, inflation (the implicit deflator), and exchange rate, ϕ_i is a matrix of moving average (MA) coefficients, μ is a constant with zero mean, and u_{t-1} is a vector of shocks (innovations). The infinite MA representation could be rewritten and standardized as an MA 1 process without loss of generality:

$$y_t = \mu + u_t \phi_1 u_{t-1}, \qquad 4.5$$

where u_t is zero mean white noise with non-singular covariance matrix Σu and $\Sigma(y_t) = \mu$.

Therefore,

$$u_t = y_t - \phi_1 u_{t-1}. \qquad 4.6$$

Equations 4.4 through 4.6 are without a structure. Accordingly, orthogonalization is required to isolate the effects of shocks (innovations) to uniquely relate the shocks to responses. A lower triangular matrix or a symmetric positive matrix ($\sum$ = P) gives the VAR a structure that is sensitive to causal ordering, otherwise known as *Cholesky decomposition*.[14] An MA VAR (Equation 4.4) could then be written in terms of orthogonalized (structural) innovations:

$$y_t = \mu + \sum_{i=0}^{\infty} \phi_i P u_{t-i}. \qquad 4.7$$

The *u* variables that are susceptible to shocks (innovations) now become uncorrelated with each other for a *k x 1* vector of the form $\gamma = (1 \ldots 0)$. The impulse response to the disturbance in the first equation (*n*) is then denoted as

$$\psi_j^0(n) = \phi'' P \gamma_j$$
$$\frac{\partial \psi_j^0(n)}{\partial \gamma_j} = \phi'' P;\ where\ P = 1. \qquad 4.8$$

Pesaran and Shin (1998) proposed a generalized impulse response that sidesteps the Cholesky limitation of causal ordering:

$$\psi_j^0 = \frac{1}{\sqrt{\sigma_j^2}} \phi'' \sum \gamma_j, \qquad 4.9$$

where σ_j^2 is for variance of the *jth* innovation. Equation 4.8 is insensitive to the order in which the variables are situated in the VAR and the BVAR.

The results of the generalized impulse response functions for the incremental effects of shocks to each of the endogenous variables are reported in Appendix B of this chapter.

The response of GDP growth to a positive import shock is immediate, and it tends to last for a long time (a decade or more). The GDP growth progressively and negatively declines because there does not seem to be a feedback effect from the imports to the productive capacity of the economy (see panel (i)). Countries tend to do better when imports are linked to their export capacities of generating national income. The eventual discussion of export-led growth (ELG) in this chapter sheds light on strategic imports.

Analogously, panel (ii) shows that a positive unit shock to exports progressively contributes to a negative decline in GDP growth. Invariably, Sierra Leone is not an export-oriented economy, which makes such a finding intuitive. Net exports have been persistently negative because imports have continuously exceeded exports. Consequently, exports are not strong enough to have a positive impact on GDP growth.

The depreciating value of the local currency has a progressively negative impact on GDP growth. A unit standard deviation shock to the market value of the local currency has a negative and explosive impact on GDP growth (panel (iii)). This result underscores the contractionary effects of currency depreciation. The general price level increases as the propensity to export diminishes and imports become enlarged and expensive. Krugman and Taylor (1978), with the aid of a Keynesian model, discussed the contractionary effects of currency devaluation, which are not unlike those of currency depreciation for a country that is experiencing increases in costly imports and falling export values with taxes on exports. They argue that a depreciation leads to a reduction in national output if: (i) imports initially exceed exports; (ii) there are differences in consumption propensities from profits and wages; and (iii) government revenues are increased by devaluation, for example, when there are significant export taxes.

The response of the general price level (inflation) to export shock is particularly noteworthy. The general price level increases on impact for at least six years before it starts to fall, suggesting that price stability is intimately contingent on the trade balance or the export of goods and services as a percentage of GDP (panel iv). Appendix B reports the stationarity preconditions (stability criteria) for analyzing the innovations and forecasting the performance of the endogenous international trade variables (Appendix D).

Several empirical studies have shed light on international shocks for large and small open economies. In the case of Australia, Jääskelä and Smith (2011) found that positive terms-of-trade (TOT) shocks tend to be expansionary but are not always inflationary. Whether the TOT shocks are inflationary depends on both the source of the shock and the response of monetary policy. They also find that the floating exchange rate provides an important buffer against foreign shocks that move the TOT. The bulk of variation in the real exchange rate in Australia is attributed to world shocks without widespread effects on other Australian variables. Notably, the Australian economy is larger than that of Sierra Leone it is much export oriented.

Determining the underlying source of variation in the terms of trade is shown to be important for understanding the impact on the Australian economy as all three shocks propagate through the economy in different ways. The relative contribution of each shock to inflation, output, interest rates, and the exchange rate has also varied over time. The main conclusion of the paper is that higher terms of trade tend to be expansionary but are not always inflationary. A key result is that the floating exchange rate has provided a convenient important buffer for the external shocks that move the terms of trade.

A small open economy is not entirely unmoored from international markets and transactions, but its participation in such markets is relatively inconsequential. The value of local currency in international markets gives valuable feedback information on matters of international trade (exports and imports), inflation, and prospective national income growth. I examine the effects of shocks on the variables and the policy implications for proactive considerations. Invariably, variance decomposition gives an idea of the interactive nature of the variables and the power of the endogenous variables to explain variations in each other for a given period. The results of the findings can be found in Appendix B.

Unexpected changes in import and export prices have been one of the most pronounced international trade perturbations – known as innovations in vector autoregression (VAR) language – for developing countries. When analyzing TOT (export-price-index to import-price-index) shocks, it is implicitly or usually assumed that the economy responds symmetrically to changes in export and import prices. Using a sample of developing countries, Di Pace et al. (2020) found contrary evidence. They construct export and import price indices using commodity and manufacturing price data, matched with trade shares, and separately identify export price, import price, and global economic activity shocks. In sum, export and import price shocks account for around 40 percent of output fluctuations but export price shocks are, on average, twice as important as import price shocks for domestic business cycles (Di Pace et al., 2020). The next section looks at international trade strategies that predate the 1960s.

4.8 International trade and economic growth: export- and import-led growth

For African economies that are decelerating and captured by the colonial paradigm of the 1960s (a steady state), the academic and political conversations in the literature about economic growth and development might be very instructive for post-colonial reconstruction (lessons of the past). Two tracks of conversations in the literature became very pronounced in the 1950s and the 1960s, export-led growth (ELG) and import-substituting industrialization (ISI). Some afterthoughts (postmortem) would suggest that the two approaches need not be dichotomous, binary, or mutually exclusive. A modified combination of the two approaches could foster rapid economic growth and economic relief for millions of disappointed and suffering Africans who have been waiting for economic progress since the 1960s. The East Asian countries, including Singapore, adopted ELG, while some Latin American countries embraced ISI.

Significantly, Sierra Leone and Singapore have common political and historical experiences. Singapore became a crown colony on April 1, 1867, about 59 years after Sierra Leone became a crown colony on January 1, 1808. The structure of the Crown Colony government of Singapore was not any different from that of the Africans. The Executive Council consisted of the Governor, the senior military official, and other officials. The Legislative Council consisted of the members of the Executive Council, the Chief Justice, and non-official members nominated by the Governor. Unlike Sierra Leone, Singapore is not well endowed with gold, diamonds, iron ore, bauxite, rutile, and piassava (natural resources). Commerce and fishing were the primary sources of revenue for Singapore, Singapore became an entrepôt for the resources of Malay, and it facilitated the disembarkation of Chinese, Indians, Indonesians, Malays, and others *en route* to other countries of the world. Singapore became a major center for ships moving between Europe and East Asia. It became a major sorting and export center for the trade in rubber as the rubber trade boomed after the 1870s (Warburton, 2005, p. 53).[15]

Unlike Sierra Leone, Singapore has a very checkered history of colonial domination.

In 1941, after the initiation of the WWII hostilities, Singapore fell under the control of the Japanese. It was subsequently recaptured by the British about three years later, but without full political rights of the Singaporeans to participate in the governance of their country. Limited participation in colonial governance was a generic practice, which gave the natives very limited exposure to the art of governance. Yet, unlike Sierra Leone, which benefitted in limited ways from the Slatter Constitution of 1922, limited participation of Singaporeans in governance of their country did not occur until March 1948.

The movement toward independence was equally volatile in both countries. It was arduous and challenging to bring factious elements in the countries together to form a common front for independence. In Sierra Leone, the Colony and the Protectorate (hinterland) had been ruled as separate entities under the colonial administration. There was widespread dissention over the unification of the Colony and Protectorate as one country and one people. In Singapore, the moderates of the People's Action Party (PAP) and the pro-Communists could not easily reconcile their political differences, and ethnic and racial riots broke out in Singapore in 1964. Sierra Leone had a coup d'état about 3 years later. On August 9, 1965, Singapore was separated from Malay, and it became a member of the United Nations on September 21, 1965, about four years after Sierra Leone (April 27, 1961).

The reconstruction tasks confronting both countries were very similar. By the mid-1960s, it became apparent that both countries had to chart a path for economic growth and human prosperity, with one country, Sierra Leone, in possession of lopsided natural wealth, and another, Singapore, with strategic geographic location. Singapore preferred unity or nationalism at the outset, "Singaporean identity," and anti-corruption and economic policies went hand in hand with nation building. It is unsurprising that countries with cleaner and transparent policies tend to grow faster than countries with preferences for personal aggrandizement and outsized levels of corruption. Singapore deliberately targeted educational policies for the acquisition of human capital and long-term foreign investments. Countries with cleaner and transparent policies, investment opportunities, and domestic human capital for investment are always capable of attracting long-term capital inflows.

Accordingly, one is tempted to pose a rather intriguing but unavoidable question: with an abundance of natural resources in Sierra Leone – gold, diamonds, iron ore, bauxite, rutile, and piassava, inter alia, why has Sierra Leone lagged behind Singapore, an entrepôt with a paucity of natural resources? The theories of underdevelopment are abundant, not the least of which are resource curse, geography (adverse geographic locations), public policies, external interference in the domestic matters of Africans, and unrestrained human incontinence. Fortunately, some of the theories are beyond the scope of this work (for further reading, see Humphreys et al. and Gallup et al.). This section merely focuses on growth strategies (ELG and ISI) with some overlapping or ancillary accommodations of the abundant theories.

4.9 Intentional public policies and Export-Led Growth (ELG)

From 1965 to 1990, East Asia grew faster than all other regions of the world. Most of the achievement has been attributed to a miraculous growth of eight economies, Japan and Four Tigers – Singapore, Hong Kong, the Republic of Korea, and Taiwan China (World Bank,1993, p. 1). What caused the "East Asian Miracle"?

The high-performing Asian economies (HPAEs) did not grow by chance or accident. Private domestic investment and growing levels of human capital were identified as the major drivers of economic growth. High investment levels came from robust domestic savings [capital formation] (World Bank, 1993, p. 5). Additionally, high productivity was encouraged in the agricultural sector. A country develops well when equity and economic growth are interdependent.

The HPAEs formulated a policy of shared growth by ensuring that the prosperity of all groups was correlated with the expansion of the macroeconomy. This is very much unlike the plutocratic and predatory systems that are so prevalent in the post-colonial African systems with rare exceptions. Explicit mechanisms were used to demonstrate the stakeholder theorem of shared prosperity that incorporated the middle class and the poor. Korea and Taiwan China carried out comprehensive land reform programs (World Bank, p. 13). Sierra Leone is still stuck with the ancient land tenure system of agriculture, which discourages private investment in mechanized agriculture and industrialization; fundamentals of economic growth and development that the public sector has been incapable of satisfactorily providing since the 1960s.

The growth of the HPAEs was not just contingent on the internal post-colonial reconstruction but deliberate policy choices for international trade, a mechanism to increase national income. The HPAEs embraced ELG, a theory that advances the view that export expansion is one of the main determinants of growth. The theory of ELG maintains that the overall growth of countries can be accelerated not only by increasing the domestic amounts of labor and capital but also by expanding exports. Accordingly, exports should naturally be perceived as an "engine of growth." Of course, a closer examination of a basic macro identity is intuitively revealing the thought that growth induced by export orientation is not a far-fetched theory. Consider Equation 4.10:

$$\mathrm{Y = C + I + G + NX,\ C = f(Y - T),\ I = f(r),\ and\ NX = f(\varepsilon),} \qquad 4.10$$

where consumption (C) is a function of disposable income (Y-T), investment (I) is a function of real interest rate (r), government spending (G) is autonomous, and net exports (NX), the difference between the value of exports (X) and the value of imports (M), is a function of exchange rate (ε). The variables individually and collectively affect the response variable Y (national income measured in terms of national expenditures) directly.

The relationship between exports and economic growth (positive change in Y) is often attributed to the positive externalities accruing to the domestic economy from selling goods, services, and assets in international markets. Nations specialize in reducing per unit long-run costs (average total costs) and improving the quality of human capital. It is extremely difficult to argue that the acquisition of income via export channels is not a growth and welfare developmental predicate. It is rather unfortunate that some econometric models have not been able to capture this truism, possibly because of the frequent (frequentist) approaches to parameter estimates that have characterized functional trade theories and models.

Imports (expenditures) without concomitant acquisition of income could barely stabilize growth at lower levels without necessarily increasing export (income) capacities. Additionally, export orientation encourages transnational operations that reduce domestic unemployment, foster technological transfer, leverage national saving, and foster foreign investment.

High growth rates, increasing trade shares in GDP, and dramatic structural change have fostered industrialization in export-oriented countries. Chenery et al. (1986) found that countries pursuing ELG strategies had rapid structural changes characterized by (1) rapid increases in the use of intermediate inputs ("deepening" of their input–output structure) and (2) unbalanced growth led by increased demand for tradable goods. Typically, the early phase of ELG industrialization is led by light manufacturing, followed by development of the intermediate and capital goods sectors (de Melo and Robinson).

Export-oriented countries have a peculiar appetite for imports. They tend to heavily concentrate on the importation of capital (investment) goods and selected intermediates rather than consumer goods that do not generate income. Furthermore, ELG countries like Korea and Taiwan experienced very rapid increases in the import content of exports. Korea and Taiwan doubled the import content of their exports within a decade (de Melo). Competitive trade forces exporters to become more innovative to reduce per unit cost and produce superior quality goods for international consumption.

Governments can create comparative advantages for firms by creating, to the greatest extent permitted by international trade law, the right kinds of environments and resources. I have dealt with the issue of international trade law much more extensively elsewhere (Warburton, 2021, pp. 363–459). In Korea, which first started with an import strategy (ISI), the government revised its procedures for collecting tax revenue to ensure a high revenue-to-GNP (gross national product) ratio, and purposive measures were taken to hold down current government spending.

An increase in commercial bank deposit and lending rates together with a price stabilization program raised the real (long-term) interest rate to approximately 10 percent per annum. By substantially increasing domestic savings rate, the government was able to finance the higher investment rates that were required for an accelerated growth of GNP (Westphalia, p. 350).

Case studies indicate that ELG strategies have taken place with active government participation, well beyond simply preventing the development of an

> *anti-export bias through dismantling policies to limit imports. On the export side, governments used large direct subsidies and, in addition, employed non-price policies, including the extensive use of export targeting and the establishment of "trade promoting organizations" (TPOs). In Korea, for example, the Korea Trade Promotion Corporation (KOTRA) was established as early as 1962 with government funds. During the early period of ELG industrialization in Korea, indicative export targets were set jointly by the government and various exporters' associations (with the government exerting leverage through its control of credit and other regulatory instruments).*
>
> (de melo and Robinson, p. 6, see also Westphal)

By 1967, South Korea provided significant incentives to foreign exporters; one of the most significant of which was unrestricted access to tariff exemptions on intermediates and capital goods (Westphal, p. 350). While South Korea and Singapore were charting pathways from the periphery, Sierra Leone had its first tribal coup détat[16] in 1967. Tribalism is like a genie in a bottle; it cannot be put back into the bottle without deconfiguration and long memory once it is permitted to get out of the bottle for self-fulfilling and nefarious purposes. In the 1960s, the East Asians (Malays and Singaporeans) quickly realized that tribalism is antithetical to economic growth and national development; they arduously kept the genie in a bottle.

As Sierra Leonean leaders fought over the spoils of post-colonial power in the 1960s, they ignored national progress and concomitantly failed to develop or adopt a coherent and serious long-term developmental strategy (or program) akin to that of the East Asians or even the Latin Americans. Consequently, Sierra Leone has unsurprisingly lagged behind countries with which it shared adverse colonial experiences in the 1960s (similarly situated countries); for example, Singapore, an entrepôt and historical counterpart of Sierra Leone with a paucity of natural resources, is now reporting eye-popping economic indicators of national progress (see Table 4.11).

Evidently, Table 4.11 reveals patterns of progress and disturbing deterioration. While Singapore started to generate exports as a percentage of GDP at a higher level in the 1960s, Sierra Leone started at a lower level and progressively declined. That is, Sierra Leone has not increased its exports of goods and services to obtain foreign exchange earnings (reserves) or income. The levels of GDP per capita between Singapore and Sierra Leone are disconcertingly incongruous. For the last decade (2000 and 2010), Singapore had GDP per capita of about $56K, while Sierra Leone regressively made $623. Sierra Leone increased its GDP per capita by about US$85 in a decade; Singapore more than doubled its GDP per capita by the 1970s.

Both countries have increased life expectancy, but Singaporeans could now live about 26 years longer than Sierra Leoneans who have a lot of work to do with food security and health care. Labor force participation rates and adult literacy show disconcerting disparities. The proportion of the population that is economically active in the last decade (2000–2010) of comparison is far lower in Sierra Leone. The labor force participation rate somewhat mirrors the adult literacy rate. Human

Table 4.11a, 11b, 11c Economic indicators of Sierra Leone (SLE) and Singapore

	A. 1960–1970 (average)		
	Export	*GDP pc*	*Life Exp.*
Singapore	132	4,737.38	67
Sierra Leone	28	544.04	36

Data source: World Bank's (World Bank, 2023).

Note: Export = Export of goods and services as a percentage of GDP; SLE exports = 1964–1970.

GDP pc = GDP per capita (2015 US$), and Life Exp. = Life expectancy at birth, *the number of years a newborn infant would live if prevailing patterns of mortality at the time of its birth were to stay the same* (World Bank, 2023).

	B. 1971–1980 (average)					
	Export		*GDP pc*			*Life Exp.*
Singapore	150		10, 571			71
Sierra Leone	24		629			41
	C. 2000-2010 (average)					
	Export	*GDP pc*	*Life Exp.*	*LFPR*	*ALitR*	*CPI*
Singapore	185	55, 723.39	83	70	97	83 (5)
Sierra Leone	22	623.1	57	57	32	110 (34)

Source: LFPR = Labor force participation rate: *The proportion of the population ages 15 and older that is economically active: all people who supply labor for the production of goods.*ALitR = adult literacy rate: *The percentage of people ages 15 and above who can both read and write with understanding a short simple statement about their everyday life* (WDI). The value for Sierra Leone corresponds to the 2013 value. Current value may be higher or lower than 2013.CPI = corruption perception index (2022) (global ranks in parenthesis, with lower ranking scores for cleanliness).

capital in the form of adult literacy is much higher in Singapore, almost 100 percent, putting Singaporeans in a position where they could quickly absorb foreign investments in search of skilled domestic labor that increases labor force participation rates. Significantly, the labor force of Singapore is undoubtedly more skilled and innovative because of investments in education and educational institutions. The Singaporean leaders have also increased domestic investments by discountenancing public corruption. Sadly, the theory of governance in Africa can hardly be told without allusion to public corruption, the proverbial elephant in the room since the 1960s.

Various studies now affirm the deleterious effects of corruption on economic activity, even when corruption is perceived as a grease of commerce – the so-called grease hypothesis that is supposed to speed up the wheels of commerce. Public corruption is the abuse of power for personal gain that provides no national benefit. At least three scholarly renditions are pedagogically adequate for clean public policies: (i) Wei (2000), (ii) Abed and Gupta (2002), and (iii) Svesson (2005). The corrosive effects of corruption on the progress of any nation cannot be overemphasized. Pointedly, higher levels of corruption cannot facilitate the economic growth and prosperity of any nation. In relative terms, the post-colonial performance of Sierra Leone and many African countries is both degrading and discouraging. Yet, the unseemly performance of the African countries reveals some disturbing subterranean global problems that had long existed in international relations.

> *Even [some]countries with high CPI scores play a role in the threats that corruption poses to global security. For decades, they have welcomed dirty money from abroad, allowing kleptocrats to increase their wealth, power and destructive geopolitical ambitions.*
>
> (Transparency International)

Evidently, corruption is a reciprocal crime, meaning that it takes two to tangle. Corruption is an interdependent or reciprocal crime because it involves a conspiracy of two or more people to execute a corrupt act; for every briber (one who bribes) there is a willing recipient. Therefore, a briber cannot be singularly corrupt without a recipient or counterpart of a corrupt transaction. Analogously, illegal capital flight from Africa has always found safe repositories (placeholders) abroad for credit expansion to third parties and foreign investments. The tragedy of a long history of corruption in Africa is that poorer Africans in various parts of Africa are now the casualties of concerted public corruption (Table 4.6 merely provides a snapshot of what is wrong in most parts of Africa).

Regrettably, after a lengthy period of embezzlement, inadvertence (or indifference), profligacy, and overindulgence, it took the world a very long time to start clamping down on international corruption. Though various conventions against corruption or ancillary transactions exist, the United Nations Convention Against Corruption, which entered into force on December 14, 2005, is the only legally binding universal anti-corruption instrument.

> *The Convention's far-reaching approach and the mandatory character of many of its provisions make it a unique tool for developing a comprehensive response to a global problem. The Convention covers five main areas: preventive measures, criminalization and law enforcement, international cooperation, asset recovery, technical assistance and information exchange. The Convention covers many different forms of corruption, such as bribery, trading in influence, abuse of functions, and various acts of corruption in the private sector.*
>
> (United Nations)[17]

If Sierra Leone did not opt for export-oriented economic growth (ELG), why not ISI? Does a preference matter anyway?

4.10 Lessons of the past: Import-Substituting Industrialization (ISI) and economic growth

In contradistinction to the East Asian economies, many Latin American countries opted for import substitution. Notably, even if Sierra Leone had adopted the less attractive ISI (second best), the odds of attaining better economic indicators would have been better or promising. Some might argue that the distinction between ELG and ISI is rather nuanced. However, a restatement of the net exports component of Equation 4.11 and sources of revenue for financing national economic growth are indispensable considerations:

$$NX = (X - M), \tag{4.11}$$

where X is for the value of exports and M is for the value of imports. Export-oriented economies focused on driving up the value of exports. Import-oriented countries focused on reducing imports but not without first increasing the value of imports to satisfy domestic and international markets. That is, imports were not necessarily intended to generate exports during the first phase of ISI. Clearly, export-oriented economies also imported capital goods and intermediates to boost exports. Therefore, the difference was merely a matter of export intensity, sources of financing, and the rationale (philosophy) behind the propensity to import.

From the 1930s to the early 1960s, the theory of import substitution industrialization dominated the economic planning of Latin America (Cardoso and Helwege, p. 84). As the Latin American economies lost revenues (reserves) from the plummeting agricultural prices in the 1930s, they turned to import substitutes to compensate for the shortfall in revenues (foreign exchange). Balance of payment problems and the specter of rising domestic unemployment initially pushed the Latin American leaders to ISI by default.

The intellectual revulsion against dependence was of significant coincidence with development theory. The theory that colonial authorities had structured the economies of their colonies to be perpetual sources of raw materials and consumption entities of industrial products had a great appeal in the intellectual circles of Latin America and Africa. The theory was influentially regarded as "dependency" in Africa and *dependentia* in Latin America.[18] There was a thirst to be unmoored from colonial domination, and industrialization was perceived as a defiant development against the theory of dependence. Raúl Prebisch, an Argentine economist, who argued for a change in the structure of the periphery in 1949, was probably the most influential thinker against the theory of *dependentia.*

The insufficiency of foreign exchange and the constraining impact of inadequate reserves on economic growth brought about an unlikely coalition of academics and public policymakers in Latin America. Significantly, adverse price movements of agricultural goods and loss of reserves necessitated the need to domestically produce nonessential imports to save precious and dwindling (scarce) reserves. Accordingly, it was perceived that structural diversification could shift unemployed farmers to an industrial sector that can generate employment, productivity, and income.[19] The coexistence of the two sectors (agricultural and industrial) became tenuous.

The circumstantial apprehensions of the Latin Americans were not any different from those of the post-colonial Africans in the 1960s. Despite the shift from agriculture to mining in Sierra Leone, mineral prices were equally volatile with variable elasticities in the international (industrialized) markets of the world. But the agricultural displacement of farmers in Sierra Leone was accompanied by illicit leakages of revenue from the mining stream (sector), largely attributable to unsavory public corruption. The advocates of ISI directed attention to linkages and externalities. Industries generate external demands for their inputs; but most importantly, the private sector is never suitable for massive structural changes with national proportions.

Confronted with trade imbalances, the goal of ISI was to establish new industries rather than protect existing ones (the infant industry theory) by using trade policies such as tariffs, import licenses, overvalued exchange rates, and direct government investment in key industries. Governments constructed plants in heavy industries – steel, cement, utilities, and airplanes with exorbitant overhead costs. New plants in automobiles, pharmaceuticals, and grain processing were set up as joint ventures with foreign firms. Foreign firms provided access to technology, while government ownership limited the repatriation of profits abroad (Cardoso and Helwege, p. 90).

The uniqueness of ISI was its preference for self-sufficiency (based on the revulsion against *dependentia*), which linked domestic resources to industrialization for domestic consumption. As a result, ISI was an inward-oriented trade theory and policy of self-sufficiency with limited prospects for international competition. Equations 4.10 and 4.11 show that a mere reduction in M without significant increases in X is not a very sustainable policy. In fact, for M to fall in the long run, it must first rise without corresponding increases in X, thereby creating some undesirable trade frictions in the immediate period. Todaro and Smith (2015) identify two significant stages of ISI.

During the first stage of ISI, developing economies were encouraged to substitute previously imported consumer goods by domestic production to staunch the bleeding of reserves. The preliminary phase could then be expanded to the domestic production of more sophisticated imported manufactured goods (stage 2) (Todaro and Smith, p. 631). However, the financial architecture for achieving emancipation from *dependentia* without reserves and revenue were rather elusive.

While the South Koreans raised long-term interest rate to incentivize savings and capital formation, the Latin American governments lowered interest rates for credit expansion and provided publicly owned enterprises to subsidize intermediate goods for endangered companies in the energy and steel sectors. Factor prices were stabilized by government regulation to protect poorer consumers and workers. In the final analysis, while ISI did not provide a panacea for economic growth and development, it laid the foundation for a diversified and structured economy that mistakenly monetized public debt in the search of revenue to finance economic growth and development.

Three major problems confronted the policymakers of ISI: (i) Protection adversely affected exchange rates without compensating pass-through effects on international trade – the effects of trade policies could also be exogenous. (ii) In sectoral terms, import substitution exaggerated industrial progress at the expense of the agricultural sector – the industrial sector was incapable of robustly absorbing the labor force with the displacement and migration of farmers to cities. (iii) Revenue from export taxes on primary goods failed to generate sufficient revenues to subsidize the industrial sector, and monetization of deficits – expanded government responsibilities for employment and finance of industrialization – led to spells of inflation (Cardoso and Helwege p. 91). It is probably revealing that the sources of revenue to finance economic growth and development made a fundamental difference between the viability of ELG and ISI.

This section and the chapter highlight the fact that economic growth and development cannot occur on their own accord. Policymakers must proactively develop national policies that are oriented toward national progress. Clearly, targeted national objectives are incompatible with personal aggrandizement that impoverishes others. It is the collective responsibility of all nations to ensure collective prosperity in an interdependent world. No nation is well ensconced from the failures or doom of other nations, and the ubiquitous spillover effects of lost decades of growth and prosperity are always pending and inevitable.

Notes

1 Mercantilists did not consider velocity to be constant. Moderately rising prices were seen as a reflection of robust economic activity (Kurz, p. 13). The transaction theory has been replaced by national (nominal) income in current theories.

2 The model suggests that industry resembles agriculture because "advances" were needed for production, and in a later edition of the Tableau *Économique* (after 1758/9) the advances (principally raw materials which must be bought in advance) were estimated to be about half of industrial costs, so output was about twice annual advances in both the "productive" and the "sterile" sectors. The choice of the word "sterile" to describe the artisan and manufacturing sectors of the economy was not very well received by many nineteenth- and twentieth-century economists, given the productive capacity of manufacturing (Eltis, p. 176).

3 See the work of Trebilcock et al., pp. 172–226, for discussions about trade disputes; see also Warburton, pp. 402–425.

4 See Warburton (2021) for a comprehensive analysis of international trade law appertaining to PTAs, equitable investment, and expropriation of foreign property (pp. 397–460).

5 Plurilateral treaties have limited reservations members cannot be parties to such treaties while objecting to the legal effects of some of the provisions of the treaties. Multiple reservations can be found in multilateral treaties. Plurilateral treaties have a narrower group of signatories, usually a subset of multilateral members.

6 The gravity model is a theoretical expansion of Newton's gravitational model, which postulates that the attraction between two heavenly bodies is proportional to the product of their masses and inversely related to the distance between them (Frankel, p. 50).

7 Imports, except for firearms, require documentation. In 2009, a pre-shipment inspection was replaced by a destination inspection. Inspections are usually okay as long as they do not become instruments of discrimination and harassment.

8 Goods that qualified for temporary entry and the regulations concerning temporary entry procedures are listed in Section 44 of the Customs Act No 9 of 2011.

9 See Section 63 of the Customs Act No 9 of 2011.

10 A small open economy, with relatively liberal trade orientation, can neither affect the volume of trade nor influence the prices of goods and services in the global economy.
11 In this chapter, overvaluation is used to describe a market situation where the price of a local currency is operating above its market clearing equilibrium – more of a domestic currency will be required to purchase foreign currencies. This definition may not have the same connotation or implication elsewhere.
12 *The 968.9-carat (193.78 g) Star of Sierra Leone diamond was discovered by miners on February 14, 1972, in the Diminco alluvial mines in the Koidu area of Sierra Leone. It ranks as the fourth-largest gem-quality diamond and the largest alluvial diamond ever discovered* (Internet Stones.com). The diamond was allegedly purchased for *$2.5 million dollars* (Third Biggest Diamond Bought by Dealer Here, *NY Times*, October 3, 1972). Miraculously, the very wealthy country profligately and overindulgently borrowed money from international financial institutions to rack up sovereign debt (national debt that is binding on subsequent generations). The investments in economic growth and national prosperity that were found in serious countries at the time were never an option for the impoverished country.
13 See www.worldstopexports.com/sierra-leones-top-10-exports.
14 If the variance of a standard matrix takes the form $V=E(e,e')=\sum$, pre-multiplication of the standard VAR by P^{-1} gives $P^{-1}y_t = P^{-1} Ay_{t-1} + P^{-1}e_t$. The lower triangular matrix then becomes: $P=PP'=\sum$ (an identity matrix).
15 See Warburton (pp. 54–60) for political challenges and post-colonial reconstruction, including nationalist policies in Singapore.
16 For discussions about political instability and coups état in Sierra Leone, see (Warburton, 2005, pp. 44–52).
17 See *www.unodc.org/unodc/corruption/tools_and_publications/UN-convention-against-corruption.html* Notice that Africa has been dogged by corruption since the 1960s. Impoverished Sierra Leoneans must have lost billions of dollars in illegal capital flight since the 1960s.
18 Prebisch became Executive Director of the Economic Commission for Latin America in 1950. Argentina's situation in the 1930s forced Prebisch to reevaluate David Ricardo's theory of comparative advantage, by separating theoretical economics from the actual practice of international trade and the power structures that underpin trading institutions and agreements.
19 In Sierra Leone, the displacement of farmers came much later as a result of the boom in the diamond trade, political migration to the city, and dismantling of the perfunctory marketing board. But for the ephemeral linkage of agriculture with an agro-based Mabole fruit processing factory of the late 1970s, there was no serious public policy to diversify the structure of the macroeconomy. From 1968 to 1991, there was a heavy reliance on mining, resulting in the importation of rice, which was once exported from the country, as farmers abandoned farms and turned to mining diamonds.

Further reading

Abed, G.T. & Gupta, S. (Eds.) (2002). Governance, corruption, and *economic performance*. International Monetary Fund.

Amadeo, K. (2021). What the Smoot Hawley Act can teach protectionists today. *The Balance*. www.thebalancemoney.com/smoot-hawley-tariff-lessons-today-4136667

Baier, S. & Standaert, S. (2020). Gravity models and empirical trade. Economics and Finance. https://doi.org/10.1093/acrefore/9780190625979.013.327

Balassa, B. (1978). Exports and growth: Further evidence. *Journal of Development Economics*, 5, 181–189.

Bhagwati, J. (1978). *Foreign Trade Regimes and Economic Development: Anatomy and Consequences of Exchange Control Regimes*. Ballinger.

Blaug, M. (1997). *Economic theory in retrospect* (5th ed.). Cambridge University.

Carbaugh, R.J. (2015). *International economics* (15th ed.). Cengage.

Cardoso, E. & Helwege, A. (1992). *Latin America's Economy*. Massachusetts Institute of Technology.

Congressional Budget Office. (2016). *How preferential trade agreements affect the US economy.* Congressional Budget Office.

de Melo, J. & Robinson, S. (1989). Productivity and externalities: Models of export-led growth (Working Paper No. 520). https://ageconsearch.umn.edu/record/198501?ln=en

Di Pace, F., Juvenal, L. & Petrella, I. (2020). *Terms of trade shocks are not all alike* (International Monetary Fund Working Paper, WP/20/280). International Monetary Fund. www.imf.org/-/media/Files/Publications/WP/2020/English/wpiea2020280-print-pdf.ashx

Eltis, W.A. (1975). Francois Quesnay: A Reinterpretation 1. The Tableau Economique.*Oxford Economic Papers*,27(2), 167–200.

Feder, G. (1983). On exports and economic growth. Journal of Development Economics, 12, 59–73.

Frankel, J.A. (1997). *Regional Trading Blocs in the World Economic System*. Institute for International Economics.

Fusfeld, D.R. (2002). *The age of the economist* (9th ed.). Pearson Education.

Gallup, J.L., Sachs, J.D. & Mellinger, A. (1999). Geography and *economic development* (CID Working Papers). Harvard University. www.hks.harvard.edu/sites/default/files/centers/cid/files/publications/faculty-working-papers/001.pdf

Heller, P. & Porter, M. (1978). Exports and growth: An empirical reinvestigation. *Journal of Development Economics*, 5(2), 191–193.

Humphreys, M., Sachs, J.D. & Stiglitz, J.E. (Eds.) (2007). *Escaping the resource curse*. Columbia University Press.

Jääskelä, J. & Smith, P. (2011). *Terms of trade shocks: What are they and what do they do*? (Research Discussion Paper, RDP 2011-05). Reserve Bank of Australia. www.rba.gov.au/publications/rdp/2011/pdf/rdp2011-05.pdf

Jung, W. & Marshall, P. (1985). Exports, growth and causality in developing countries. *Journal of Development Economics*, 18, 1–12.

Kilian, L. (2009). Not all oil price shocks are alike: Disentangling demand and supply shocks in the crude oil market. *American Economic Review*, 99(3), 1053–1069.

Krugman, P. & Taylor, L. (1978). Contractionary effects of devaluation. *Journal of International Economics*, 8(3), 445–456.

Kurz, H.D. (2017). *Economic thought: A brief history*. Columbia University.

Little, I.M.D. (1982). *Economic development: Theory, policy, and international relations*. Basic Books.

Lloyds Bank. (2023). Sierra Leone: Trade profile. www.lloydsbanktrade.com/en/market-potential/sierra-leone/trade-profile

Lubik, T.K. & Teo, W.L. (2005). *Do world shocks drive domestic business cycles? Some evidence from structural estimation*. Mimeo. Johns Hopkins University.

Meade, J. (1955). *The theory of customs unions*. North-Holland.

Michaely, M. (1977). Exports and growth: An empirical examination. *Journal of Development Economics*, 4(1), 49–53.

Mitchener, K.J., Wandschneider, K. & O'Rourke, K.H. (2021). The Smoot-Hawley Trade war. National Bureau of Economic Research. www.nber.org/system/files/working_papers/w28616/w28616.pdf,

Peersman, G. & Van Robays, I. (2009). Oil and the Euro area economy. *Economic Policy*, 24(60), 603–651.

Pesaran, H.H. & Shin, Y. (1998). Generalized impulse response analysis in linear multivariate models. *Economics Letters*, 58(1), 17–29.

Reinert, K.A. (2021). *An introduction to international economics* (2nd ed.). Cambridge University Press.

Salvatore, D. (2010). *International economics* (10th ed.). John Wiley & Sons.
Schmitt-Grohé, S. & Uribe, M. (2018). How important are terms-of-trade shocks? *International Economic Review,* 59(1), 85–111.
Smith, A. (1776 [1994]). *An inquiry into the nature and causes of the wealth of nations*. Random House.
Svesson, J. (2005). Eight questions about corruption. *Journal of Economic Perspectives,* 19(3), 19–42.
Todaro, M.P. & Smith, S.C. (2015). *Economic development* (12th ed.). Pearson.
Totty, M. (2023). Higher demand from U.S. and China means expanding into new markets. *UCLA Anderson Review.* https://anderson-review.ucla.edu/in-u-s-china-trade-war-bystander-countries-increase-exports/
Trebilcock, M., Howse, R. & Eliason, A. (2013). The *regulation of international trade* (4th ed.). Routledge.
UCLA Anderson Review. https://anderson-review.ucla.edu/in-u-s-china-trade-war-bystander-countries-increase-exports/
United States Department of State (n.d.). 2023 investment climate statements: Sierra Leone. www.state.gov/reports/2023-investment-climate-statements/sierra-leone/
US International Trade Administration. (2021). Sierra Leone – country commercial guide. *US of Commerce*. www.trade.gov/country-commercial-guides/sierra-leone-trade-barriers.
Viner, J. (1953). *The customs union issue*. The Carnegie Endowment for International Peace.
Warburton, C.E.S. (2005). *The evolution of crises and underdevelopment in Africa*. University Press of America.
Warburton, C.E.S. (2010). International trade law and trade theory. *Journal of International Trade Law and Policy*, 9(1), 64–82.
Warburton, C.E.S. (2016). The international law and economics of coercive diplomacy: Macroeconomic effects and empirical findings. Applied Econometrics and *I*nternational *D*evelopment, 16(1), 36–52.
Warburton, C.E.S. (2021). *Economic analysis and law*. Routledge.
Wei, S.-J. (2000). How taxing is corruption on international investors? *The Review of Economics and Statistics,* LXXXII(1), 1–11.
Westphal, L. (1978). The Republic of Korea's experience with export-led industrial development. World Development, 6, 347–82.
World Bank. (1993). *The East Asian Miracle: Economic growth and public policy*. Oxford University Press.
World Bank. (2023). *World development indicators*. World Bank.
World Trade Organization. (2007). *World trade report 2007*. World Trade Organization.

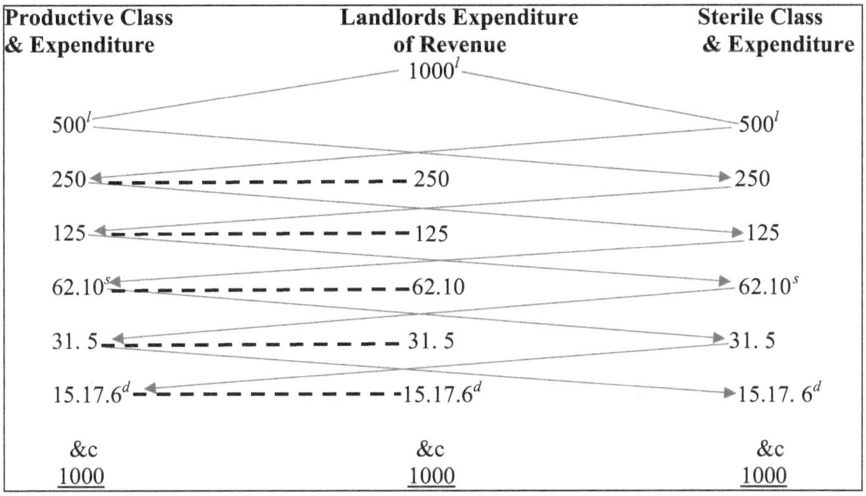

Appendix 4.1A Quesnay's *Tableau Ȇconomique*

Source: Eltis p. 181; slight modifications by author

Note: Superscript = Livres, sous, and deniers (currency units). There are various versions of the *Tableau Ȇconomique*, including leakages from the income stream. See Eltis for a comprehensive discussion of the *Tableau Ȇconomique*.

Quesnay structured the feudal French society into three categories, the productive farmers who provided revenues for the affairs of state (the middle column), the landlords who were consumers of rent (the productive revenue of the farmers) and artisan products, and the sterile or unproductive artisan class that did not provide revenue (taxes) for the affairs of the state. In this circular flow depiction of the closed macroeconomy, the landlord started off by consuming 500 from farmers and artisans.

Both farmers and artisans retain a fraction of income (half) for the next round of spending until the initial injection (1000^l) of the unproductive landlords is exhausted. The farmers pay rent to the landlords and save seeds for the next round of production. The initial spending is doubled in this multiplier system, which was subsequently revised downward, before the next round of spending. This closed economy model makes some convenient but unrealistic assumptions that are incompatible with modern macroeconomic models; for example, productive capital is taxed, modern economies are open, a fraction of national income is saved or invested, and farmers obtain loans from financiers. Financing production by equity, bonds, or loans is much more sophisticated in contemporary economies. In effect, by utilizing some simplifying assumptions, Quesnay was modeling the feudal realities of his time to the best of his ability and knowledge of the operations of the feudal system. The farmers provided livelihood in the form of food, and taxes to finance the operations of government, but taxes crushed farming and depopulated some provinces of France.

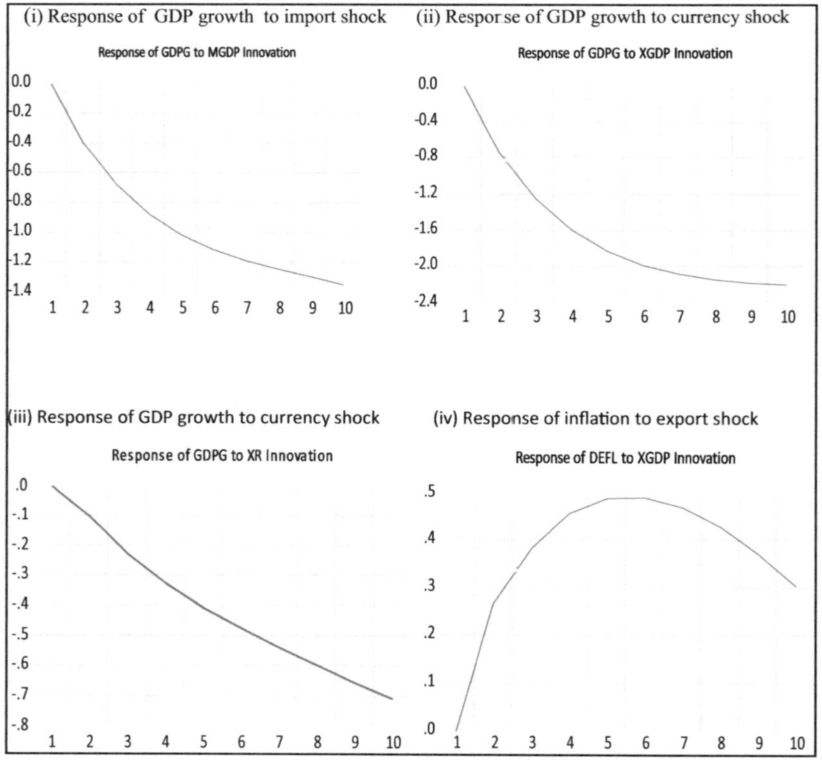

Appendix 4.1B Responses of GDP growth to perturbations

Note: *GDPg* = GDP growth, *MGDP* = Import of goods and services as a percentage of GDP, *XGDP* = Export of goods and services as a percentage of GDP; *XR* = Implied PPP conversion rate of the leone (national currency per international dollar), and *DEFL* = inflation in terms of the GDP deflator. *The GDP implicit deflator is calculated as the ratio of GDP in current local currency to GDP in constant local currency* (WDI). All innovations have been estimated by Eviews 12.

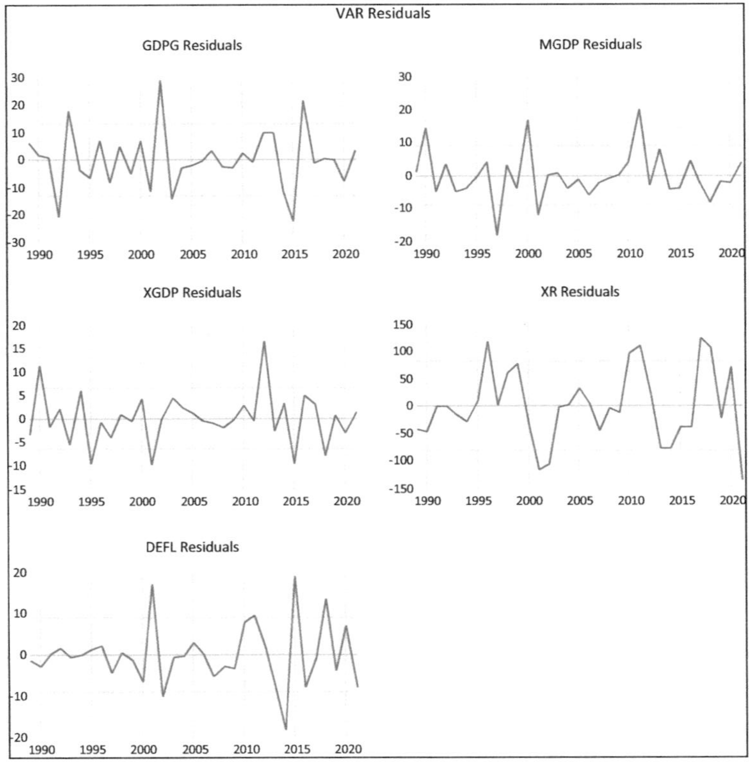

Appendix 4.1C The stationarity of residuals

Note: *GDPg* = GDP growth, *MGDP* = Import of goods and services as a percentage of GDP, *XGDP* = Export of goods and services as a percentage of GDP; *XR* = Implied PPP conversion rate of the leone (national currency per international dollar), and *DEFL* = inflation in terms of the GDP deflator. *The GDP implicit deflator is calculated as the ratio of GDP in current local currency to GDP in constant local currency* (WDI).

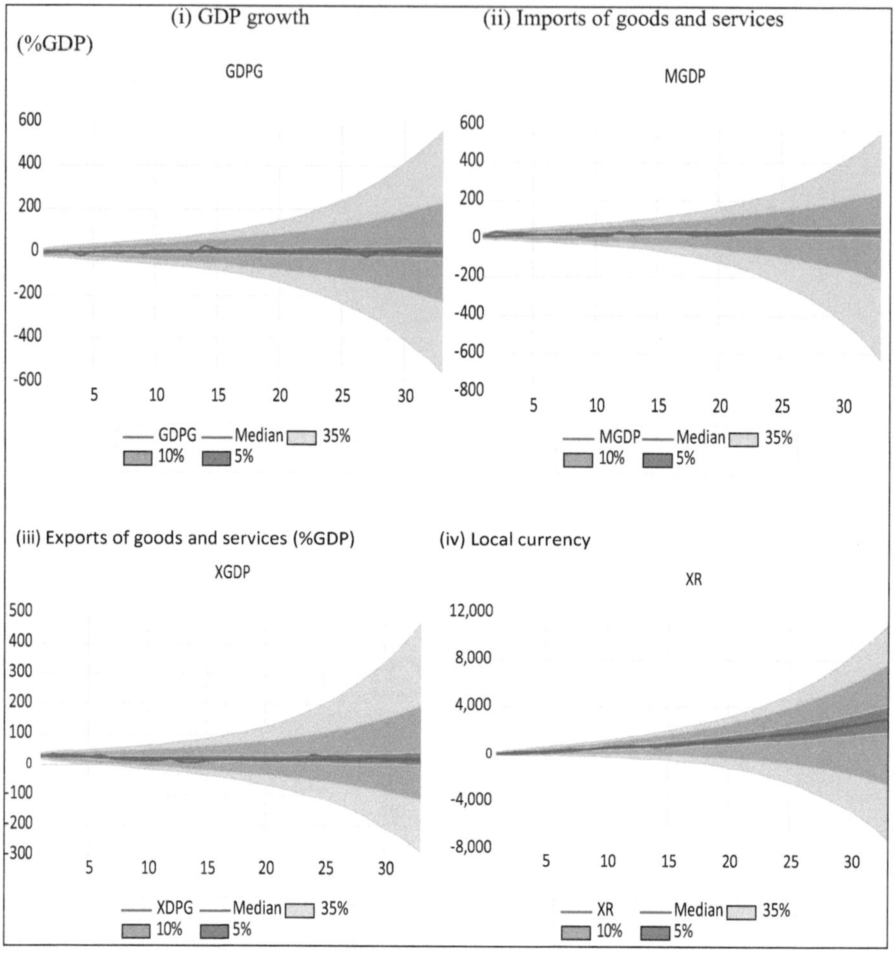

Appendix 4.1D Bayesian forecasts

5 External threats to macroeconomic stability

5.1 Volatility of commodity prices

Technically speaking, the volatility of the prices of assets can be associated with the standard deviation or variations from expected values. It is also plausible to characterize the volatility of asset values in terms of the rate at which asset prices change.

It is paramount to determine the factors that cause volatility to consider appropriate policy measures or regulations to control excessive price fluctuations. Volatility is a highly complex issue, whose effects may have undesirable implications for food security, financial markets, and trade flows. The aftermath of the last commodity crisis (2006–2008) provoked sprawling debates about the causative factors. The main lesson emanating from the debates is that commodity price volatility could be triggered by the combination of multiple variables, though it has been impossible to find a major cause or determinant.

Irwin and Sanders (2010) do not support the financial bubble hypothesis. In their view, the fundamentals hold persuasive explanations because they push prices up. They also consider the strong demand from China, India, and other developing countries, a leveling out of crude oil production, US monetary policy, the increased biofuel production and the weather shocks that affected the production of certain commodities.

It is believed that futures markets have a long-standing existence and that they have evolved because of volatility. Volatility causes farmers to hedge against price movements associated with their crops. Consequently, a volatility level exceeding the average would attract more speculators to financial markets for profits. However, if greater speculative activity proves to be correlated with higher prices and higher volatility, speculation more as a symptom of volatility rather than as a cause of it (Miguez and Michelena).

Chicago Mercantile Exchange's (CME's) historical volatility (v) estimate is equal to the annual standard deviation (sd) of the first differences in the logarithm (ln) of monthly prices (p_t-pt_{-1}). The standard deviation of the logarithm of prices in differences (SDD) is volatility adjusted for monthly variations:

$$v = sd\left(\ln\left(\frac{p_t}{p_{t-1}}\right)\right) * \sqrt{12}. \qquad 5.1$$

DOI: 10.4324/9781003518464-6

Volatility may also be defined as high deviations from a global tendency; but a large part of the variation in commodity prices could also be attributed to variations of a trend rather than around a trend (Dehn et al., 2005). An alternative measure is the coefficient of variation (CV), which controls for variations in expected values across different asset categories (Equation 5.2)

$$cv = \frac{sd}{\overline{P}} \rightarrow \sqrt{\frac{\sum_{i=1}^{n}\left(P_i - \overline{P}\right)^2}{n-1}}, \qquad 5.2$$

where P is for prices $\overline{P}$ is for the average value of prices in a series, and n is for the number of observations.

Agricultural commodity price volatility is an unavoidable phenomenon. Practitioners and policymakers, especially in advanced economies, have routinely followed the vagaries of the financial market prices. Matthews (2010) observes that farmers in some countries now face several risks that were formerly absorbed by market and price support policies. OECD (2009) finds that agriculture remains exposed to many risks like production, market, institutional, personal, and financial risks. Market risk, which is related to uncertainty about price movements and prices that farmers will receive for their products or pay for their inputs, is situated among the most important risk exposure.

Some researchers who have spent some time studying agricultural price volatility have concluded that agricultural price volatility was relatively low in the 1960s compared to the 1970s. Though agricultural prices fell during the second half of the 1980s and 1990s, they did not fall below the level of the 1960s (Gilbert, 2006). This finding affirms the theory that the 1960s was a favorable period to establish the basis of food security and the agricultural basis for industrialization. Rice production is a special case of insecurity. Gilbert and Morgan (2010) investigated 19 products over the period 1970–2009 and concluded that volatility has generally been lower over the two last decades than previously, except for rice. However, Balcombe (2009) finds persistent volatility in agricultural price series.

Huchet-Bourdon (2011) recounts the evolution of price volatility, which is integrally related to changes in the market forces of demand and supply. The most frequent drivers of the interaction of supply and demand are economic growth and underinvestment in agriculture. On the demand side, the fast economic growth in Asian economies and particularly in China is often emphasized. On the supply side, the underinvestment in agriculture as well as low commodity inventory levels of recent years is often cited as contributory factors. Increase in the production of biofuels is a relatively new source of volatility in commodity markets, as much as other macroeconomic and financial factors apart from specific commodity market fundamentals. Other factors include changes in oil prices, changes in world money supply, and changes in the value of the dollar since many agricultural commodity prices are denominated in terms of the US dollar.

Now, farmers must also worry about climate change, changing weather conditions, and restrictive trade policies (alluded to in the previous chapter) confronting agrarian economies. There is lack of consensus on the primacy of speculation as a contributing factor to price volatility, but the motive and practice of speculation cannot be controversial. Gilbert and Morgan (2010) and De Schutter (2010) highlight the role of speculation in futures and options trading on food commodity markets. Irwin and Sanders (2010) draw attention to market fundamentals as drivers of price volatility. Notably, interests in commodity markets are variegated, and profit-seeking activities cannot be eliminated from market transactions in commodities markets.

It has been found that movements of prices in commodity markets may have important implications for resource allocation and the general welfare of consumers and producers. Volatility may have undesirable macroeconomic effects on growth and poverty, with devastating consequences for the poor in underdeveloped and poorer countries (Aizenman and Marion, 1993; Ramey and Ramey, 1995; Rodrick, 1999). Therefore, policymakers in agrarian economies must continuously understand that price volatility is a fundamental feature of agricultural markets and probably one of the main sources of risk in international agricultural trade (Houchet-Bourdon, p. 10).

Huchet-Bourdon (2011) identifies two kinds of volatility in literature: (i) an historical (realized) volatility, and (ii) an implicit future volatility an historical (realized). The historical volatility is based on observed past prices, and it reveals the prices in the past. Implicit volatility corresponds to future expectations of volatile market prices based on the value of price options (Matthews, 2010, and European Commission, 2009).[1]

The historical (realized) volatility and the coefficient of variation could be used to estimate the risks that are associated with oil and rice prices or imports. Sierra Leone is heavily reliant on oil and rice imports (review the previous chapter and Table 4.5). I evaluate the comparative risk exposures of the country to price volatility of two products with far-reaching socio-economic effects on the country (see Figures 5.1 and 5.2). Recall that cereal was a high-ranking cohort of imports to the country in 2018 (see Table 4.5).

It is reasonable to scientifically conclude that crude oil prices are more volatile than the price of rough rice, reiterating the concept that energy diversification could attenuate the effects of price instability that comes from external disturbances. Invariably, undesirable energy prices pose a severe threat to the stability and vitality of the Sierra Leonean economy. This finding has been supported. A comparison of the volatility of the prices of selected commodities within four commodity groups (food; agricultural raw materials; minerals, ores, and metals; energy) shows that the price of oil is usually more volatile than the price of copper, wheat, or cotton (UNCTAD, 2023)

Sierra Leone is a net exporter in the top commodity categories of iron ore ($209 million, 25% of GDP), titanium ore ($141 million, 17% of GDP), diamonds ($104 million, 12% of GDP), and cocoa beans ($72.3 million, 8.6% of GDP), as of 2017. The bulk of imports comprise rice, petroleum, and machinery. When prices

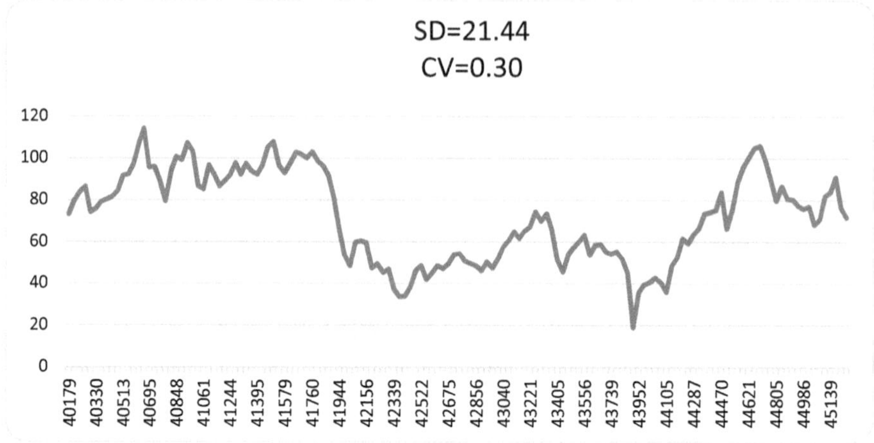

Figure 5.1 Monthly closing prices for crude oil (Jan. 2010–Dec. 2023, USD).

Data source: Yahoo Finance (New York Mercantile Exchange; 1,000 barrels per contract)
Note: SD = Standard deviation; CV = Coefficient of variation (mean =71.78).

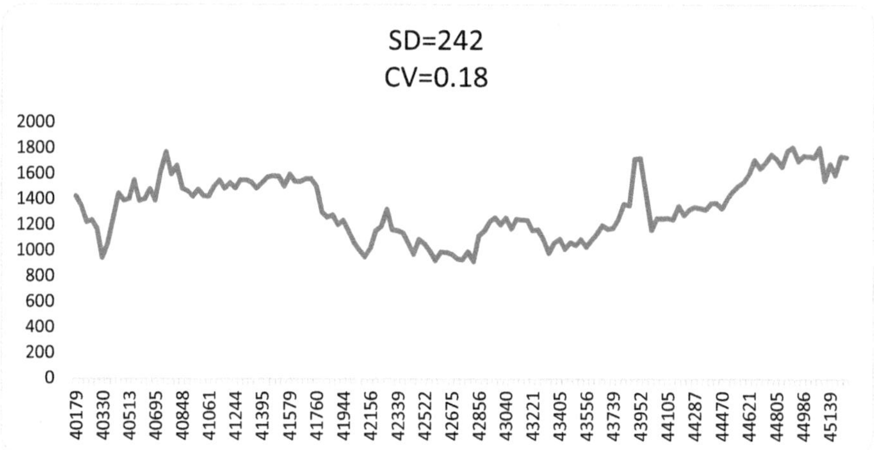

Figure 5.2 Monthly closing prices for rough rice (Jan. 2010–Dec. 2023, USD).

Data source: Yahoo Finance (Chicago Board of Trade (CBOT); 2,000 cwt (Hundredweight) per contract); mean value = 1344.51

of these commodities plummet, the country's exports generate insufficient foreign exchange to import rice, which forms part of the staple Sierra Leonean diet.

Srivatsa and Mchenga (2020) report that exports brought in $4.8 million worth of foreign exchange in 2019, but that exports, which make up 17.5 percent of GDP, could fall by half because of falling international prices and a halt to production and extraction activities. The value of exports in the second half of 2019 was $556.6.9 million, largely owing to increases in mineral and agricultural exports. The slowing down of activity in both these sectors means that exports will likely reduce by half in the worst-case scenario. That is, fragile economies could not be insulated from disruptive international price movements, but they could certainly work to attenuate the effects of disruptive international prices by maintaining healthy foreign reserves and managing imports properly through technological innovation and domestic production. From a public policy point of view, understanding the causes of price volatility is unavoidable.

In 2023b, UNCTAD provided a very interesting and compelling schematic representation of the causes of price volatility in commodity-dependent developing countries. The schematic representation has been provided for ease of reference and discussion of the causes of commodity price volatility (see Figure 5.3).

Commodity price volatility could be associated with at least eight factors: (i) market demand, (ii) market supply, (iii) climate change, (iv) the level of market transparency, (v) technological change, (vi) exchange rates, (vii) trade policy, and (viii) geopolitical events (Figure 5.3). Notably, climate change, exchange rates, trade policy, and geopolitical events are occurrences with shared responsibilities.

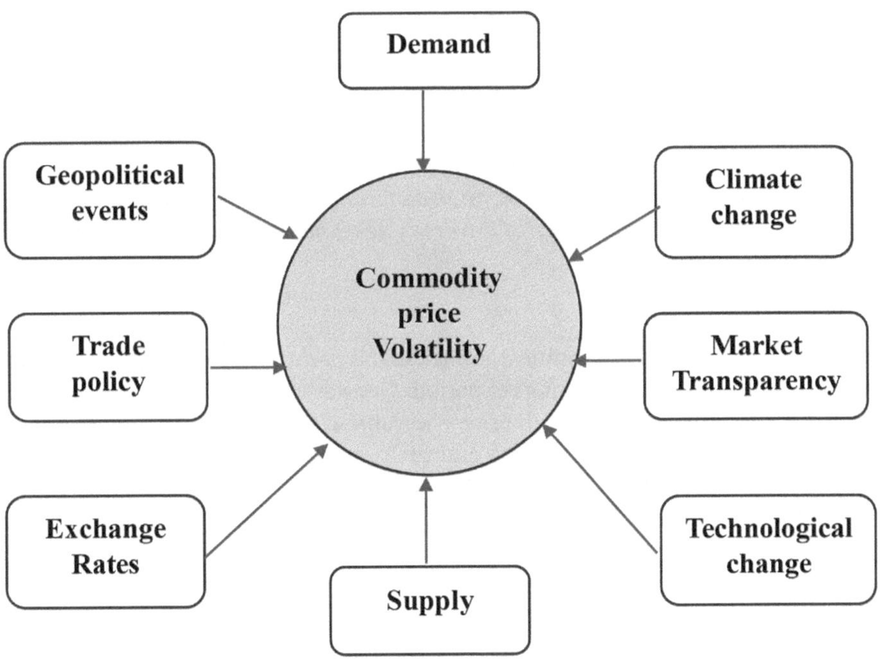

Figure 5.3 Drivers of commodity price volatility.

Source: UNCTAD (2023b), p. 4

Small open economies like Sierra Leone are incapable of influencing market demand and supply, technological advances in other areas of the world, and lack of market transparency elsewhere. However, the effects of climate change cannot be constrained to any country. Countries have a collective responsibility to achieve sustainable development. Policymakers could also influence the appreciation and depreciation of their currencies through trade policies and fiscal and monetary policies to mitigate exchange rate risks. The values of currencies (convertible and inconvertible) are inevitably going to change.

Accordingly, Sierra Leone could neither influence the depreciation or appreciation (price) of the US dollar in international markets nor control the effects of US dollar-denominated prices for commodities. However, Sierra Leone could reduce its reliance on commodities as a source of foreign exchange earnings to avoid the disastrous effects of exchange rate risk. Analogously, underdeveloped and developing economies alike could not easily penetrate the agricultural markets of advanced economies. The impenetrability exposes the poorer economies to loss of revenue and exchange rate risks via the net exports channel. This issue will be examined subsequently.

Naturally, price movements are not always unfavorable, meaning that farmers and their trade representatives must also exploit booms to defray the cost of busts. Price volatility is just a natural occurrence of market transactions. Pointedly, intense international trade in commodities requires intense risk mitigation planning.

> *These price changes allow producers and consumers to allocate resources more efficiently and contribute to the proper functioning of markets. However, if commodity prices fluctuate by significant amounts and are driven by non-fundamental forces, price signals get distorted, which can cause uncertainty and inefficiency. The potential consequences of market failure and uncertainty include a number of adverse effects impacting the real economy and people's livelihoods.*
>
> (UNCTAD, 2023b, p. 2)

Market sensitivities (elasticities) influence the prices of essential goods that do not have substitutes during a market period. Consumers are seldom threatened by price changes for goods with high price elasticities. Yet the supply of, and demand for many commodities, such as food and fuels, are generally inelastic in the short term or market period, relatively small supply or demand changes can lead to significant price swings. A longer time horizon is required for readjustments to such price swings, especially when products could be substituted after a relatively long period. Agricultural products are generally susceptible to seasonality, meaning that their yields and market availability are contingent on time periods within a year. Shortfalls of agricultural production could occur for any number of reasons that could cause seasonal variations in prices and unexpected shortfalls in production (supply shocks). Invariably, the supply of agricultural products is intricately linked to climatic conditions.

Climate change creates weather conditions – through extreme temperatures, heavy rainfall, and droughts – that affect agricultural output (crop yield) and the quality of agricultural harvest. I alluded to domestic environmental threats in Chapter 3 of this book. Increases in the frequency and severity of extreme weather events have been found to impact commodity price volatility because of too much water, lack of water in some areas, and rising temperatures that are unsuitable for crops. The unavailability of products increases product prices to reflect the desired demand. While focus is normally place on agricultural products, *mining and energy supply chains can also be affected by climate change through disruptions due to extreme weather events or changes in temperature and precipitation patterns that can affect the availability of water and other resources required for mining operations; the latter can result in increased resource competition, higher costs, and reduced efficiency* (UNCTAD, 2023b, p. 5).

Since extreme weather events are not very predictable, they often cause supply shocks in commodity markets for agricultural goods. Crop yields are sensitive to weather conditions, including temperature and precipitation patterns, and to impacts from extreme weather events.

> *[I]n Australia, a major wheat exporter, the drought in 2018–2019 caused a significant shortfall in wheat production; and in Thailand, the largest rice exporter in the world at the time, floods severely reduced the rice crop in 2011. In addition, local supply shocks due to inclement weather conditions can cause retail food prices to rise suddenly (even if international prices remain unaffected). Extreme weather events can also impact mining supply. For example, in Australia, floods in* Queensland in 2010–*2011 led to significant disruptions in coal mining operations, including at Goonyella Riverside Mine, one of the world's largest coal mines, and contributed to a 22 per cent increase in unit costs of thermal coal mines in Australia in the first half of 2022.*
>
> (UNCTAD, 2023b, p. 5)

Data from the African Development Bank show that Sierra Leone's Green Growth Index deteriorated from 45.3 percent in 2010 to 44.9 percent in 2021 though there are ongoing initiatives to enhance natural capital (see Box 5.1). Between 1995 and 2018, the nonrenewable natural capital rose 94 percent in real terms, and its renewable natural capital rose 70 percent.

Market opacity and information asymmetry create market uncertainties that lead to volatile prices of goods. International markets could be rattled when market participants know little or nothing about inventory of commodities and speculate about the availability of commodities. Therefore, information asymmetry (friction) could be expected to lead to volatility. Without adequate information, purchasers hedge by making contracts based on their expected value of prices in the future. Intense price volatility could then cause ethical lapses in the form of price gouging or fixing, and fraud.

Box 5.1 Climate change issues

Sierra Leone's Green Growth Index deteriorated from 45.3 percent in 2010 to 44.9 percent in 2021, highlighting the challenges associated with achieving the green growth target. This was due to weak performance in green economic opportunities. Despite this, supported by green growth policies and strategies, Sierra Leone has the potential to foster economic growth while reducing vulnerability to climate change. Its national and sectoral green growth policies and strategies are aligned with its Nationally Determined Contribution, whose financing need is an estimated $276 million. Inflows amounted to $164 million, 12 percent of which came from the private sector. Sierra Leone can mobilize private climate finance through innovative instruments, including a carbon market, debt for-climate swaps, and climate-related debt. Between 1995 and 2018, its nonrenewable natural capital rose 94 percent in real terms, and its renewable natural capital rose 70 percent. This provides a major chance to leverage private climate finance with natural resources. Ongoing initiatives to enhance natural capital include pursuing oil and gas exploration and strengthening the legislative framework around forest protection and related environmental issues to leverage climate finance from forests, including carbon credits [Reducing emissions from deforestation and forest degradation in developing countries], REDD+ payments, and grants for forest conservation or reforestation.

Source: African Development Bank

Technological changes and innovation could also impact commodity prices. Such changes create *new sources of demand for commodities, such as the growing demand for the lithium-ion batteries used in electric vehicles. This can increase the price of critical battery materials and create price volatility if supply cannot keep up with demand. On the supply side, new technologies can facilitate the discovery and exploitation of new oil, gas, and mineral deposits, by reducing operating costs. For example, the development of new technical processes to extract shale oil and gas led to a significant increase in oil production in the United States* (UNCTAD, 2023b, p. 8).

In the previous chapter, it was revealed that import restrictions could adversely affect national welfare through the loss of surpluses that could otherwise accrue to a nation. Export restrictions have implications of their own. Export tariffs and NTBs like quotas contribute to price volatility because of apprehensions and shortages in international markets.[2] There seems to be an inverse relationship between commodity prices and the value of the US dollar, possibly through the foreign demand channel for US dollars (see Figure 4.11 and imagine an inward shift of the supply curve for a dollar-foreign currency exchange rate). Higher commodity prices seem to suggest less foreign demand for US dollars, and therefore a depreciation of the US dollar. However, this correlation has been rather tenuous after the COVID-19 pandemic for reasons that might be unrelated to foreign demand. *With this shift in the relationship between commodity prices and the strength of the dollar, the exchange rate shifted from being a shock absorber to a shock amplifier in many net commodity-importing developing countries* (UNCTAD, 2023a, p. 8).

Disruptive geopolitics – a confluence of politics, geography, economics, and demography that impacts international relations – is also a major determinant of commodity price volatility. Hostile incidents are particularly prominent in the Middle East, Eastern Europe, and Southeast Asia. Conflicts in these regions involve major players that are very capable of causing supply shocks and destabilizing prices in global markets. Some major incidents with significant economic consequences in the twentieth and twenty-first centuries include the Yom Kippur War (the Fourth Arab-Israeli War, or Ramadan War) from October 6 to 25, 1973, between Israel and a coalition of Arab states under the auspices of Egypt and Syria, the 1980 Iran oil embargo, the 1990 Gulf war, the 2012 threat by Iran to close the Strait of Hormuz, and the 2022 Russian invasion of Ukraine. Looming threats exist over the international passage of the South China Sea and the controversy over Taiwan's autonomy.

International food and energy crises are always harmful to poorer countries.

> *The economies of all the non-oil-exporting poor countries were hard hit by the increase in oil prices in 1973–74. Worldwide, the net increase in their payments to oil sellers [have] been estimated at over $12 billion during the first year. The overall increase in their current accounts deficits was $20 billion, bringing the total to $32 billion. Thus, the net amount of the oil bill increase was about a third of the total LDC deficit in 1974, but perhaps half of its increase.*
>
> (Johnson & Wilson, 1982, p. 214)

It was estimated that the increased deficit associated with the cost of oil imports into 29. African countries amounted to $797 million for the first year of the crisis. Further, the oil bills of the "Black African" states increased by $1.3 billion (Johnson & Wilson, 1982, p. 214).

> *[T]he balance-of-trade position of the LDCs deteriorated by about $20 billion during the first year of the crisis. The combination of direct and indirect petroleum cost increases apparently could be blamed for all of this. In reality, however, two other factors must be added in. Stagflation in the industrial countries continued; the cost of industrial goods imported from them by the LDCs rose by about 40 percent between 1973 and 1975.16 Markets for exported goods from Africa and the other LDCs were likewise depressed. Overall, the LDC terms of trade were estimated by the Overseas Development. . . . Oil as a percentage of imports increased 8 to 18 percent during the first wave, and some of the hardest hit states, like Kenya, found themselves paying a quarter of their import bill for oil by the end of 1974.*
>
> (Johnson & Wilson, 1982, pp. 215–216)

By 1975, the changes in the total cost of the poorer oil-importing countries had increased astronomically (see Table 5.1), with outsized changes in the percentage of national income that was allocated to oil imports. The total cost for Sierra Leone increased from 57 percent by the end of 1973 to 218 percent by the end of 1975.

Table 5.1 Changes in total costs for imported petroleum products for selected African countries (in percentages) (1972–1978)

Total cost change in percent of GDP							
	1972–73	*1973–75*	*1975–78*	*1972–73*	*1973–75*	*1975–78*	*1972–78*
Ethiopia	70	271	27	50	100	25	650
Ghana	63	227	188	50	244	16	500
Kenya	59	237	16	63	235	15	525
Malawi	35	300	31	43	290	31	629
Morocco	62	249	255	67	247	25	622
Sierra Leone	57	218	11	54	215	11	439
Sudan	59	222	13	43	230	15	443
Tanzania	57	232	23	50	233	20	525
Uganda	33	258	19	40	271	19	520
Zaire	57	236	17	43	250	14	471
Zambia	54	230	6	67	220	6	467

Source: Compiled from figures given by *African Contemporary Record*, 1977–78, p. C198, and Johnson and Wilson (1982, p. 217)

Note: Original figures in current market prices; GDP = Gross Domestic Product.

The severity of geopolitical effects on commodity prices is ultimately contingent on the perception of market participants about price movements, and the intensity and duration of the market disturbances. Figure 5.4 depicts the trajectory of imported crude oil prices into the US, which corresponds to some frictional geopolitical events.

The price of imported crude oil started its ascent round about 1973 (the period of the Arab-Israeli War) and reached a temporary (non-global peak) in 1981. In 1980, an oil embargo was placed on oil shipments from Iran to halt Iran's nuclear program. The former US President, Jimmy Carter, announced the economic against Iran on April 7, 1980. Ultimately, the US convinced its European allies to impose the sanctions. West Germany and the nine Common Market members announced in Luxemburg on April 22 that they intend to implement an embargo on exports to Iran. On April 1, Iran had declared a \$2.50 per barrel surcharge on its oil, lifting the price to \$35 a barrel.

However, oil companies refused to pay the surcharge, and The National Iranian Oil Company responded by shutting off shipments to BP and Shell (which together had been importing 205,000 barrels a day) on April 8. Seven Japanese companies were also included on April 21. As a result of the oil price dispute, European Community (EC) imports from Iran fell from \$829 million in January 1980 to \$100 million in October – a drop that was far more significant than any related to the sanctions (Shehadi, 1981).

Another significant geopolitical threat occurred in 2012 after Iran threatened to close the Strait of Hormuz. The Strait is situated off the coast of Iran, and it is a strategic global trade route (see Box 5.2). It is a strait between the Persian Gulf and the Gulf of Oman, and it is the only sea passage from the Persian Gulf to the Indian Ocean. Consequently, it is one of the world's most strategic trade routes. About 30 percent of the world's trade in crude oil (approximately 17 million barrels of oil each day) passes through the Strait of Hormuz.[3]

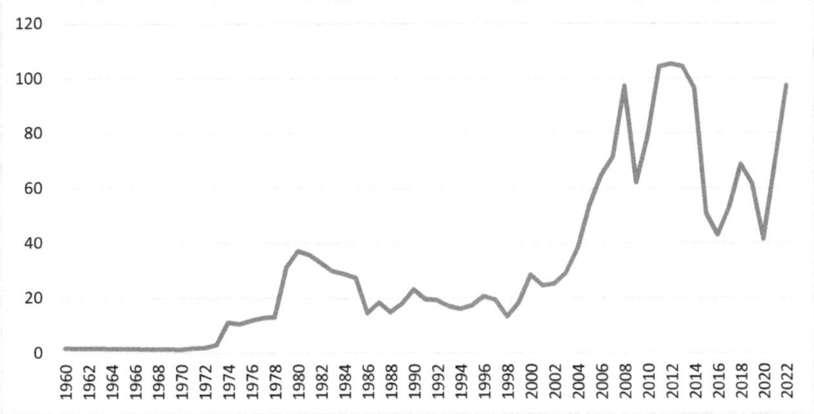

Figure 5.4 Average value of the US-imported crude oil prices (1970–2022Q1).

Data source: US Energy Information Administration and The Balance

Note: Real Petroleum Prices are computed by dividing the nominal price in a given month by the ratio of the Consumer Price Index (CPI) in that month to the CPI in some "base" period. The Real Petroleum Prices spreadsheet and charts are updated every month so that the current month is the base period in the monthly price series. Consequently, all real prices are expressed in "current" dollars and any current month price may be compared directly with any past or projected real prices.

Box 5.2 The strait of Hormuz

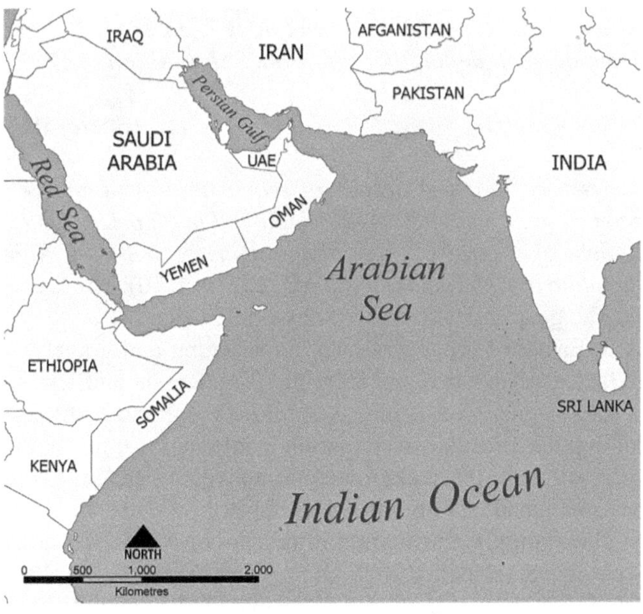

Source: NormanEinstein, Ras67, CC BY-SA 3.0, via Wikimedia Commons.

The threat was not necessarily disastrous for the commodities markets as one might expect but given the significance of the volume of crude oil trade that was routed through the Strait, the threat itself posed a risk to market price stability.[4] Figure 5.4 shows that the geopolitical frictions of 1980 and 2012 were not as disastrous as one might expect, given the downward trend of prices. Yet it might be a mistake to conclude that perturbations in the region do not have significant consequences for energy prices. In fact, the initiation of hostilities is sufficient to speculatively bid up oil prices, and the upward movement of prices prior to the incidents may reflect that reality. In effect, the initiation of hostilities generates market and price signals. Significantly, Brazil diversified its sources of energy to include ethanol after the crisis of the 1970s – a very significant lesson of innovation and diversification to fend off looming threats.

In the 1980s, many developing countries were plunged into a massive debt crisis because of the prohibitive cost of oil. Two important shocks that are not readily apparent in the data triggered the debt crisis – the second oil crisis of 1979 (see also Table 5.1 for a prelude), and disinflationary measures to slow down the growth of inflation in the developed economies.

> *Two external shocks hit the developing countries between 1979 and 1981. First, the second oil crisis of 1979 caused a surge in the price of oil to a high of $35 in 1981 [see also Table 5.1, there may be quarterly variations]. Second, anti-inflationary policies in the developed countries and a steep recession caused a precipitous drop in commodity prices and an adverse shift in the [least developed countries'] LDCs' terms of trade . . . . The effects of these shocks were an increase in the trade deficit of the developing countries from $22.2 billion in 1979 to $41.8 billion in 1981; and a current account deficit that rose from $31.3 billion in 1979 to $118.6 in 1981.*
>
> (Spero, 1990, p. 175)

This debt crisis led to a lost decade of economic growth and development in many low-income countries. In 2014–2016, the fall in oil prices led to an increase in the public debt of several oil-exporting countries, including Nigeria and the Bolivarian Republic of Venezuela (UNCTAD, 2023a, p. 10). The Eastern European crisis is unlike the geopolitical crises in the Middle East.

The crisis in Eastern Europe has been far-reaching and gravely destabilizing. In February 2022, Russia's invaded Ukraine. Both Russia and Ukraine are major exporters of natural gas, wheat, maize, sunflower oil, and fertilizers. The invasion had a buildup that created consternation in international financial markets that caused the price of crude oil to skyrocket far above prepandemic prices (see Figure 5.4). War signals had already placed an upward pressure on prices because of apprehension about supply and market prices. As of April 2022, oil was trading around $104 per barrel (price for 2022 Q1).

The African Development Bank estimates that the Russian invasion of Ukraine triggered a shortage of about 30 million tons of grains on the continent, along with a sharp increase in cost. The unspectacular adversity affects a continent that has over 65 percent of the world's uncultivated land and very favorable climatic conditions for agriculture in multiple countries. Not only did African countries fail to get the much-needed food that constitute a colossal fraction of their budgets, but they could also not even get sufficient access to fertilizers for farming that is already suboptimal. In the interim, the continent has the highest prevalence of food insecurity in 2020 (see Box 5.3).

Box 5.3 Shocks to Africa's food system

- While Africa has over 65 percent of the world's uncultivated land, it is a net food importer, and as such, has been severely impacted by the rise of global food prices, resulting in increased food insecurity.
- In 2020, 15 African countries imported over 50 percent of their wheat products from the Russian Federation or Ukraine. Six of these countries (Eritrea, Egypt, Benin, Sudan, Djibouti, and Tanzania) imported over 70 percent of their wheat from the region.
- Food items take up about 42 percent of African household consumption, reaching as high as 60 percent in countries affected by conflict and insecurity. In France and the United States, food items represent 13 percent and 6 percent of household consumption, respectively, notes the United Nations.
- According to the African Development Bank (AfDB), African countries spend over $75 billion to import over 100 million metric tons of cereals annually. In 2020, 15 African countries imported over 50 percent of their wheat products from the Russian Federation or Ukraine. Six of these countries (Eritrea, Egypt, Benin, Sudan, Djibouti, and Tanzania) imported over 70 percent of their wheat from the region.
- The UN's 2023 World Economic Situations and Prospects Report shows that Africa already had the highest prevalence of food insecurity globally in 2020 with 26 percent facing severe food insecurity and 60 percent of the population affected by moderate or severe food insecurity according to the Food and Agriculture Organization (FAO).
- Supply chain disruptions of primary farm inputs, including fertilizer imports from Russia, Ukraine, and Belarus, further threatened Africa's food security. The World Food Programme (WFP) reported that global fertilizer prices have risen by 199 percent since May 2020, with prices for fertilizers more than doubling in Kenya, Uganda, and Tanzania in 2022.
- The WFP notes that "while this is partly a consequence of the war in Ukraine, prices of food, fuel, and fertilizers had already reached record highs by the end of 2021."

Source: Yohannes-Kassahu (2023, February), *African Renewal*.

Therefore, highly volatile commodity prices have been found to be negatively correlated with economic growth, particularly in low-income countries that are exposed to the negative effects of commodity price volatility on growth. Van der Ploeg and Poelhekke (2009) put some emphasis on the transmission of price volatility to poor investment. Higher volatility in commodity prices and revenue shortfalls also induce greater volatility in government finances of investment and social programs.

The eight factors (Figure 5.3) necessarily induce price volatility, but they are not necessarily all-encompassing. Phytosanitary problems, collective work stoppages, and availability of liquidity could easily disrupt commodity prices.[5] There are various reasons why underdeveloped economies must not be complacent about external shocks and their transmissions to economic performance. Some of the main reasons have been provided in Figure 5.5.

Commodity price volatility causes multiple volatilities and uncertainty that impinge on investment and economic growth. Economic growth, terms of trade, public revenue, capital flow, and exchange rate become volatile, meaning that commodity price volatility has a multiplier effect of volatilities that generate uncertainty. The volatilities that are transmitted from commodity price volatility generate uncertainty that unfavorably impinges on investment, capital accumulation through

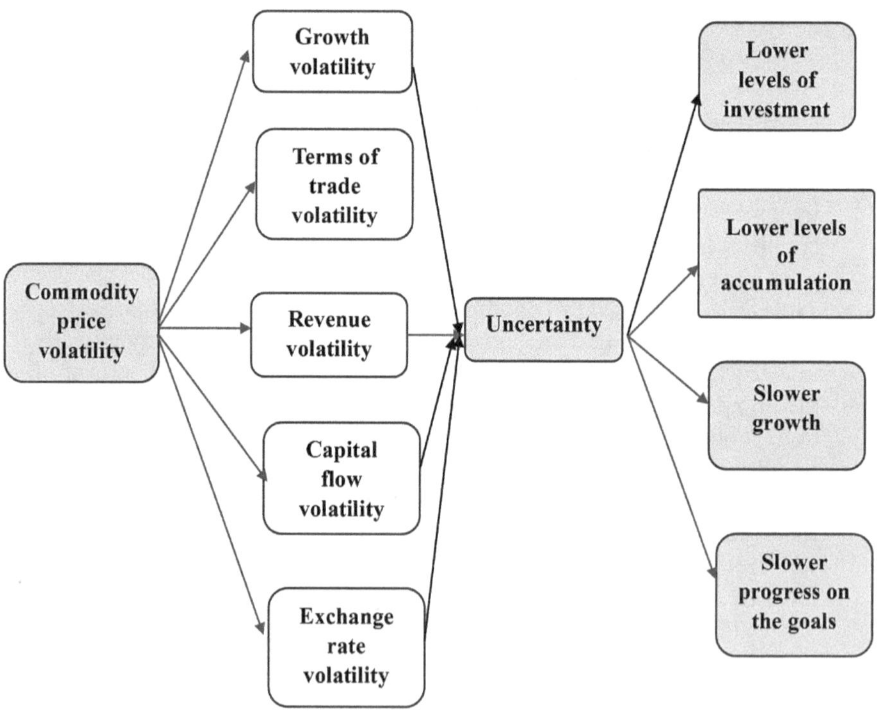

Figure 5.5 Transmission channels of volatility in commodity-dependent developing countries.
Source: UNCTAD (2023b, p. 9)

the national saving channel, slower economic growth, and tardiness to achieve targeted policy objectives.

When businesses in countries that heavily trade agrarian and mining products contend with volatile commodity prices, the businesses become exceedingly exposed to speculative market outcomes. The businesses deal with uncertainty about production costs and the price of end products for profitable market operations. Notably, poorer countries tend to specialize in more volatile sectors such as agriculture and mining (Koren & Tenreyro, 2007).

Accordingly, higher volatility in commodity prices is negatively correlated with economic growth, especially in low-income countries where commodity price volatility with the negative effect on growth could be attributed to the impact on investment and productivity (Van der Ploeg and Poelhekke).

In an underdeveloped economy like Sierra Leone where the longevity of business operations can be precarious (see Chapter 2 of this book), commodity price volatility could easily increase attrition rates of business operations and loss of public revenue. Attrition of business operations causes greater variability of government revenue and the capacity of a government to consistently fulfill its social obligations. Variability in revenue leads to instability in public spending on social services, infrastructure, and other areas of social need. Poorer governments that are already struggling with the provision of vital services like education, health care, infrastructure, and healthy drinking water could least afford to be unprepared for the consequences of commodity price volatility.

The rise and fall of commodity prices determine the fortunes of exporting nations that are dependent on the sale of primary products. Price instability positively correlates with the value of currencies and the prospects of capital inflows. Increases in foreign exchange earnings shore up the value of currencies and vice versa (see Figure 4.10). Currencies are equally prone to speculative attack, especially when their performances become reasonably predictable.

Erratic movements in commodity prices can prompt investors to adjust their portfolios and seek more stable opportunities elsewhere, leading to volatile capital flows and affecting exchange rates.

Underdeveloped economies with high sovereign debts are particularly vulnerable to commodity price volatility. The relationship between net exports and sovereign debt was explored. In the previous chapter of this book, unanticipated drops in commodity prices exacerbates debt distress in highly indebted underdeveloped economies that are commodity dependent. When commodity prices decline precipitously, export earnings in commodity-dependent countries plummet significantly, thereby reducing revenue streams and compromising the ability of indebted countries to generate sufficient revenues to satisfy debt obligations and nondiscretionary social spending. Dwindling revenue and foreign reserves elevate the difficulty of servicing external debt. In addition, due to falling revenues, these countries must borrow more to refinance existing debt, which leads to serial acquisition of sovereign debt. The risk (cost) of unsustainable sovereign debt will be discussed in Section 5.3 of this chapter. The next section takes a look at the threat of impenetrable markets for a commodity-dependent underdeveloped economy.

5.2 Loss of competitiveness and inaccessible global markets

The collapse of the Doha Round of talks clearly reveals one of the main problems with the trade preferences of underdeveloped and commodity-dependent economies. Commodities should be used for cash and food security to reduce the expensive imports of cereals. This means that there is an urgent need for underdeveloped economies to rethink the logic that underlies their preferences for international trade in contradistinction to their domestic needs.

Countries that are heavily reliant on agricultural products to penetrate the agricultural markets of advanced economies do not stand a chance of accessing such markets on a sustainable basis for economic growth and the acquisition of foreign reserves. Accordingly, they expose themselves to the assorted categories of risks that have already been discussed in the previous section of this book. Sierra Leone must start to focus on diversification of its articles of trade and food security to reduce expensive imports and shore up its foreign reserves. The prospects of attaining food security are dwindling in the light of climate change and exogenous geopolitical disturbances already alluded to.

Obviously, this does not mean that agricultural products are not tradeable goods. Countries that cannot penetrate industrial markets with competitive agrarian products merely need to find strategic trading partners beyond the impenetrable northern markets. It is worthwhile to revisit the gravity theorem, trade diversion, and the utility of PTAs that were discussed in the previous chapter. It strains credulity to understand why Sierra Leone has consistently increased its propensity to import costly agricultural products while depleting its reserves because of reliance on products with very volatile prices in international markets.

Over 70 percent of the poor in developing countries live in rural areas, and agriculture is the largest employer in low-income countries. Farm employment accounts for about 60 percent of the labor force, and it produces about 25 percent of GDP for developing countries. During the Doha Round of Talks, developing countries focused on the need to reduce and eliminate trade-distorting subsidies in developed countries and to reduce tariffs for market access to their products.

According to the US Trade Representative (USTR, 2005), focusing on market access is where the biggest gains to global trade liberalization are to be realized.[6] The World Bank estimates that 93 percent of the global benefits from removing distortions in agriculture would come from market access. For developing countries, nearly all the benefit they receive from liberalization is from the global reduction of import tariffs.[7]

After several years of mixed successes, trade negotiations stalled during the Doha Round of negotiations (2001–2015). Recall that the most significant impasse between the developed countries led by the European Union (EU), the United States (US), Canada, and Japan, and the major developing countries led and represented mainly by India, Brazil, China, and South Africa revolved around the maintenance of agricultural subsidies in the EU and the US.

The participants had a very good understanding of the contours of their negotiations. The United States knew that it would have to subscribe to more cuts of farm subsidy.

The European Union had to reduce agricultural tariffs, and the larger emerging countries had to offer deeper industrial and agricultural tariff cuts of their own. Yet none of the players could meet the expectations of their declared versions of liberalized trade.

Beyond the economic theories that tend to glamorize trade liberalization, and righteously so, the political consequences of trade agreements are more objectionable and untidier than they might seem. While some of the leaders of developing countries are not accountable to their voters or citizens, leaders of industrialized economies or Western "democracies" are more accountable to their voters for the positions that they take on trade agreement (review the political economy of international trade policies in the previous chapter). Therefore, they are neither going to infuriate the farmers of their countries who rely on farm subsidies nor annoy their consumers who depend on relatively cheaper agricultural products for food security. Sierra Leone might do well to readjust to the changes that are taking place in the global economy and rationalize why the industrialized economies are protecting their agricultural sector and targeting food security. Table 5.2 and Figure 5.6 show the prospects for Africa's export trade.

Evidently, Africa is losing competitiveness and revenue in global markets. The dominant importers of Africa's exports are reducing their absorption of Africa's exports. While Africa will continue to do well in the mining sector, the agricultural sector is losing competitiveness in the global economy. The future of petroleum exports is precarious because some countries are moving toward cleaner energy with a propensity to utilize domestic supply. The US can use a fraction of its reserves for domestic consumption; for example, increases in domestic oil and natural gas production in the US have reduced African petroleum imports. In fact, there are alternative sources from which countries could fetch petroleum, and Sierra Leone is not a prime exporter of petroleum. Aforesaid, the agrarian sector of the advanced economies is very robust, and Africa cannot possibly gain competitive advantage in the agrarian markets of advanced economies. Of course, there are opportunities for limited exports because of variations in climatic conditions

Table 5.2 Countries with more than 1% share of Africa's total export value (1995–2020)

	US	*China*	*Italy*	*Spain*	*France*	*Germany*	*UK*	*Canada*	*Australia*
1995	14	1	11	6	11	8	5	1	0
2000	18	3	9	7	8	7	6	1	0
2005	20	6	8	7	7	5	5	2	1
2010	15	11	8	6	6	4	4	2	1
2015	5	12	5	6	6	4	4	1	0
2020	5	15	4	6	5	5	3	1	1

Data source: Sebastian Gräff (June 26, 2023), *Visual Capitalist*.

Note: All values are in percentages. *Data are from Harvard University's Atlas of Economic Complexity, the World Bank, and Bloomberg. They are used to track total exports from African countries over the years. Countries receiving a 1% or greater share of total exports have been included, and percentages have been rounded.*

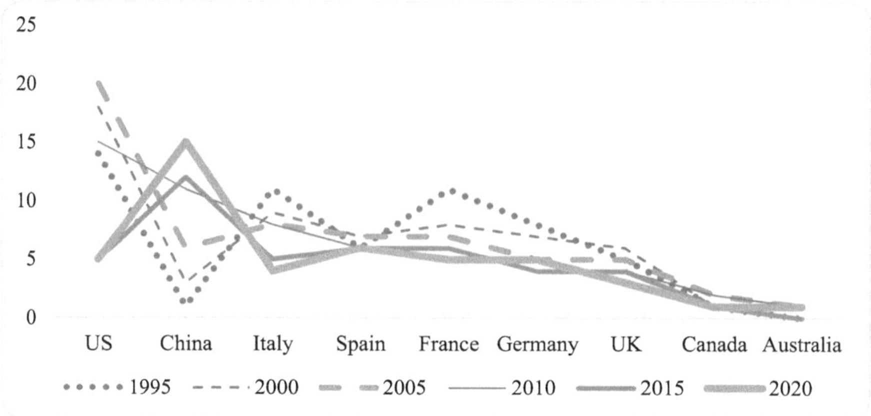

Figure 5.6 Loss of competitiveness and the trajectory of Africa's exports.

Data source: Sebastian Gräff (June 26, 2023), *Visual Capitalist*

and foreign demand. The movement to intra-regional trade has presented attractive prospects, but it must be complemented by innovation for competitiveness in the global economy and improvements in the service sector. The opportunities for competitiveness are heavily dependent on the availability of human capital.

What can Sierra Leone do? The country must diversify its articles of trade through innovation, intensify its efforts to target and obtain food security, desist from unnecessarily importing costly food items that could otherwise be produced locally, and intensify its efforts to create human capital. Perverse trade imbalances deplete the foreign reserves of the country, cause inflation, and diminish the value of the country's currency. Inaccessible foreign markets are beyond the control of a small open economy but increasing domestic production is within the control of the country. Loss of revenue increases the poverty of domestic investment and reduces social spending. Sovereign debt and interest payments become unsustainable (review the previous section for the concomitant risks or threats).

5.3 Cost of unsustainable sovereign debt

African countries that cannot generate income will eventually amass unsustainable sovereign debts, debts that enjoin subsequent generations when they cannot be paid by current governments or generations. Sovereign debts are hardly legally odious because their benefits can partially be transferred to unborn generations. Unsustainable debts are acquired because of the avid consumption of foreign products that could not be used to generate national income while the cost of the debts is increasing. Unsustainable sovereign debts compromise the ability of countries and subsequent generations to grow. Invariably, sovereign debtors do not have control over the interest payments that are most responsible for leakages of financial assets from their national income streams. Leakages make it impossible for governments to make social investments for subsequent growth.

> *A new dataset from the Kiel Institute paints a detailed picture of Africa's government debt. On average, African countries pay much higher interest rates to foreign bondholders and Chinese lenders than to international financial institutions such as the World Bank. The gap in borrowing conditions has grown over the past 10 years, suggesting substantial cross-creditor subsidies . . . .*
>
> *On average private external bonds carry interest rates of 6.2 percent. By contrast, loans by international public institutions like the World Bank, carry a much lower average interest rate, of only around 1 percent. Loans from bilateral, government lenders tend to have somewhat higher interest rates, with Germany and France charging average rates of 1.7 percent, while loans from Japan are the cheapest at an average of 0.5 percent.*[8]
>
> (Trebesch, 2023)

Trebesch (2023) finds that data on African sovereign debt are aggregated and in inaccessible form. The data only provide information on average interest rates vis-à-vis all creditors but not generally on the terms of individual contracts and individual creditors. Individual debt instruments have enormously high interest rates, while many others have little or no interest costs. The differences across different creditors are reportedly large, and the interest rate gap across creditors to African states has widened significantly over the past 20 years.

> In the 2000s, *the interest gap between loans by state-owned lenders and debt raised from foreign bondholders averaged only 0.5 to 1 percentage points, but in recent years it has been around 5 percentage points. The reason is that the coupon on African bonds in the international capital market rose significantly, while public lenders now charge even lower interest rates than they did then . . . .*
>
> *The interest burden on private bonds has risen significantly in recent years and is putting increasing pressure on the national budgets of poorer African countries in particular. It is not so much the difference in interest rates that is remarkable, because public lenders often have a political mandate and the goal of helping African countries to develop. In contrast, private investors focus on financial returns.*
>
> (Trebesch, 2023)

What is particularly worrying is the adoption of what Hyman Minsky considered to be "Ponzi finance" to finance the debt obligations of some African countries – the intertemporal shift of liability from one category to another or borrowing new loans to make interest payments on older ones because of mismatching maturities (see the work of Merhling, 1999, p. 148; Minsky, 1991, and Roubini & Mihm, 2010, p. 51). Some African leaders simultaneously borrow money both from private investors and, on a large scale, from public lenders so that the low-cost loans from the public sector – ultimately taxpayers' money – could be used to cross-finance the high returns of private investors such as hedge funds. The same is true of Chinese loans from African countries, some of which are serviced with the help of cheap development loans from Western countries (Trebesch, 2023). Apart from enjoining subsequent generations, high sovereign debts make government-issued securities very risky and costly.

> *Minsky's Financial Instability Hypothesis had another dimension. He categorized the debtors in a given economy into three groups, according to the nature of the financing they used; hedge borrowers, speculative borrowers, and Ponzi borrowers. Hedge borrowers are those who can make payments on both the interest and the principal of their debts from their current cash flow, Speculative borrowers are those whose income will cover interest payments but not the principal; they have to roll over their debts, selling new debts to pay off old.*
>
> *Ponzi borrowers are the most unstable; their income covers neither the principal nor the interest payments. Their only option is to mortgage their future finances by borrowing still further, hoping for a rise in the value of the assets they purchased with borrowed money.*
>
> (Roubini & Mihm, 2010, p. 51)

Sovereign debts are conventionally considered to be unsustainable when the debt-to-GDP ratio is above 60 percent. In 2020, there were 27 countries in Africa with a debt-to-GDP ratio above 60 percent, an increase of nine countries compared to the previous year.

> *While this number receded to 24 by 2022, compared to other developing countries, those in Africa have been slower to reduce their levels of debt. From a regional perspective, Central Africa is the only region with an average debt level below the 60% threshold in 2022.*
>
> (UNCTAD, 2023b)[9]

Naturally, the cost of servicing debt is positively correlated to debt unsustainability.

UNCTAD's data (information) reveal that the interests of the creditors are not necessarily aligned with the needs of the African continent. The debts that some of the African countries owe generally belong to creditors who are out of the African continent, suggesting that there is more work to be done by regional and continental organizations. This work starts with a lot of introspection and collective housekeeping responsibilities. A logical outcome of unsustainable indebtedness, apart from other problems, is the diminishing value of some local currencies that are evidently inconvertible and without any market share in the global economy. Figure 5.7 and Table 5.3 are indicative of the number of African countries with unsustainable sovereign debt that threatens macroeconomic stability, economic growth, and sustainable development.

Line graph shows the increasing number of African countries with high debt levels.

Apart from the volume and unsustainability of sovereign debt, the ownership of debt is equally important for financial stability and economic growth. Africa's creditor composition is evolving to be very complex. Whereas historically a large share of African debt was held by multilateral or bilateral creditors, such as the Paris Club, today the share of private creditors holding African debt has grown

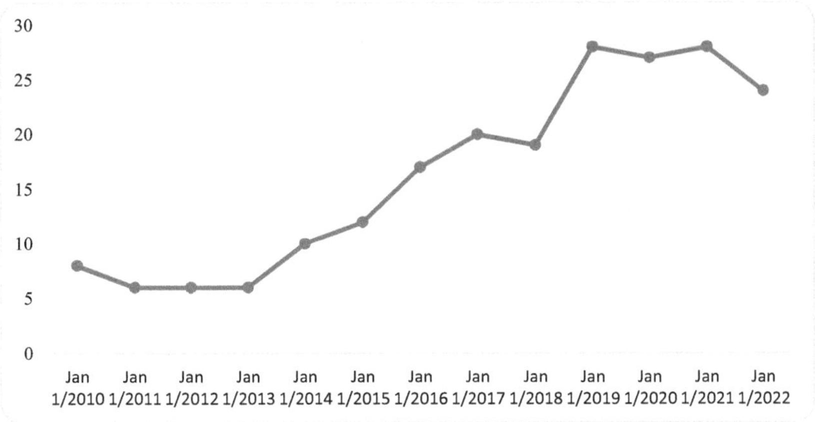

Figure 5.7 Number of African countries with high debt levels.

Source: UN Global Crisis Response Group calculations, based on IMF World Economic Outlook (April 2023)

Note: Public debt exceeding 60% of GDP.

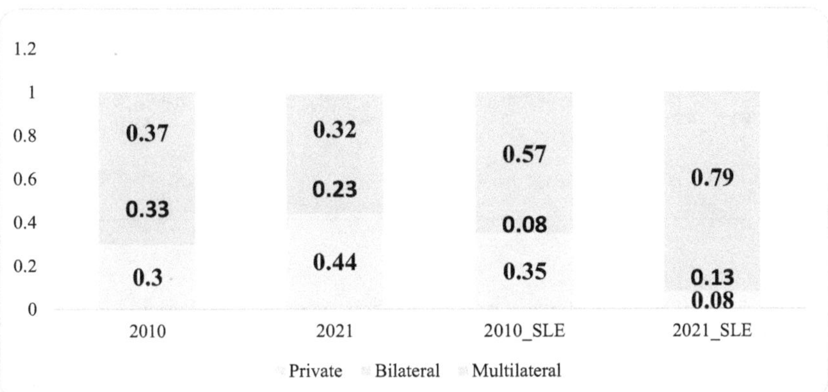

Figure 5.8 Creditor compositions of external debt (Africa and Sierra Leone, SLE).

Data sources: IMF and UN Global Crisis Response Group calculations, based on World Bank International Debt Report 2022

Note: Multilateral lending for Sierra Leone includes the Islamic Development Bank, Arab Bank for Economic Development in Africa, and African Development Bank ordinary capital; *P* = Private, *B* = Bilateral, and default = multilateral.

significantly. In 2010, only 30 percent of Africa's debt was held by private creditors. By 2021, this figure had increased to 44 percent of its debt. The share of private creditors grew faster in Africa than in other developing regions (UNCTAD, 2023a); see also Box 5.3[10] and Figure 5.8. Between 2010 and 2021, Sierra Leone reduced its composition of private sources of sovereign debt.

Box 5.4 Sources and threats of Sovereign Debt

[The sources of debt] raise several issues. First, a timely and orderly restructuring of Africa's debt is limited by differing interests and creditor concerns. Since private creditors may be banks or other market-based lenders, their interest in extracting more market-based returns differs from more traditional, concessional-based financing. Having a bigger share of private creditors also raises the price of African debt since many private loans are made on market terms. Second, coordination among creditors is limited since there is no formal creditor coordination mechanism to bring together all private actors. And third, many creditors and nations are reluctant to undergo debt-sustainability talks since the stigma associated with restructuring could limit a country's ability to find sources of future funding. In the case of banks or other private creditors, the potential of losses for interested parties also lessens the likelihood of debt restructuring agreements.

As a percentage of GDP, Africa's share of external debt has risen from approximately 19 percent in 2010 to nearly 29 percent in 2022. Simultaneously, its external debt as a share of exports has risen from 74.5 percent to 140 percent over the same period. This latter point is important in Africa since many countries are reliant on exports, especially exports from the extractive industries with little value-added. The imbalance between debt and exports has made it more difficult for Africa to service its external debt as its ability to obtain foreign currency has grown at a rate lower than its debt-servicing costs.

Source: UNCTAD (2023a), see fn. 10.

Under normal circumstances, bad debts do not generate revenues (income) or returns. Therefore, when countries embark on the solicitation and receipt of sovereign debts that do not generate returns, they are accumulating bad and odious debts (liberally defined). The revenue stream of the incurrence of debt must be apparent and predictable, meaning that debtors and creditors alike have contractual responsibilities to ensure that loans can be repaid without hardship. At the micro level, character, capacity, capital, conditions, and collateral mean something to creditors. Sovereign debts take a life of their own, partly because they are binding on subsequent generations. Of course, there are exigent circumstances that do not fall neatly into a paradigm of specific rules. These exigent hocks, which are usually the results of natural disasters or health crises, are unavoidable occurrences and usually require concessionary funding of their own.

Invariably the magnitude of funding may also be contingent on the quality of investment decisions preceding the occurrences of natural adversities; for example, the neglect of healthcare expenditures to save lives before crisis periods, and poor environmental planning that results in mudslides and flooding are costly failures of apathy and inadequate foresight. Migration and urbanization have placed unreasonable pressures on the use of environmental resources. That is, policy failures interact with natural adversities in a very costly way that is not entirely surprising. The net result of inadequate foresight is the increasing accumulation of sovereign debt because of inadequate and untimely investments. Consequently, the allocation and sequencing of government expenditures is critically important to prevent explosive and unsustainable levels of public indebtedness. The acquisition of public revenue and national saving and investment are unavoidable aspects of economic growth and development.

Table 5.3 shows unsustainable levels of sovereign debt that threaten current and future economic growth and development of some countries in Africa. Clearly, the indebted countries have no control over the cost of their debts, but they do have control over some of the factors that lead them to contract odious debts that enjoin subsequent generations.

Between 2010 and 2021, Sierra Leone reduced its composition of private sources of sovereign debt (Figure 5.8), but it increased its share of multilateral debt, and its indebtedness has progressively increased from Le 6.03 trillion in 2016 to Le30.71trillion in 2020 (see Figure 5.9). As should be expected, increases in the level of debt positively correlate with increases in debt service on total external debt as a percentage of export of goods and services (see Figure 5.10). Sierra Leone does not have control over its cost of debt once its sovereign debt has been contracted. Revenue and debt challenges bring into sharper focus spending on social programs and preparations to deal with natural disasters.

Table 5.3 African countries with the highest debt-to-GDP ratios (2021)

Country	*Ratio*	*Country*	*Ratio*
Eritrea	171.5	Guinea-Bissau	79.1
Cabo Verde	160.7	Rwanda	74.8
Mozambique	133.6	Burundi	72.4
Angola	103.7	Gabon	72.1
Mauritius	101	Senegal	71.9
Zambia	101	Sierra Leone	71.1
Republic of Congo	85.4	Namibia	69.9
Ghana	83.5	Kenya	69.7
The Gambia	82.3	South Africa	68.8
Seychelles	81.9	South Sudan	64.4

Data source: Business Insider Africa, Benson (2022)

Benson, E.A. (2022). Twenty countries with the highest debt-to-GDP ratio in Africa. *Business Insider Africa*.

Note: Debt-to-GDP ratio greater than 60%. Sierra Leone's domestic debt amounted to 20 percent of GDP at the end of 2009. Around 80 percent of outstanding domestic debt is in the form of treasury instruments (IMF).

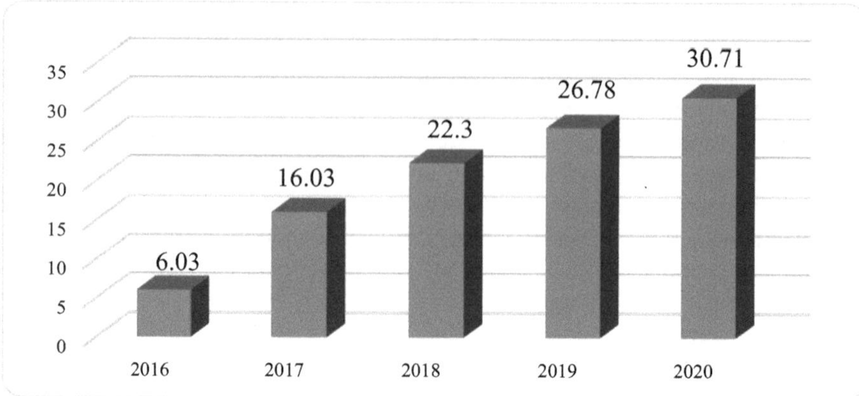

Figure 5.9 Trend in total public debt 2016–2020 (Le trillions).

Source: Public Debt Bulletin 2020

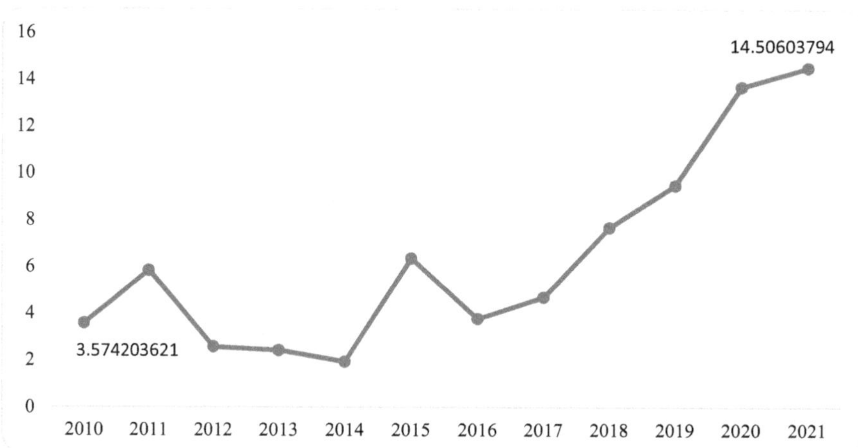

Figure 5.10 Sierra Leone's debt service on total external debt as a percentage of export of goods and services (2010–2021).

Data source: World Bank's WDI (2023)

Note: Exports of goods and services represent the value of all goods and other market services provided to the rest of the world. They include the value of merchandise, freight, insurance, transport, travel, royalties, license fees, and other services, such as communication, construction, financial, information, business, personal, and government services. They exclude compensation of employees and investment income (formerly called factor services) and transfer payments. Data are in constant local currency (export of goods and services evaluated at constant 2015 US$). Total debt service is the sum of principal repayments and interest actually paid in currency, goods, or services on long-term debt, interest paid on short-term debt, and repayments (repurchases and charges) to the IMF. Data are in current US dollars.

5.4 Pandemics and health infrastructure

Africa's increased debt is not solely a result of the conflict in Europe. Indeed, the additional need to source personal protective equipment (PPE), pharmaceutical products, medicines, and vaccines, amongst other goods, during the COVID-19 pandemic became a major impetus for higher levels of debt (UNCTAD, 2023a).

Pandemics have extraterritorial origins. They come from outside the frontiers of a country and might quickly spread to other countries with deadly effects. They are large-scale outbreaks of infectious diseases that can greatly increase morbidity and mortality over a wide geographic area and cause significant economic, social, and political disruptions. Evidence suggests that the likelihood of pandemics has increased over the past century because of increased global travel and integration, urbanization, changes in land use, and greater exploitation of the natural environment (Jones et al., 2008; Morse, 1995). Table 5.4 gives an historical context of pandemics and their inevitability. Pandemics have a historical presence, and they appear to be increasing in frequency.

The scientific literature makes a distinction between an epidemic and a pandemic. An epidemic is defined as "the occurrence in a community or region of cases of an illness . . . clearly in excess of normal expectancy" (Porta, 2014). A pandemic is defined as "an epidemic occurring over a very wide area, crossing international boundaries, and usually affecting a large number of people" (Porta, 2014). Pandemics are, therefore, identified by their geographic scale rather than the severity of illness (Madhav et al., 2017, p. 315).

Over the years, the international community has made progress toward the mitigation of the impact of pandemics. The 2003 severe acute respiratory syndrome (SARS) pandemic and growing concerns about the threat posed by avian influenza led many countries to devise pandemic plans (U.S. Department of Health and Human Services, 2005). Delayed reporting of early SARS cases also led the World Health Assembly to update the International Health Regulations (IHR) to compel all World

Table 5.4 Incidence of pandemics (1957–2019)

Starting year	*Event*	*Geographic extent*
1957	Asian flu influenza	Global
1968	Hong Kong flu influenza pandemic	Global
1981	HIV/AIDS pandemic	Global
2003	SARS pandemic	4 continents, 37countries
2009	Swine flu influenza pandemic	Global
2012	MERS epidemic	22 countries
2013	West Africa Ebola virus disease epidemic	10 countries
2015	Zika virus pandemic	76 countries
2019	COVID-19 pandemic	Global

Source: Madhav et al. (pp. 317–318)

Note: The West Africa Ebola virus outbreak occurred from 2013 to 2016, but the peak and international response efforts began in 2014; see the source for earlier occurrences, dating back to the Middle Ages, fatalities associated with epidemics and pandemics, and partial economic consequences of epidemics and pandemics (author's inclusion of COVID-19).

Health Organization member states to meet specific standards for detecting, reporting on, and responding to outbreaks (WHO, 2005; Madhav et al., 2017, p. 315).

Despite the proactive measures to defray the social costs of pandemics, significant gaps and challenges exist in global pandemic preparedness. Vulnerable economies with poor healthcare facilities are naturally exposed to danger. Scientists have concluded that pandemic risk is driven by the combined effects of spark risk (the likely source of a pandemic) and spread risk (the likelihood that a pandemic will be broadly diffused through human populations). Geographic regions like Central and West Africa have been identified as regions with a high spark risk (Madhave et al., p. 316), meaning that countries in the regions should embark on enhanced safeguards to protect their populations from deadly pandemics (see Box 5.5 for the origins of pandemics).

Progress toward meeting the IHR has been uneven, and many countries have been unable to meet basic requirements for compliance (Fischer & Katz, 2013, and WHO, 2014). Multiple outbreaks, notably the 2014 West Africa Ebola epidemic, have exposed gaps related to the timely detection of disease, availability of basic care, tracing of contacts, quarantine and isolation procedures, and preparedness outside the health sector, including global coordination and response mobilization (Moon et al., 2015; Pathmanathan et al., 2014). These gaps are especially evident in resource-limited settings and have posed challenges during relatively localized epidemics, with dire implications for what may happen during a full-fledged global pandemic (Madhav et al., 2017, p. 315).

A preparedness index is usually utilized as a stress-test indicator of a country's defenses against the spark and spread of pandemics. An influential index has been provided by Oppenheim et al. (2017), which also shows variations in global institutional readiness to detect and respond to a large-scale outbreak of infectious disease. Box 5.6 provides examples of pandemic preparedness and response activities by time periods. It is believed that the contents reflect the core capacity metrics of IHR and other publicly accessible cross-national indicators.

Box 5.5 The origins of pandemics

Most new pandemics have originated through the "zoonotic" transmission of pathogens from animals to humans (Murphy, 1998; Woolhouse & Gowtage-Sequeria, 2005), *and the next pandemic is likely to be a zoonosis as well. Zoonoses enter into human populations from both domesticated animals (such as farmed swine or poultry) and wildlife. Many historically significant zoonoses were introduced through increased human–animal interaction following domestication, and potentially high-risk zoonoses (including avian influenzas) continue to emerge from livestock production systems (Van Boeckel et al., 2012;* Wolfe et al., 2007*). Some pathogens (including Ebola) have emerged from wildlife reservoirs and entered into human populations through the hunting and consumption of wild species (such as bushmeat), the wild animal trade, and other contact with wildlife (Pike et al., 2010;* Wolfe et al., 2007*).*

Urbanization and Spread Risk

After a spark or importation, the risk that a pathogen will spread within a population is influenced by pathogen-specific factors (including genetic adaptation and mode of transmission) and human population-level factors (such as the density of the population and the susceptibility to infection; patterns of movement driven by travel, trade, and migration; and speed and effectiveness of public health surveillance and response measures). . . . (Sands et al., 2016).

Dense concentrations of population, especially in urban centers harboring overcrowded informal settlements, can act as foci for disease transmission and accelerate the spread of pathogens (Neiderud, 2015).

Moreover, social inequality, poverty, and their environmental correlates can increase individual susceptibility to infection significantly (Farmer, 1996). Comorbidities, malnutrition, and caloric deficits weaken an individual's immune system, while environmental factors such as lack of clean water and adequate sanitation amplify transmission rates and increase morbidity and mortality (Toole & Waldman, 1990). *Collectively, all these factors suggest that marginalized populations, including refugees and people living in urban slums and informal settlements, likely face elevated risks of morbidity and mortality during a pandemic.*

Source: Madhav et al. (pp. 318–320)

Box 5.6 Stress-test indicators

Prepandemic period (before a pandemic starts)

- Stockpile building
- Continuity planning
- Public health workforce training
- Simulation exercises
- Risk transfer mechanism setup
- Situational awareness[a]

Spark period (as a pandemic starts)

- Initial outbreak detection
- Pathogen characterization or laboratory confirmation
- Risk communication and community engagement
- Animal disease control
- Contact tracing, quarantine, and isolation
- Situational awareness[a]

Spread period (after a pandemic starts)

- Global pandemic declaration
- Risk communications
- Contact tracing, quarantine, and isolation
- Social distancing
- Stockpile deployment
- Vaccine or antiviral administration
- Care and treatment
- Situational awareness[a]

a/Situational awareness includes passive and active animal and human disease surveillance and monitoring of public health facilities and resources.

Source: Madhav et al. (p. 326)

Situational awareness is critically recurrent and applicable to all phases – prepandemic, spark, and spread. It can be contextually defined as having an accurate, up-to-date view of potential or ongoing infectious disease threats (including through traditional surveillance in humans and animals), and the resources (human, financial, informational, and institutional) available to manage those threats (ASPR, 2014).

> *Well-prepared countries have effective public institutions, strong economies, and adequate investment in the health sector. They have built specific competencies critical to detecting and managing disease outbreaks, including surveillance, mass vaccination, and risk communications. Poorly prepared countries may suffer from political instability, weak public administration, inadequate resources for public health, and gaps in fundamental outbreak detection and response systems.*
>
> (Madhav et al., p. 320)

In terms of effective communications, the effects of poverty and urbanization are crippling. Poverty retards or prevents the acquisition of human capital, and it equally retards or prevents the attainment of health security. The urbanized environment in the Western area (see Chapter 1 of this book) is ripe for the incubation of superspreaders of diseases. Urbanization and population density pose serious health threats to the country. The socio-economic consequences of epidemics and pandemics on underdeveloped economies are nontrivial. Hazardous environmental conditions are conducive to the spread of diseases. The persistence of slums, unresponsive health systems, higher prevalence of comorbidities, weaker sanitation, and aging populations are enhancing factors (Arimah, 2010; UNDESA, 2015).

> *When pandemics cause large morbidity and mortality spikes, they are much more likely to overwhelm health systems. Overwhelmed health systems and other indirect effects may contribute to a 2.3-fold increase in all-cause mortality during pandemics, although attribution of the causative agent is difficult (Simonsen et al., 2013). If indirect deaths are taken into account, the average annual global deaths from influenza pandemics could be greater than 520,000, although there is a significant uncertainty in the estimate.*
>
> (Madhav et al., p. 323)

During the 2014 West Africa Ebola epidemic, lack of routine care for malaria, HIV/AIDS, and tuberculosis led to an estimated 10,600 additional deaths in Guinea, Liberia, and Sierra Leone (Parpia et al., 2016). This indirect death toll nearly equaled the 11,300 deaths directly caused by Ebola in those countries. Additionally, diversion of funds, medical resources, and personnel led to a 30 percent decrease in routine childhood immunization rates in affected countries (UNDP, 2014). Healthcare deficiencies are exacerbated by the lack of mechanisms for risk transfer. The underdeveloped economies seldom have robust opportunities for risk pooling, or the availability of private and public insurance to manage the cost of epidemic and pandemic risks.

Outbreaks of epidemics and pandemics naturally cause closures of facilities and trepidations of contracting illnesses. These phenomena occurred during the outbreak of the 2014 Ebola epidemic in West Africa. A study of 45 public facilities in Guinea found that the Ebola outbreak led to a 31 percent decrease in outpatient visits for routine maternal and child health services (Barden-O'Fallon et al., 2015). Among children under age five years, hospitals witnessed a 60 percent decrease in visits for diarrhea and a 58 percent decrease in visits for acute respiratory illness (ARI), while health centers saw a 25 percent decrease in visits for diarrhea and a 23 percent decrease in visits for ARI. In Sierra Leone, visits to public facilities for reproductive health care fell by as much as 40 percent during the outbreak (UNDP, 2014).

Pandemics cause monetary and fiscal disturbances that threaten economic growth and sustainable development. The disturbances have costs that are associated with the implementation of social distancing, quarantine, replacement of medical personnel, medical equipments, diminution of a labor force, provision of facilities, and loss of public revenue. Achonu et al. (2005) characterize disturbances in terms of short-term fiscal shocks and long-term damage to economic growth. Herstein et al. (2016) direct attention to the cost of medical supplies, personal protective equipment, and drugs as epidemics persist.

Countries that are already experiencing shortfalls in public revenue come under fiscal pressures during the outbreaks of epidemics and pandemics, for example, response costs surged, economic activity slowed down, and quarantines and curfews reduced government capacity to collect revenue during the 2014 West Africa Ebola epidemic in Liberia (World Bank, 2014). Though high-income countries may provide official development assistance during the inceptive phases of epidemics, they may be constrained to do so during existence of pandemics. Accordingly, underdeveloped economies must not rely on high-income countries for unlimited financial support to control pandemics. The costs of containing epidemics and pandemics are astronomical. Figure 5.11 shows the cross section of costs incurred by

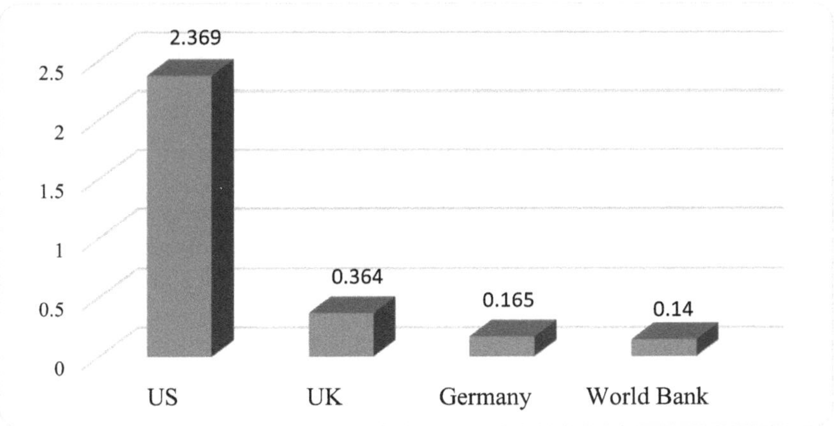

Figure 5.11 Cost of the response to the Ebola epidemic between 2014 and 2015 (US$ billion).
Data source: US' Centers for Disease Control and Prevention (CDC)

the US, the UK, Germany, and the World Bank to respond to the Ebola epidemic between 2014 and 2015. Overall, more than $3.6 billion was spent to fight the epidemic by the end of 2015.

Proactive planning and resource availability are indispensable to the preparedness of nations in a highly integrated world that could be shut down at any time. Because rich and poorer Sierra Leoneans might not be able to access the healthcare services of developing and industrialized countries during pandemics, public investment in health care is no longer optional. A baseline national health security starts with generating employment, reducing poverty, decentralizing medical facilities, and fixing the problem of undesirable urbanization. In an era of looming pandemics, public finance of health care can no longer be disregarded, except if the policymakers of a country are strong believers of the Malthusian theorem of doom. I have discussed this theory elsewhere in the context of the COVID-19 pandemic (Warburton, 2021).

The virulence of pandemics, their global threats, and the financial costs that are associated with their attenuation or control, necessitate a collective response to preparedness. Oversight of lethargic and noncompliant countries should not be casually dismissed and taken for granted, especially when countries are in a high-risk zone. The punishing global costs of pandemics are just too staggering to be disregarded.

Lack of preparedness leads to discombobulated responses, untimely interventions, unnecessary fatalities, and increasing costs.

> *The initial response to the [Ebola] outbreak [in Sierra Leone] was characterized by confusion, chaos and denial. While a country can be overwhelmed by a serious outbreak, a situation in which WHO fails to mobilize the assistance needed to help a national government take control of an epidemic is unusual. The rest of the international community was, meanwhile, slow to rally. The window of opportunity to contain the outbreak through conventional control approaches closed, and the outbreak became a humanitarian crisis.*
>
> (Ross et al., 2017, p. 2)

Inadequate healthcare facilities, poverty, and comorbidities have negative external effects.

> *The reduction in access to healthcare services because of Ebola caused an estimated 10,600 additional deaths due to untreated conditions in Guinea, Liberia, and Sierra Leone 17,300 children lost one or both parents to Ebola. More than 33 weeks of education were lost due to school closures.*
>
> (Centers for Disease Control and Prevention)[11]

Incomes of poorer countries are depressed. The Ebola epidemic is estimated to have reduced GDP growth by 2.3 percent in Guinea, 2.2 percent in Liberia, and 1.7 percent in Sierra Leone (UNDP, 2014, p. 16). The World Bank estimated further macroeconomic losses. It is estimated that epidemic increased the budget deficits of Liberia, Guinea, and Sierra Leone by $500 million in 2014 (World Bank, 2014). The decline in business activity and in imports, combined with declines in employment, reduced taxes on incomes, sales, and external trade.

The Ebola epidemic mentally prepared Sierra Leoneans to deal with the COVID-19 pandemic. The country had not been exposed to an epidemic for over five decades. As such, it was least prepared to deal with the Ebola epidemic in an environment of inadequate health facilities. Sierra Leone reported its first case of the COVID-19 pandemic on March 31, 2020, after observing the devastating effects of the pandemic on developed economies. The country was merely equipped with knowledge of the Ebola epidemic and COVID-19 pandemic, for which it promptly made a timely decision to restrict traveling from abroad in addition to lockdowns and social distancing. The effects of the pandemic on the country were less destructive than Ebola, and much less than the effects on the epicenters of the advanced economies (see also the work of Srivatsa & Mchenga, 2020). Significantly, the idea that prompt responses are required to drastically limit the virulent effects of epidemics and pandemics was validated – an idea that would have reduced the fatalities and cost of the Ebola epidemic.

The COVID-19 pandemic also disrupted the macroeconomic stability of the country. It affected all sectors of the economy (see Figure 5.12). About 30 percent of households reduced daily intake of meals, farmers reduced their inputs by 50 percent, businesses lost profits,[12] firms lost consumers, and about 50 percent shutdown on impact. The next section looks at the instability of long-term investment when an economy is precarious.

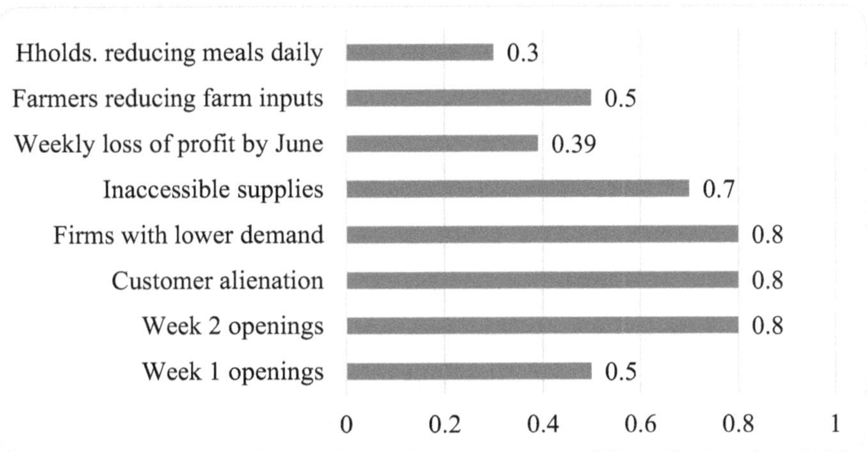

Figure 5.12 Partial effects of the COVID-19 pandemic on firms and households.

Data source: Merrigi et al. (2020, pp. 1–14)

Note: Five weeks of data collection, spanning April 30–June 6, 2020, were used for this study, and the values reflect national averages and changes over time. In total, 4,515 unique people were called (Phone Survey), of which 2,261 unique respondents (approximately 50%) answered the phone as willing participants of the survey. Data collection was made on a rolling basis. Respondents answered various questions that were intended to conceptualize the results of pre-COVID-19 and COVID-19 time dynamics. The first case of COVID-19 was reported in Sierra Leone on March 31. During the duration of the survey, the Government of Sierra Leone implemented two national lockdowns (April 5–7 and May 3–5) and a series of announced restrictions (effective on April 11) that included restrictions on inter-district movements. The survey covered five different topics: (i) economic indicators, (ii) food security, (iii) COVID-19 knowledge and behaviors, (iv) health-seeking behaviors, and (v) migration. Figure 5.12 is representative of extrapolated information from the first 14 pages (about two months after the pandemic); *Hholds* = Households.

5.5 Sustainability of long-term investments

In Chapter 2, I presented a workable definition of FDI and highlighted its importance. It was defined as the sum of equity capital, reinvestment of earnings, and long-term capital with an ownership of 10 percent or more voting shares that flows into a foreign country. FDI is very important for underdeveloped economies with a paucity of national saving and insufficient human and physical capital. Unlike capital inflows that are highly reversible, FDI is relatively long-lasting. This section discusses the push factors of FDI flows, or those factors abroad that could prevent FDI from flowing into Sierra Leone. Though FDI has been flowing into Sierra Leone and other countries of Africa, long-term capital flows have competing avenues, and Figure 5.13 shows alternative avenues that compete with Africa for long-term flows.

Notably, flows to Africa and other regions have fluctuated in the past. However, FDI flows to Africa dropped by 44 percent between 2021 and 2022. Europe also lost a considerable number of inflows (107%). FDI flows to the Latin American and Caribbean (LAC) countries increased by 56 percent. North America and the developed economies lost 26 percent and 7 percent, respectively. Developing economies gained 4 percent, but long-term flows to Asia remained constant. The top recipients of FDI flows are rather consistent – the US, China, Hong Kong, Singapore, Canada, Brazil, Australia, and India (UNCTAD, 2023, p. 8).

Figure 5.13 shows that African countries must contend with Latin America, Asia, and emerging economies to attract long-term capital inflows. That is, it is not certain that the African countries, including Sierra Leone, will consistently receive long-term inflows to augment national saving and the inadequacy of physical and human capital. In fact, for countries that are not already receiving a significant share of FDI, the long-term prospect of receiving long-term investments could be very doleful. The top recipients normally have relatively advanced human capital, a reasonable amount

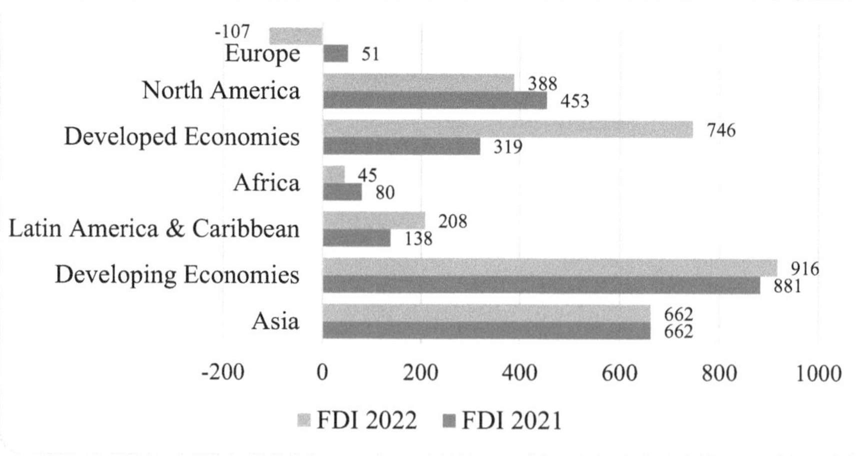

Figure 5.13 FDI inflows, by region, 2021 and 2022 (US$ billions).

Source: UNCTAD, FDI/MNE database (www.unctad.org/fdistatistics).

UNCTAD, *World Investment Report* (2023, p. 5)

of political stability, and a stronger reputation for adherence to the rule of law. Their domestic firms tend to be very innovative, and their consumers are informed and demanding (review Porter's Diamond model in Chapter 2 of this book).

Though Africa is rich in natural resources, there are push factors in the form of relatively high taxes (see Chapter 2), macroeconomic instability, loss of assets due to nonenforceability of contracts, and physical destruction of assets caused by armed conflicts (see Box 5.7). The reduction of investment risk is essential to attract long-term investment in the future. Sierra Leone stands to considerably benefit from long-term investment (see Figure 5.14).

Box 5.7 Inward FDI in Africa

The main factors motivating FDI into Africa in recent decades appear to have been the availability of natural resources in the host countries (e.g., investment in the oil industries of Nigeria and Angola) and, to a lesser extent, the size of the domestic economy. The reasons for the lackluster FDI in most other African countries are most likely the same factors that have contributed to a generally low rate of private investment to GDP across the continent. Studies have attributed this to the fact that, while gross returns on investment can be very high in Africa, the effect is more than counterbalanced by high taxes and a significant risk of capital losses. As for the risk factors, analysts now agree that three of them may be particularly pertinent: macroeconomic instability, loss of assets due to nonenforceability of contracts, and physical destruction caused by armed conflicts.

The second of these may be particularly discouraging to investors domiciled abroad, since they are generally excluded from the informal networks of agreements and enforcement that develop in the absence of a transparent judicial system.

Several other factors holding back FDI have been proposed in recent studies, notably the perceived sustainability of national economic policies, poor quality of public services, and closed trade regimes. Even where the obstacles to FDI do not seem insurmountable, investors may have powerful incentives to adopt a wait-and-see attitude. FDI (and especially greenfield investment) contains an important irreversible element, so where investors' risk perception is heightened the inducement would have to be massive to make them undertake FDI as opposed to deferring their decision. This problem is compounded where a deficit of democracy, or of other kinds of political legitimacy, makes the system government prone to sudden changes. Finally, a lack of effective regional trade integration efforts has been singled out as a factor. Due to this, national markets remained small and grew at a modest pace (and, in some cases, they even contracted).

Source: OECD (2002), *Foreign Direct Investment for Development: Maximizing benefits, minimizing costs*, p. 8

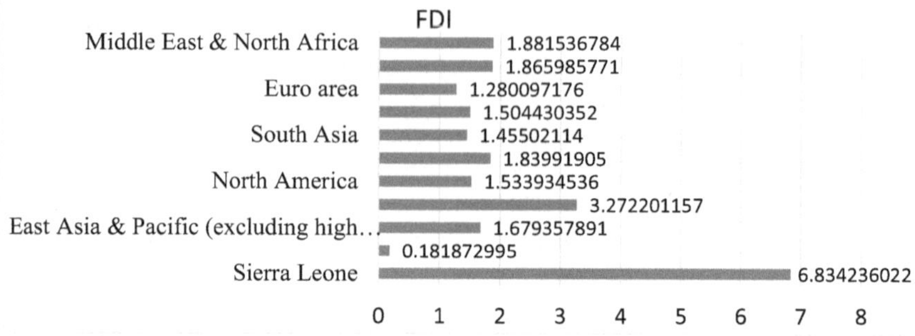

Figure 5.14 Average net inflows of FDI as a percentage of GDP (2017–2022).

Data source: World Bank's World Development Indicators (2023)

Note: Foreign direct investments are the net inflows of investment to acquire a lasting management interest (10 percent or more of voting stock) in an enterprise operating in an economy other than that of the investor. It is the sum of equity capital, reinvestment of earnings, other long-term capital, and short-term capital as shown in the balance of payments. This series shows net inflows (new investment inflows less disinvestment) in the reporting economy from foreign investors and is divided by GDP. High-income countries are excluded from the East Asia & Pacific cohort.

The average net inflows of FDI as a percentage of GDP into Sierra Leone extravagantly exceed the regional flows of FDI to other regions between 2017 and 2022 (Figure 5.14). This inflow may not be sustainable if other countries or regions outcompete Sierra Leone for long-term capital inflows. It could also be disrupted by external shocks. The asymmetry of net long-term investment suggests that the country financially benefited from long-term investments if profits were not disproportionately repatriated. To be clear, the FDI flows to regions are aggregated, which means that skewed receipt of average net FDI inflows could have been redistributed among the countries in a regional cohort. Yet the value of the inflow is outstanding by any measure. Therefore, a significant diversion of long-term investment could be problematic for economic growth.

FDI flows are highly contingent on geopolitical stability, which was discussed in the introductory section of this chapter, and screening for national security purposes. As such, the discussion will not be repeated here. It is noteworthy that external crises, natural or man-made, could ultimately affect the volume and direction of long-term investment. However, some developed economies are now introducing new layers of regulation to screen FDI flows for security reasons and tax windfall profits of investment. It is currently unclear how these newer measures will ultimately determine the direction of long-term investments.

Notes

1 *Several historical volatility measurements have been used in the literature. Economists have employed measures based on the price levels. They have focused on the standard deviation of prices or of logarithmic prices or on the coefficient of variation which expresses the standard deviation as a percentage of the sample mean. The main*

advantage of the latter is that it does not depend on the unit of measurement. Second, some measures take into account the fact that most economic series exhibit some form of trend and permit the removal of trend movements in the volatility measures. In that context, some authors use the standard deviation of the first difference in the logarithmic value of prices (Clem, 1985; and Gilbert, 2006) (Houchet-Bourdon, p. 11). Others controversially estimate a volatility model for conditional variance of innovation derived from the auto-regressive process of a time series by using a GARCH (Generalized Auto Regressive Conditional Heteroscedasticity) (Bollerslev, 1986).

2 *For example, during the food price crisis of 2007/08, Argentina, a major wheat producer, temporarily raised export taxes on wheat and other agricultural products; and India and Viet Nam, two key rice exporters, limited rice exports*. In 2010, *key exporters temporarily restricted wheat, maize, and barley exports. More recently, in the context of the pandemic and the war in Ukraine, many countries have implemented food and fertilizer export restrictions* (UNCTAD, 2023b, p. 5).

3 See *Strait of Hormuz: Assessing the threat to oil flows through the Strait*. Strauss Center for International Security and Law, The University of Texas at Austin, www.strauss-center.org/strait-of-hormuz-about-the-strait/

4 The dispute started when the European Union sanctioned (banned) oil exports from Iran to Europe on January 23, 2012, to deter Iran from continuing with their nuclear program. Oil exports accounted for about 80 percent of Iranian public revenue; see "Iran threatens new war games in the oil lanes of the Gulf." *The Telegraph* (January 6, 2012). On December 27, 2011, Iranian Vice President, Mohammad-Reza Rahimi, threatened to close the Strait of Hormuz. In late April 2019, Iran threatened to block shipping through the Strait if it was barred from using the strategic waterway and sanctioned by the US. The threat sparked off episodic military hostilities in the region and preparations for war by major stakeholders.

5 See *Managing commodity price volatility in commodity dependent developing countries* (UNCTAD, 2023b) for a comprehensive discussion of the triggers of commodity price volatility.

6 See USTR (2005, October). Facts on the Doha Round. Doha Development Agenda Policy Brief. *www.ustr.gov*

7 *Ibid*.

8 *China plays a special role as a creditor. Although the loans are also granted by the state or through state-owned banks, Beijing charges on average 3.2 percent interest rates and therefore significantly more than the other state creditors. The analysis is based on the new and freely accessible Africa Debt Database (Who Lends to Africa and How? Introducing the Africa Debt Database) of the Kiel Institute for the World Economy. It contains more than 7,400 loans and bonds from over 50 different public and private external lenders between the years 2000 and 2020 with a total volume of USD 790 billion* (Trebesch, 2023).

9 See *A World of debt*, https://unctad.org/publication/world-of-debt/regional-stories

10 Loc. cit.

11 See www.cdc.gov/vhf/ebola/outbreaks/2014-west-africa/cost-of-ebola.html.

12 The business respondents are typically small and informal. Petty traders and processors of agricultural goods are about 45 percent and 15 percent, respectively. The majority (64%) of wageworkers are employed by the government, and 14 percent are employed as construction workers (Merrigi et al., p. 4).

Further reading

Achonu, C., Laporte, A. & Gardam, M.A. (2005). The financial impact of controlling a respiratory virus outbreak in a teaching hospital: Lessons learned from SARS. *Canadian Journal of Public Health*, 96(1): 52–54.

African Development Bank. (2023). Sierra Leone economic outlook. www.afdb.org/en/countries-west-africa-sierra-leone/sierra-leone-economic-outlook

Aizenman, J. & Marion, N. (1993). Policy uncertainty, persistence and growth. *Review of International Economics*, 1(9), 145–163.

Arimah, B.C. (2010). The face of urban poverty: Explaining the prevalence of slums in developing countries. In B. Jo, G.-K. Basudeh & K. Ravi (Eds.), *Urbanization and development: Multidisciplinary perspectives* (pp. 143–164). Oxford University Press.

ASPR (Assistant Secretary for Preparedness and Response). (2014). *Public Health and Medical Situational Awareness Strategy. Strategy document for situational awareness implementation plan.* U.S. Department of Health and Human Services.

Balcombe, K. (2009). *The nature and determinants of volatility in agricultural prices: An empirical study from 1962–2008. A report.* Food and Agriculture Organization of the United Nations.

Barden-O'Fallon, J., Barry, M.A., Brodish, P. & Hazerjian, J. (2015, August). Rapid assessment of Ebola-related implications for reproductive, maternal, newborn, and child health service delivery and utilization in Guinea. *PLoS Currents Outbreaks*.

Barrett, P., Das, S., Magistretti, G., Pugacheva, E. & Wingender, P. (2021). *After-effects of the COVID-19 pandemic: Prospects for medium-term economic damage* (IMF Working Paper WP/21/203). IMF.

Benson, E.A. (2022, March). Twenty countries with the highest debt-to-GDP ratio in Africa. Business Insider Africa. https://africa.businessinsider.com/local/markets/20-countries-with-the-highest-debt-to-gdp-ratio-in-africa/8qdmrsq

Blanchard, O.J., Eugenio, C. & Summers, L. (2015). *Inflation and activity – two explorations and their monetary policy implications* (NBER Working Paper 21726). National Bureau of Economic Research.

Bollerslev, T. (1986). Generalized autoregressive conditional heteroskedasticity. *Journal of Econometrics*, 31(3), 307–27.

Bteish, C., Jain, S., Mowatt, R., Newiak, M. & Saffa, M. (n.d.) *The longer-term impact of the COVID-19 crisis and mitigating policies for Sierra Lone*. IMF.

Chandy, L., Kato, H. & Kharas, H. (Eds.) (2015). *The last mile in ending extreme poverty*. Brookings Institution Press.

Charu, V., et al. (2011). Burden of the A/H1N1, pandemic in Mexico: A comparison of deaths and years of life lost to seasonal influenza. *Clinical Infectious Diseases*, 53(10), 985–993.

Chen, W., Mico, M. & Malhar, N. (2019). The *global economic recovery 10 years after the 2008 financial crisis* (IMF Working Paper 2019/83). International Monetary Fund.

Clem, A. (1985, June). Commodity price volatility: Trends during 1975–84. Monthly Labor Review.

Cohn, S.K. (2007). The black death and the burning of Jews. Past and Present, 196(1), 3–36.

Colizza, V., Barrat, A., Barthelemy, M., Valleron, A.J. & Vespignani, A. (2007). Modeling the Worldwide spread of pandemic influenza: Baseline case and containment interventions. *PLoS Medicine,* 4(1), 95–110.

Dehn, J., Gilbert, C.L. & Varangis, P. (2005). Agricultural commodity price volatility. In J. Aizenman & B. Pinto (eds) *Managing economic volatility and crises: A practitioner's guide*. Cambridge University Press.

De Schutter, O. (2010, September). *Food commodities speculation and food price crises: Regulation to reduce the risks of price volatility* (Briefing note 02). United Nations Special Rapporteur on the Right to Food. www.srfood.org/

European Commission. (2009). *Historical price volatility. Directorate – General for Agriculture and Rural Development.*

Farmer, P. (1996). Social inequalities and emerging infectious diseases. *Emerging Infectious Diseases*, 2(4), 259–269.

Fischer, J.E. & Katz, R. (2013). Moving forward to 2014: Global IHR (2005) implementation. *Biosecurity and Bioterrorism: Biodefense Strategy, Practice, and Science*, 11(2), 153–156. [PubMed]
Gilbert, C.L. (2006). Trends and volatility in agricultural commodity prices. In A. Sarris and D. Hallam (eds) Agricultural *commodity markets and* trade. Edward Elgar.
Gilbert, C.L. & Morgan, C.W. (2010, January), Has food price volatility risen? revised version 8 April 2010. Workshop on Methods to Analyse price volatility.
Global IHR. (2005). Implementation. Biosecurity and bioterrorism. Biodefense Strategy, Practice, and Science, 11(2), 153–156.
Herstein, J.J., Biddinger, P.D., Kraft, C.S., Saiman, L., Gibbs, S.G., et al. (2016). Initial costs of Ebola Treatment Centers in the United States. *Emerging Infectious Diseases,* 22(2), 350.
Huchet-Bourdon, M. (2011). *Agricultural commodity price volatility: An overview* (OECD Food, Agriculture and Fisheries Papers No. 52). OECD Publishing. http://dx.doi.org/10.1787/5kg0t00nrthc-en
International Health Regulations. (2005). *Document, reference WHO/HSE/GCR/2014.10.* WHO.
Irwin, S.H. & Sanders, D.R. (2010). *The impact of index and swap funds on commodity futures markets. Preliminary results* (OECD Food, Agriculture and Fisheries Working Papers 27).
Jacks, D.S., O'Rourke, K.H., & Williamson, J.G. (2009). Commodity price volatility and world market integration since 1700 (NBER Working paper series 14748).
Johnson, W.R. & Wilson III, E.J. (1982). The "Oil Crises" and African Economies: Oil Wave on a Tidal Flood of Industrial Price Inflation. Daedalus, 111(2), 211–241. www.jstor.org/stable/20024792
Jones, K.E., Patel, N.G., Levy, M.A., Storeygard, A., Balk, D., Gittleman, J.L., & Daszak, P. (2008). Global trends in emerging infectious diseases. *Nature,* 451(7181), 990–993.
Jordà, Ò., Sanjay, R., Singh, R.S. & Taylor, A.M. (2020). *Longer-run economic consequences of pandemics* (NBER Working Paper 26934). National Bureau of Economic Research.
Koren, M. & Tenreyro, S. (2007). Volatility and development. *The Quarterly Journal of Economics,* 122(1), 243–287.
Madhav, N., Oppenheim, B., Gallivan, M., Mulembakani, P., Rubin, E. & Wolfe, N. (2017). Pandemics: Risks, impacts, and mitigation. In D.T. Jamison, H. Gelband, S. Horton, P. Jha, R. Laxminarayan, C.N. Mock & R. Nugent (eds) *Disease control priorities: Improving health and reducing poverty* (3rd ed.). World Bank.
Matthews, A. (2010). *Perspectives on addressing market instability and income risk for farmers* (Joint AES and SFER conference on The Common Agricultural policy post 2013). The Institute for International Integration Studies.
McCoy, T. (2014, September 19). Why the brutal murder of several ebola workers may hint at more violence to come. *Washington Post.*
Merhling, P. (1999). The vision of Hyman Minsky. *Journal of Economic Behavior &* Organization, 39, 129–158.
Meriggi, N., Humphreys, M., Kamara, A.B., Krupoff, M., Levine, M., Mcleod, H., Mobarak, M., Prichard, W., Shridhar, A., van der Windt, P. & Voors, M. (2020). *Tracking the economic consequences of COVID-19.* International Growth Center.
Miguez, I.D. & Michelena, G. (2011). *Commodity price volatility: The case of agricultural products* (Documentos de trabajo, No. 1e). Centro de Economía Internacional (CEI).
Minsky, H.P. (1991). The financial instability hypothesis: A clarification. In M. Feldstein (ed.) The *risk of economic crisis* (pp. 158–166). University of Chicago Press.
Moon, S., Sridhar, D., Pate, M.A., Jha, A.K., Clinton, C., Delaunay, S., Edwin, V., Fallah, M., Fidler, D.P., Garrett, L., Goosby, E., Gostin, L. O., Heymann, D.L., Lee, K., Leung, M.G., Morrison, J.S., Saavedra, J., Tanner, M., Leigh, J.A., Hawkins, B., Woskie, L.R.,

& Piot, P. (2015). Will ebola change the game? Ten essential reforms before the next pandemic. The report of thc Harvard – LSHTM Independent Panel on the Global Response to Ebola. *The Lancet*, 386(10009), 2204–2221.

Morse, J.M. (1995). The significance of saturation. *Qualitative Health Research*, 5(2), 147–149.

Murphy, F.A. (1998). Emerging zoonoses. *Emerging Infectious Diseases,* 4(3), 429–435.

Neiderud, C.J. (2015). How urbanization affects the epidemiology of emerging infectious diseases. Infection Ecology and Epidemiology, 5. 27060. doi:10.3402/iee.v5.27060.

OECD. (2002). *Foreign direct investment for development: Maximizing benefits, minimizing costs*. OECD.

OECD. (2009). *Managing risk in agriculture: A holistic approach*. OECD.

Oppenheim, B., Gallivan, M.D., Madhav, N., Brown, N., Serhiyenko, V., et al. (2017). Global preparedness for the next pandemic. Unpublished manuscript.

Parpia, A.S., Ndeffo-Mbah, M.L., Wenzel, N.S. & Galvani, A.P. (2016). Effects of response to 2014–2015 Ebola outbreak on deaths from malaria, HIV/AIDS, and tuberculosis, West Africa. *Emerging Infectious Diseases,* 22(3), 433–441.

Pathmanathan, I., O'Connor, K.A., Adams, M.L., Rao, C.Y., Kilmarx, P.H., et al. (2014). Rapid assessment of ebola infection prevention and control needs – six districts, Sierra Leone, October 2015. *Morbidity and Mortality Weekly Report (MMWR)*, 63(49), 1172–1174.

Person, B., Sy, F., Holton, K., Govert, B., Liang, A., Garza, B., Gould, D., Hickson, M., McDonald, M., Meijer, C., Smith, J., Veto, L., Williams, W., & Zauderer, L. (2004). Fear and stigma: The epidemic within the SARS outbreak. *Emerging Infectious Diseases*, 10(2), 358–363.

Pike, B.L., Saylors, K.E., Fair, J.N., Lebreton, M., Tamoufe, U., et al. (2010). The origin and prevention of pandemics. *Clinical Infectious Diseases*, 50(12), 1636–1640.

Porta, M. (ed.) (2014). *A dictionary of epidemiology* (6th ed.). Oxford University Press.

Pritchett, L., Woolcock, M. & Andrews, M. (2013). Looking like a state: Techniques of persistent failure in state capability for implementation. *Journal of Development Studies*, 49(1), 1–18.

Ramey, G. & Ramey, V.A. (1995). Cross-country evidence on the link between volatility and growth. *American Economic Review*, 85(5), 1138–1151.

Rodrick, D. (1999). Where did all the growth go? External shocks. social conflict and growth collapse. *Journal of Economic Growth*, 4(4), 385–412.

Ross, E., Welch, G.H. & Angelides, P. (2017, March). *Sierra Leone's Response to the Ebola outbreak management strategies and key responder experiences. Centre on Global Health Security*. Chatham House, The Royal Institute of International Affairs.

Roubini, N. & Mihm, S. (2010). *Crisis economics: A crash course in the future of finance*. The Penguin Press.

Rubinson, L., Mutter, R., Viboud, C., Hupert, N., Uyeki, T., et al. (2013). Impact of the Fall 2009 Influenza A(H1N1) pdm09 Pandemic on US Hospitals. *Medical Care,* 51(3), 259–265.

Shehadi, P. (1981, July/August). Economic sanctions and Iranian Trade. Middle East Research and Information Project: Critical coverage of the Middle East Since 1971. https://merip.org/1981/07/economic-sanctions-and-iranian-trade/

Simonsen, L., Spreeuwenberg, P., Lustig, R., Taylor, R.J., Fleming, D.M., et al. (2013). Global mortality estimates for the 2009 influenza pandemic from the GLaMOR project: A modeling study. *PLoS Medicine,* 10(11), e1001558.

Siu, J.Y.M. (2015). Influence of social experiences in shaping perceptions of the ebola virus among African Residents of Hong Kong during the 2014 outbreak: A qualitative study. *International Journal for Equity in Health*, 14(1), 88.

Spero, J.E. (1990). *The politics of international economic relations* (4th ed.). St. Martin's Press.

Srivatsa, S.I. & Mchenga, M. (2020, April). Economic impacts of and policy responses to the coronavirus pandemic: Early evidence from Sierra, Leone. Supporting Economic Transformation. https://set.odi.org/wp-content/uploads/2020/04/Economic-impacts-of-and-policy-responses-to-the-coronavirus-pandemic-early-evidence-from-Sierra-Leone-1.pdf
Tilman, D. & Clark, M. (2014). Global diets link environmental sustainability and human health. *Nature*, 515(7528), 518–522.
Tizzoni, M., Bajardi, P., Poletto, C., Ramasco, J.J., Balcan, D., et al. (2012). Real-time numerical forecast of global epidemic spreading: Case study of 2009 A/H1N1pdm. *BMC Medicine*, 10(1), 165.
Toole, M.J. & Waldman, R.J. (1990). Prevention of excess mortality in refugee and displaced populations in developing countries. *Journal of the American Medical Association,* 263(24), 3296–3302.
Trebesch, C. (2023, February). Sovereign debt in Africa: Large interest rate differences across creditors. *Kiel Institute for the world Economy*. www.ifw-kiel.de/publications/news/sovereign-debt-in-africa-large-interest-rate-differences-across-creditors/
UNCTAD. (2022). *World Investment Report: International tax Reforms and sustainable development*. United Nations.
UNCTAD. (2023a). A world of debt. United Nations.
UNCTAD. (2023b). *Managing commodity price volatility in commodity-dependent developing countries*. United Nations.
UNCTAD. (2023c). *UNCTAD handbook of statistics* 2023. United Nations.
UNCTAD. (2023d). *World investment report 2023: Investing in sustainable energy for all.* United Nations.
UNDESA (United Nations Department of Economic and Social Affairs). (2015). World Population Prospects: The 2015 Revision, Key Findings and Advance Tables (Report ESA/P/WP.241). UNDESA.
UNDP (United Nations Development Programme). (2014). *Assessing the socio-economic impacts of Ebola virus disease in Guinea, Liberia, and Sierra Leone: The road to recovery. Synthesis report*. UNDP.
UNDP. (2014, December). *Assessing the socio-economic impacts of Ebola Virus Disease in Guinea, Liberia and Sierra Leone: The road to recovery*. UNDP.
U.S. Department of Health and Human Services. (2005). *"HHS Pandemic Influenza Plan." Strategic, guidance, and operational planning document*. U.S. Department of Health and Human Services.
U.S. Energy Information Administration. (2020, September). *The impact of COVID-19 on businesses in Sierra Leone: A synthesis of various surveys. Policy Brief No. 1.* Ministry of Finance, Government of Sierra Leone.
U.S. Energy Information Administration. (2024, January). Short-term energy outlook. www.eia.gov/outlooks/steo/realprices/
US Trade Representative. (2005, October). Facts on the Doha. *Round*. https://ustr.gov/archive/assets/Document_Library/Fact_Sheets/2005/asset_upload_file93_8213.pdf
Valerie, C. & Saxena, S.C. (2008). Growth dynamics: The myth of economic recovery. *American Economic Review*, 98(1), 439–457.
Van Boeckel, T.P., Thanapongtharm, W., Robinson, T., Biradar, C.M., Xiao, X., et al. (2012). Improving risk models for avian influenza: The role of intensive poultry farming and flooded land during the 2004 Thailand epidemic. *PLoS One*, 7(11), e49528.
Van der Ploeg, F. & Poelhekke, S. (2009). Volatility and the natural resource curse. *Oxford Economic Papers*, 61, 727–760.
Wallinga, J. & Teunis, P. (2004). Different epidemic curves for severe acute respiratory syndrome reveal similar impacts of control measures. *American Journal of Epidemiology*, 160(6), 509–516.
Warburton, C.E.S. (2021). Positive check: The Malthusian theorem and the Covid-19 pandemic. *Journal of Smart Economic Growth,* 6(3), 1–7.

WHO (World Health Organization). (2005). *International health regulations*. WHO.
WHO (World Health Organization). (2014). Summary of states parties 2013 report on IHR core capacity implementation: Regional profiles. WHO/HSE/GCR/2014.8. https://iris.who.int/bitstream/handle/10665/112839/WHO_HSE_GCR_2014.8_eng.pdf?sequence=1
Wolfe, N.D., Dunavan, C.P. & Diamond, J. (2007). Origins of major human infectious diseases. *Nature*, 447(7142), 279–283.
Woolhouse, M.E.J. & Gowtage-Sequeria, S. (2005). Host range and emerging and reemerging pathogens. *Emerging Infectious Diseases*, 11(12), 1842–1847.
World Bank. (2014). The *economic impact of* the 2014 Ebola epidemic: Short and *medium term estimates for* Guinea, Liberia, and *Sierra Leone* (Working Paper 90748). World Bank.
World Bank. (2021). *Sierra Leone 2021 economic update: Welfare and poverty effects of the COVID-19 pandemic*. World Bank.
Yohannes-Kassahu, B. (2023, February). One Year Later: The impact of the Russian conflict with Ukraine on Africa. *Africa Renewal*. www.un.org/africarenewal/magazine/february-2023/one-year-later-impact-russian-conflict-ukraine-africa
Zell, R. (2004). Global climate change and the emergence/re-emergence of infectious diseases. *International Journal of Medical Microbiology Supplements*, 293(Suppl 37), 16–26.

Index

Kolibri 360 GmbH
Ferdinand-Jühlke-Straße 7
99095 Erfurt, Deutschland
produktsicherheit@kolibri360.de